SOCIOLOGY
TODAY

GERARD O'DONNELL

Principal, West Thames College

CAMBRIDGE
UNIVERSITY PRESS

Published by the Press Syndicate of the University of Cambridge
The Pitt Building, Trumpington Street, Cambridge CB2 1RP
40 West 20th Street, New York, NY 10011–4211, USA
10 Stamford Road, Oakleigh, Melbourne 3166, Australia

© Cambridge University Press 1993

First published 1993

Printed in Great Britain by Scotprint Limited, Musselburgh

A catalogue record for this book is available from the British Library

ISBN 0 521 42670 7 paperback

Cover illustration by Elaine Cox

Notice to teachers

CONTENTS

Acknowledgements		vi
Introduction		vii
	About the GCSE	viii
	Coursework for GCSE	ix
	Key to research techniques and methodology	xiv

UNIT 1

COUNTING | 1.1 | Living together | 1
PEOPLE | 1.2 | Groups today – belonging | 2
| 1.3 | The development of urban culture | 7
| 1.4 | Population in Britain | 13
| 1.5 | The world outside – the future | 17

	Discussion	19
	Additional assignments and investigations	21
	Outline of an appropriate GCSE investigation/project	24
	GCSE question	25
	Self-test questions	26

UNIT 2

FAMILY LIFE | 2.1 | What a family is | 27
| 2.2 | Why families? | 29
| 2.3 | Different sorts of family | 31
| 2.4 | The changing family pattern | 35
| 2.5 | Family roles | 40
| 2.6 | Young people in the family | 45

	Discussion	48
	Additional assignments and investigations	49
	Outline of an appropriate GCSE investigation/project	50
	GCSE question	52
	Self-test questions	57

UNIT 3

LEARNING FOR | 3.1 | Informal education | 58
LIFE | 3.2 | Learning our roles | 59
| 3.3 | Intelligence | 61
| 3.4 | Environment | 63
| 3.5 | The British education system | 67

3.6	The future of education	71
3.7	Youth culture	73
3.8	Youth activities	78
	Discussion	81
	Additional assignments and investigations	83
	Outline of an appropriate GCSE investigation/project	86
	GCSE question	88
	Self-test questions	90

UNIT 4

US AND THEM

4.1	Minorities	91
4.2	Race and ethnic groups	94
4.3	Racism	96
4.4	Ethnic minorities in Britain	99
4.5	Social class	107
4.6	Social differences in Britain	111
	Discussion	115
	Additional assignments and investigations	119
	Outline of an appropriate GCSE investigation/project	120
	GCSE question	123
	Self-test questions	125

UNIT 5

A BETTER LIFE?

5.1	Poverty	126
5.2	The welfare state	131
5.3	Benefits and services	133
5.4	Health	136
5.5	Housing	140
5.6	Planning	142
5.7	Environment and pollution	146
	Discussion	149
	Additional assignments and investigations	150
	Outline of an appropriate GCSE investigation/project	152
	GCSE question	154
	Self-test questions	156

UNIT 6

CHANGING THE RULES

6.1	Power	157
6.2	Dictatorship	160
6.3	Democracy	163
6.4	Political parties in Britain	165
6.5	Elections	169
6.6	Pressure groups	177
6.7	Supranational authority	180
	Discussion	185
	Additional assignments and investigations	187

Outline of an appropriate GCSE investigation/project   191
GCSE question   193
Self-test questions   194

UNIT 7

THE MEDIA AND   7.1   Communicating   195
POWER   7.2   The media   197
                  7.3   The press   199
                  7.4   Sound and vision   203
                  7.5   Advertising   207
                  7.6   Power and censorship   209

                        Discussion   212
                        Additional assignments and investigations   214
                        Outline of an appropriate GCSE investigation/project   217
                        GCSE question   219
                        Self-test questions   221

UNIT 8

EARNING OUR   8.1   The economy   222
LIVING   8.2   Changes in industry and commerce   225
                  8.3   The world of work   227
                  8.4   Women and employment   230
                  8.5   Wages and salaries   234
                  8.6   Trade unions   237
                  8.7   Leisure   243
                  8.8   Providing for leisure   246

                        Discussion   249
                        Additional assignments and investigations   251
                        Outline of an appropriate GCSE investigation/project   253
                        GCSE question   255
                        Self-test questions   257

UNIT 9

KEEPING THE   9.1   Why have rules?   258
RULES   9.2   Religion   260
                  9.3   Why keep the rules?   263
                  9.4   Informal control   265
                  9.5   Formal control   269
                  9.6   Labels   272

                        Discussion   274
                        Additional assignments and investigations   278
                        Outline of an appropriate GCSE investigation/project   283
                        GCSE question   285
                        Self-test questions   286

APPENDIX   Answers to self-test questions   287

                  Index   295

ACKNOWLEDGEMENTS

Illustrations

1, © Mark Cator/Impact Photos; 3, Peter Frey/Survival International; 5, 112*t*, 140*l*, Philip Gordon/Impact Photos; 9, © The Daily Telegraph plc; 10, Conservation Trust/George Philip; 11*t*, Barnaby's Picture Library; 11*b*, 136*r*, © Brian Harris/Impact Photos; 17, 68, 102, 136*l*, 268*a*, *c*, *d*, Hulton-Deutsch Collection; 27, Mark Boulton/Barnaby's Picture Library; 28, 59, 69, © Peter Arkell/Impact Photos; 32, © Thomas Kelly/Impact Photos; 35, F. Popely/Life File; 40*l*, 161, 223, 228*t*, 259*b*, 268*e*, Ann Ronan at Image Select; 40*r*, © Claire Godfrey/ Impact Photos; 64*r*, 135, © Steve Benbow/Impact Photos; 64*b*, David Lurie/Impact Photos; 74, 98, 170*r*, 241, John Arthur/Impact Photos; 91, 104, 162*b*, 178*t*, 211, Popperfoto; 93, 193, courtesy of *Punch*; 112*b*, Jim Rice/Impact Photos; 123, Sheila Gray/Format; 126*l*, Chris Shelton/ Impact Photos; 126*r*, Adam Hinton/© Impact Photos; 140*r*, Michael Jenner; 145, Bill Meadows/Barnaby's Picture Library; 147, R. Baker/ Impact Photos; 157, Dod Miller/Impact Photos; 162*t*, Archiv für Kunst und Geschichte; 169 © The Observer, London; 170*l*, 231*t*, © Piers Cavendish/Impact Photos; 178*b*, Jane Skinner/Barnaby's Picture Library; 183, © Stuart Clarke/Impact Photos; 207, 267*t*, Ben Edwards/ Impact Photos; 226, courtesy of Ford Motor Co. Ltd; 228*b*, Sefton Photo Library; 230, © Homer Sykes/Impact Photos; 231*b*, David Alexander Simson/Barnaby's Picture Library; 259*t*, Ray Ward/Life File; 261*t*, © David Harden/Impact Photos; 261*bl*, Peter Sanders; 261*br*, Sally-Anne Fison/Life File; 267*b*, Michael Mirecki/Impact Photos.

Extracts

11, Canongate; 12, 30–1, Penguin Books; 19–20, 265, J. M. Dent; 21, 277, © The Observer, London; 41–3, 203 © New Statesman and Society; 60, Krieger; 66, © Times Newspapers Ltd; 67, 72, 116, 130*b*, 139*b*, 232, 233*b*, 276, 279, 280*b*, 281, © The Daily Telegraph plc; 70, 81, Open Books; 75, 269, Longman; 94, 185, Collins Fontana; 116–17, 280, Macmillan; 129, Routledge and Kegan Paul; 159, 159–60, 245–6, Jonathan Cape; 198–9, Constable; 202–3, 233 © The Guardian; 212– 13, Leicester University Press; 271 (O'Donnell), John Murray; 271 (Becker) Allen Lane; 274, Quadrangle; 277, Sidgwick and Jackson.

Every effort has been made to reach copyright holders; the publishers would like to hear from anyone whose rights they have unwittingly infringed.

INTRODUCTION

This book is intended for use by students with differing levels of ability. Less able students will find some of the exercises well within their grasp while some sections will stretch even the most able. *Sociology Today* aims to do what the assessment process seeks to do – to cater for the whole ability range from a potential level 4 to a potential level 10. (From 1994 level 4 equals the old grade G and level 9 equals the old grade A; level 10 is a new grade for the highest achievers.) This means that some questions/sections will appear ridiculously easy to some readers while others will appear very hard.

The book increases in complexity as the student proceeds but allows a variety of approaches appropriate to the age and ability of the students concerned.

It is not intended that all the projects and exercises should be carried out by all individuals – there should be an opportunity both for choice and for work in small groups. Much information is given but there is ample scope for students to discover more for themselves.

In the enthusiasm created by the development of coursework for GCSE some books and schools/colleges have concentrated on this and relegated subject knowledge to a lesser position. *Sociology Today* recognises that a large proportion of marks is awarded for knowledge and ensures a proper balance in the text between knowing and doing. (From 1994 70% of marks are for knowledge and understanding.)

Coursework is very important in all GCSE syllabuses and an understanding of the methods used by social scientists (the 'methodology') is vital for success. However, a substantial chunk of 'methodology' at the beginning of a book can be quite daunting and has been avoided in *Sociology Today*. Research methods are gradually introduced and each time the aspect of methodology described is related to a real task so that its relevance is clear.

You are *not* provided with all the information you need in this textbook – a most important aspect of GCSE is finding out for yourself rather than merely learning 'facts'. Guidance is given, but use your common sense as well – information which you have to discover is often related to source material near the question and that source material will have a note telling you where it came from; your school, college or public library is likely to have up-to-date copies of that source material. When using an index, for example that in *Social Trends*, if you cannot find 'working hours' try 'hours of work'!

In any book dealing with our society there is a danger of bias and students should always be aware that an author, like anyone else, may be unconsciously prejudiced. However, every endeavour has been made to ensure that a balanced view is presented. It may be even more important to stress that the sources from which material is drawn may not be neutral and the reader should not unthinkingly accept any statements made in the text or in the reproduced extracts – some have been included in order to be deliberately provocative!

ABOUT THE GCSE

The GCSE replaced the former GCE O Level and CSE examinations, and is intended for the range of candidates who formerly entered those examinations (assumed to be some 70 per cent of the secondary school population). The GCSE was not just an amalgamation of two examinations; it was meant as a new and positive examination experience for candidates at all levels. You will be encouraged to demonstrate what you know, understand and can do rather than what you do not know, as often seemed to be the case in the past. In the GCSE there is an emphasis on *using* your knowledge, rather than merely remembering a quantity of facts.

There are four Examining Groups in England, one for Wales and one for Northern Ireland (Scotland has a different examination system). You may, theoretically, enter through any Group regardless of where you live. In fact some schools and colleges – and some local education authorities – may have regulations limiting their entries to only one Examining Group. However, if one syllabus seems to meet your needs and it is not available in your locality you should write to the Examining Group concerned (get the address from *The Education Authority Directory* in your local library) and they will give you the address of the nearest Examining Centre through which you may enter.

What you are expected to know and do

Each Examining Group will tell you what your 'aims' should be – what you should aim to do *during* and at the *end* of the course, and also what you are expected to *know*. How well you achieve these aims will be assessed by coursework and a final examination. What your assessments and examination are seeking to find out are called 'assessment objectives'. Each Group may state its 'objectives' slightly differently but all include the following:

1. An ability to show how economic, social and political factors jointly affect social life.
2. An ability to acquire social scientific knowledge, both from personal experience and from the work of others.

3. To demonstrate skills of comprehension and communication of data presented in different ways including written and numerical data and data in the form of graphs, diagrams and pictures.
4. An ability to design and carry out research, including the ability to collect, analyse and interpret data.
5. An ability to distinguish between evidence and opinion. (Evidence is material based on systematic observation which has been subjected to careful analysis.) You should be able to recognise deficiencies in material, such as gaps, inconsistencies and bias, which reduce its value as evidence.
6. An ability to recall, organise, analyse, interpret and evaluate social scientific knowledge and to apply that knowledge, particularly in practical situations likely to fall within your own experience.

These 'objectives' will be tested in a variety of ways but all Groups are conscious of the need to ensure that all candidates are able to gain credit in each part of the assessment for what they know and can do, so that candidates of all levels of ability are able to score appropriate marks. This should mean that the assessment process is a positive one for *all* candidates rather than merely being a demonstration of failure for many.

Of course it is necessary to ensure that different levels of achievement are rewarded and the Examining Groups call this 'differentiation'. This is achieved in the written papers by the following:

1. The use of a series of questions of increasing difficulty and requiring longer answers, those at the end showing most need for evaluation by the candidate. (These may be described as 'on an incline of difficulty' or 'stepped questions' or 'structured questions'.)
2. Longer questions in which the depth of the candidate's response can be measured.
3. Question papers set for differing levels of ability (e.g. one paper for potential levels 4–7 and one for levels 7–10).

COURSEWORK FOR GCSE

I. *Requirements*

This component is designed to give an opportunity to select some aspect, or aspects, of the syllabus which are of special interest to you and to study them in greater depth, using social science skills.

You will be able to proceed at your own pace in acquiring and compiling the information and be able to use your own skills in applying your findings. Your teacher or lecturer is expected to help you select your project and guide you as it progresses, but all Examining

Groups stress that it must be your own work. For example, the Welsh Joint Education Committee states:

> The choice of topic by the candidate should be approved by the teacher and should be within the scope and spirit of the syllabus. In general the choice should take account of the candidate's interests and considerations such as availability of materials and opportunities for personal investigative activities. The choice of topic will influence final assessment insofar as it makes a *valid* contribution to the subject. In *content* the project should be original in the sense that it is the candidate's own work, that it discloses new information or considers published information in a new light or setting. The study should show a logical progression of facts and observations and should show evidence of further reading which places the study in a wider perspective. The project should be *presented* in a neat and legible form, preferably of A4 size, and be fully identifiable.

The percentage of marks awarded for coursework varies; and the percentage allocated to coursework will give you some guide as to the proportion of time which you should devote to it.

Each Examining Group includes in their published syllabus details of what they expect to see in your completed coursework and you should read this carefully yourself. Some allow you to include non-written material, for example an audio-visual presentation, a computer program presentation or an oral presentation. Make certain you know what is acceptable before you start.

You will have to choose appropriate methods with which to carry out your investigation. The Northern Group list the following investigative techniques:

- direct observation
- participant observation
- experiments
- interviews
- questionnaires
- surveys
- sampling
- case studies
- hypothesis testing
- the use of secondary sources.

Each of these techniques and their advantages and disadvantages are dealt with in this book and suggestions for possible investigations using them are given in each unit. A full list of techniques and references to where they are explained is on page xiv. The Southern Group gives the following list of 'secondary sources' from which you may draw some of your information:

- relevant pieces of social research
- statistical material

- literature, journals, newspapers, diaries, biographies/auto-biographies, etc.
- audio-visual material
- written material from interest groups, etc.
- diagrammatic material.

2.   *Sources of information for coursework investigations*

Librarians in public and school/college libraries have been trained in how to find out information, so make use of their knowledge.

You may find it useful to know some general sources of information, in addition to the obvious encyclopaedia and textbooks.

- *The British Humanities Index.* This index lists recently published articles by subject. For example, if you are making a study of the causes and effects of football hooliganism look up 'football spectators and violence'. You are likely to find references which will give you the name of newspapers which have published articles on this topic, the date of publication and the pages the articles are on. You can then ask for the relevant copy from the store of back numbers. The index is published annually, with quarterly updates. These updates are most likely to be useful to you as you may have difficulty getting older newspapers or periodicals. An up-to-date copy of the index is usually available in larger libraries (which will also keep 'back' copies of many newspapers and magazines).
- *Social Trends* (published annually by HMSO). This is packed with statistical information on most topics which you are likely to cover (e.g. numbers unemployed, causes of death, age at marriage). It tends to be a bit dated by the time it comes out but is excellent at showing trends (general movement) over a period of time.
- *Whitaker's Almanack* (published annually). This provides lots of useful addresses for source material – pressure groups, charities, etc. – and general information on a wide range of subjects, for example the votes obtained by each Member of Parliament or public school fees.
- *Family Expenditure Survey* (published annually by the Department of Employment). This gives useful information on income, employment, composition of households (e.g. family size), what money is spent on – some of which is not in *Social Trends*.
- *Annual Abstract of Statistics* (published annually by HMSO). This provides similar information to that in *Social Trends* but no explanatory articles and is less accessible. It is useful if you want more up-to-date information than that in *Social Trends*.
- *Guide to the Social Services* (usually published annually by the

Family Welfare Association). This has up-to-date information on welfare benefits, how and where to make complaints, basic law, etc.

- *Monthly Index to the Financial Times*. This is a complete index to *The Financial Times*, divided into three sections: (1) Corporate: articles about corporations; (2) General: articles on general subjects, such as drugs, smoking, etc.; (3) People: articles about specific people.

- *Applied Social Sciences Index and Abstracts (ASSIA)*. This provides an index to articles on a wide range of social science subjects and additionally provides brief summaries to them. The summaries could be used by students as a basis for some assignments.

- *Guardian Index*. This is similar to the *Monthly Index to the Financial Times* except that it indexes the *Guardian* newspaper.

- *Colour Supplement Index 1962–1987*. This indexes all major articles in *The Observer*, *The Sunday Times* and *Sunday Telegraph* magazines. It is on microfiche in many libraries.

3. *Coursework topics*

Although each Examining Group indicates a maximum or average length for coursework projects or assignments it is the quality, rather than the quantity, of the work which is being assessed.

Examples of appropriate investigations or enquiries are given in each unit, but be imaginative. In one enquiry a mature student dressed her little boy sometimes as a little boy and sometimes as a little girl and took him into a variety of situations, including playgroups. She observed the behaviour of other children and adults and her project included photographs of a variety of situations. She produced an excellent coursework project on the learning of gender roles.

Each Examining Group will specify what they want you to include in your research report. That of the Southern Group is a good example:

Presentation of the Personal Research Study

The research report must include:

- title page
- contents page
- statement of intent, including description of the area to be studied, the questions to be asked and the methods chosen to investigate these questions
- descriptions of how the research was conducted
- presentation of results and findings, including reference to secondary sources
- analysis and conclusions of results and findings
- discussion of the success or failure of the questions asked; the

methods chosen; the conduct of the research; the performance of the researcher.

The criteria for assessing the coursework will also vary but that of
the London and East Anglian Group will give you a good idea of what
is expected:

Criteria for assessment   *Max. mark*

(i)   Independent searching out of information   15
(ii)   Originality of treatment, clarity of organisation
        and presentation in candidate's own words   25
(iii)   Reasoned argument, adequate depth in
        coverage of topic and relevant conclusions   30
(iv)   Integration within the text of all types of
        supportive materials   15
(v)   Accuracy of material   10
(vi)   Summary of sources used, and bibliography   5
                                                                                         ———
                                                                                         100

Essentially, the coursework investigation tests your ability to conduct
social research in a scientific way. This is well illustrated by the Mid-
land Group's emphasis on two major objectives:

● To analyse, interpret and evaluate evidence presented in a
  variety of ways.
● To locate and select primary and secondary evidence using
  appropriate sociological methods.

4.   *When is a fact in fact a fact?*

WHY THIS ADDRESS?

To call at every address in the country would take too long and
cost too much, so we select a sample of addresses. We choose
them from the Post Office's list of addresses in a way that gives
every address the same chance of being selected.

That is how we selected your address. We did not know anything
in advance about you or your household. But while it is a matter
of chance which addresses are selected, once they have been
chosen we must contact those addresses and no others. This
ensures that all types of people are properly represented in the
sample.

That is why it is so important that everyone we approach agrees
to take part. Everyone has information to give which is needed in
the survey.

                                        Labour Force Survey 1992 (Census Office)

This extract indicates the care with which those engaged in original or
primary research select their sample – in this case the **sampling
frame**, the list from which the sample is drawn, is the largest poss-

ible, that is every address in the country. *Your* investigation will be limited by time and your samples will be limited in size and unlikely to be as representative as you would like. However, you will be aware of any shortcomings and can refer to these and give the reasons for them in your report (you will receive credit for this).

However, when you rely on **secondary** material – that is, information collected and interpreted by other people, such as diaries, books and statistics – you may have more difficulty in judging how reliable and valid they are. Books may not be **objective** or unbiased: Charles Dickens's accounts of Victorian England may be accurate, but he was writing fiction; history is usually written from the point of view of those who won. Doubts have even been cast on the reliability of much supposedly unbiased research, for example Cyril Burt's study on intelligence or Margaret Mead's accounts of tribal life in New Guinea.

The most important skill you must acquire during your Social Science course is the ability to assess the quality of the information which you receive, and to ensure that your own research receives the same critical look that you will give to other people's.

When something is stated as a **fact** consider:

- Who says so?
- How was this fact discovered?
- If a research finding, why was the research undertaken?
- Has any individual or group anything to gain as a result?

KEY TO RESEARCH TECHNIQUES AND METHODOLOGY

The numbers listed after each entry below are the numbers of the pages on which more information is given: the number in bold is the page containing a description or definition; other numbers are those pages where more information is given or suggestions for using techniques are made.

Bias **33**, 86, 153

Collating results **85**, 284

Hypothesis **24**, **51**, **85**, 87, 120, 152, 191, 217, 283

Interview **24**, 80, **84**, 87, 121, 192, 218, 254, 284

Interviewing techniques **84**, 87, 218

Longitudinal survey **46–7**

Observation **xii**, **60–1**, 86, 121, 191, **254**

  Participant observation **5**, **60–1**, 191, **284**

Opinion polls **168–9**

Pie chart **34**, 284

Pilot survey **153**

Presentation **xii–xiii**, 51, 87, 121–2, 284

Primary sources **xiii**, **24**, **83**, 191

Questioning evidence **xiv**, 83

Questionnaire 24, **33**, 47, **50–1**, 60, 80, **86–7**, **120–1**, 152, 254, 282, 283–4

  Closed questionnaire 33, **86**, 121, 254, 283

  Open questionnaire 33, **86**, 121

Random sample **xiii**, 33, 60, 121

Representative sample 24, 47, **121**, 254

Respondents **152**, 282

Sample 24, **33**, **43–4**, 47, 121, 254

Secondary sources **x–xi**, **xiv**, 24, 50, 86, 120, 191, 217, 283

Stratified sample **43–4**, 47

Survey **x**, 45–6, 49, 119, 150, 215

UNIT 1

COUNTING PEOPLE

The anonymity of living together – a crowded street in Tokyo.

1.1   LIVING TOGETHER

There are more than 4,000 million people in the world, but there is no one quite like you. You are an individual, and as an individual you are important.

It may be that you are the only person who realises just how important you are, but your family almost certainly does and your friends probably do. Your teachers or lecturers should do also, since without you, and others like you, they would be out of a job!

Other people who know you, even if only as a statistic, will also regard you as of some importance. For every person who knows you, however, there will be millions of people in the world who have never heard of you and in your home town many people will not know you personally. It is because we live mainly among strangers that we experience many of our difficulties in living with others.

In Great Britain (that is, England, Wales and Scotland) there were only about 2 million people altogether when the Normans conquered England in the 11th century. Six hundred years later, when James II fled from William of Orange, the population had risen to about 6.5 million. Today there are 58 million people living in the United Kingdom (that is, Great Britain and Northern Ireland).

Although the number of people and what they do has changed greatly in a short period of time, we have hardly changed physically. We are basically the same sort of animal that would have lived a simple life among a small group of people well known to us only a few thousand years ago. It is only in the last few hundred years that the majority of people have spent a great deal of their time among strangers. This is a very short time in the history of humankind, and we have not had very long to adjust to this new situation.

Modern man (*Homo sapiens*) appears to have developed about 100,000 years ago in Asia. We cannot be certain how many people there were or how they lived, but from their remains we do know that there were not many of them and that they lived in small groups which rarely made contact with other groups. Groups remained small because the food supply in any area was limited as long as people remained mainly hunters. Gradually people spread out to find new hunting grounds, avoid enemies and escape changing climates. The last Ice Age, about 30,000 years ago, reduced the level of the oceans and enabled people to cross into America.

Population increase was slow as the **death rate** roughly equalled the **birth rate**. (The term 'birth rate' is given to the number of live births for every 1,000 of the population in any given year, while the death rate is the number who die in every 1,000 of the population during the year.) Although the population started to increase more rapidly with the development of agriculture about 10,000 years ago, the real population boom did not start until the 18th century, so that the population of the world has increased from about 800 million to about 5,000 million during the last 200 years.

---

1. Would you like to live all by yourself? Explain the reasons for your answer.
2. Here are some of the disadvantages of living in towns:

    noise   cramped space
    polluted air   overcrowding

    Now list some of the advantages.

1.2   GROUPS TODAY – BELONGING

Most animals are gregarious, that is they like to be in the company of others of the same kind as themselves – for some of the time at least. Humans are no exception. We usually have close ties with members of our family. We often inherit our looks from our relations. Since we have shared the same background, or environ-

The tribal way of life of traditional societies.

ment, we often think and feel in the same way. We usually feel at ease in the company of our family, at least during the early years of our life.

Gradually most people make friends outside their immediate family. People are usually attracted to others who have the same interests and attitudes as themselves and who are also likely to be about the same age. This group is known as a **peer group** ('peer' meaning 'equal'), and as we grow older this group may gradually take over from our family in having most influence on us.

It is likely that our early ancestors stayed with their immediate families and that each tribe was made up mainly of members of the same family: father, mother, brothers, sisters, cousins, etc. There was some protection at least against death or being taken into slavery by other tribes, a greater possibility of food and shelter if ill or injured, and by co-operating a greater chance of overcoming the wild animals that provided meat.

The members of the pack had the security of the tribe as a protection against 'them' – the feared members of other tribes. As the tribe became larger the more powerful individuals might dominate the weaker, and life for the less fortunate might become grim, but not as grim as in the big wilderness outside. In traditional societies banishment from the tribe was and is the most terrible of penalties; even in Britain today people fear being 'sent to Coventry' by their friends or being kicked out of the gang.

As societies developed, tasks became more specialised and some people became experts at particular jobs: people became more interdependent. At the same time large numbers of people might be required to do particular jobs which would benefit everyone, for example to build an irrigation system to bring water to farm the land.

Today it would be difficult for any one person to be fully competent as a brain surgeon, a lorry driver, a computer programmer, a language teacher *and* a television comedian. We need therefore to live in a group of people who can assist us while we assist them.

It is the study of people in groups that is sociology – the 'science of society'. Sociologists try to use scientific methods to study how people behave when they are part of a group and how membership of groups affects the behaviour of individuals and that of other groups.

Today we each belong to several groups – families, gangs, political parties, nations, colleges. Most people enjoy belonging to a group and feel lost outside it, perhaps a feeling left over from the days long ago when one could not survive without belonging. This feeling of belonging can be made stronger in all sorts of ways – national anthems, football chants, flags, uniforms, special hairstyles, symbols. These might antagonise people outside the group, and even be part of their purpose or **function**. In this way the hostility of people outside the group may draw the group members closer together, giving a feeling of **solidarity**. Do you ever feel like this?

Just as groups identify themselves by particular signs, so all humans have developed rituals, codes and signs so that we can recognise those who have the same interests as ourselves, and at the same time recognise 'them' – those who do not! Certainly many leaders have realised the importance of giving the members of their group something or somebody outside the group to hate and fear (often these are the same thing).

In 1989 the Home Office produced a report on the upsurge of 'lager louts' in rural areas called 'Drinking and Disorder: A Study of Non-metropolitan Violence'. Some fifteen years before, James Patrick described a group of boys who sprayed gang slogans on walls, smashed windows and beheaded tailors' dummies – in his book *A Glasgow*

Do you identify with these unemployed young people in a store in Barnsley?

Gang Observed. In *Delinquent Boys: The Culture of the Gang* (1955) A. K. Cohen described how the boys stole things which they then gave or threw away. The hunting ground for such boys, however, is very different from that of their ancestors of long ago.

James Patrick joined a Glasgow gang in order to find out how it really behaved and the reasons for that behaviour. He had to become a real gang member and to participate in (join in) the gang's drinking and other activities. He stopped his study because he did not want to be involved in law-breaking activities.

This kind of study, known as **participant observation**, has the following advantages:

1. The researcher will not encounter resentment from the group for being a researcher.
2. Relationships in the group can be explored in depth.
3. Factors may become apparent that would otherwise be hidden.
4. The presence of the researcher may not influence the behaviour of the group if he or she is accepted as a member.
5. Non-verbal communication can be recorded.

1. No man is an *Island*, entire of itself ... any man's *death* diminishes *me*, because I am involved in *Mankind*

   John Donne, 1572–1631

   One must journey through life alone; to rely on others is to invite heartbreak

   Jawaharlal Nehru, 1889–1964

   In these quotations one writer is expressing the view that every man is rather like a cog in a machine, that we depend upon each other; the other is suggesting that each person is an individual who can only depend upon him or herself.
   a. Which of these two statements most nearly reflects the way you feel? Why?
   b. Why do you think the peer group increases in influence over us as we grow older?
   c. Would you dislike being 'sent to Coventry'? What effect do you think it would have on you?

2. People need to belong and often dress in a distinctive way in order to establish a group identity. Look at the photograph on p. 5:
   a. Do you think that the young people in this group wanted people in general to like the way they are dressed?
   b. Do you find anything offensive about the way any of the individuals look?
   c. Would you be surprised if you met any of these people dressed as in the photograph working as:
      i. a waiter or waitress?
      ii. a bank clerk?
      iii. a priest or nun?

3. Consider the way you normally dress:
   a. at college or school
   b. when a guest at a wedding
   c. at a disco or some other social event.
   Why do you dress in these ways?

4.   *Signs*
   Some of the ways we communicate with each other are not through speech, that is, they are **non-verbal**. Here are some – you may be able to think of others:

uniform	make-up	trade marks
coats of arms	fashion	gestures
flags	hairstyles	food
tattooing	shop signs	

   a. Think of some examples of each of these and say what message you think your example might convey.
   b. Think of a group – or groups – to which you belong.

What special 'signs' does your group have that show it is different from other groups?

5. GANG OF 20 STAB TWO TEENAGERS

   GANG 'LIKE PACK OF WOLVES'

   Do you think people behave in a different way from usual when they are part of a crowd or gang? If so, why?

6. Read the following poem:

   Father, Mother and Me
   Sister and Auntie say
   All people like us are We
   and everyone else is They
   And They live over the sea,
   While We live over the way
   But – would you believe it?
   They look upon We
   As only a sort of They.

   Rudyard Kipling, 'We and They'

   Make a list of the kind of people who you would think of as 'we'.
   Now make a list of some of those that you would think of as 'they'.

1.3 THE DEVELOPMENT OF URBAN CULTURE

So long as the tribe depended on food gathering and hunting for its living it had to remain fairly small for it needed a fairly large territory in which to find its food. If the number of people in the tribe increased, some members would have to set off to establish a new tribe with its own territory.

Farming, however, allowed a tribe to produce enough food in one place to permit the tribe to grow. Wild wheat and barley grew on the eastern shore of the Mediterranean, wild rice grew in Southern Asia and wild maize in Central America. These were the places where people were able to settle down as farmers and develop what we call civilisation, for not only did farming allow the tribe to stay in one place and grow, it often produced more than was actually needed. This **surplus** encouraged people to plan for the future and some no longer had to be concerned in actually producing the food and could become leaders, teachers, priests and technicians.

The first town-based civilisations developed about 5,000 years ago in desert areas which could be made fertile through irrigation. This required leaders, technical experts and fairly large numbers of people in one place. For example, the towns in the civilisation of Sumer, part of modern-day Iraq, were quite small with populations of about

7,000–20,000, the size of a small mining town in Yorkshire today or a country town in Somerset. They were, however, big enough for the people in the community not to know everyone as individuals. This impersonality is probably the most important aspect of urban life. Most people are strangers whom some will exploit or cheat without the sense of guilt that might be felt if they were dealing with relatives or friends. Generally there may be lacking a sense of responsibility for other people in the community.

On the other hand, some studies of parts of the central areas of cities such as Delhi, Cairo, East London, Lagos and Mexico City suggest that 'urban villages' can exist where most contact can still be with familiar people. **Urbanisation** does not always follow the same pattern, although certainly it has to do with people being concentrated into one place, and usually their contacts with others will be more impersonal and superficial than in the less anonymous village.

A dependency on others is another feature of urban life. For example, Birmingham needs water from Wales; ancient Rome relied upon grain from Egypt; for 600 years London required coal from Newcastle – now it needs gas from under the North Sea.

It took about 95,000 years for *Homo sapiens* to develop into the town dwellers of Sumer, but only 5,000 years for us to develop from that early urban culture into the hi-tech world of today.

Towns throughout the world continue to grow in size as a smaller percentage of people are employed in **primary** industries such as farming, fishing and mining. People are moving increasingly into **secondary** industries such as manufacturing and building, and now at an accelerating pace into **tertiary**, or 'service', occupations such as distribution, communications and the professions.

However, in Great Britain many people are now moving out of inner-city areas and away from the big conurbations. This is because of the growth of service industries, which can often be located anywhere, and because of the decline of traditional industries. London's population will have fallen from about 8 million in 1966 to an estimate of less than 7 million by 2001. Nevertheless, the population continues to be tightly compressed into urban belts, and the authorities use planning controls to try to ensure that these do not merge into each other.

By 1990 the greatest concentration of population in Britain was in the North-West (868 people per square kilometre), about a quarter more than in the South-East. However, this was considerably less than the densest population in Europe, around Brussels, with a population of 6,000 per square kilometre.

A few years ago, Desmond Morris in *The Human Zoo* (1969) suggested that to describe our teeming city world as a 'concrete jungle' is quite wrong. Wild animals under normal conditions do not develop stomach ulcers, become too fat or kill their own kind. Animals in a zoo, however, where there is plenty of spare time, no problem of survival, but often overcrowding, do develop all these peculiarly 'human' ways of behaving. The city is not a 'concrete jungle', he suggests, but a 'human zoo'.

Of course there are advantages of living in a zoo. The wild animal does not normally live as long as its captive counterpart; it is at the mercy of the predator, of famine and disease. In 1901 the average man at birth in Britain could be expected to live for 48 years (about the same as in India now), but by 1991 his **expectation of life** had increased to almost 73 years. In 1901 a woman at birth could be expected to live until she was 52, but by 1991 she could expect 79 years of life (by 2001 expectation of life should rise to 74.5 years for men and 80 years for women). Even today some countries have an expectation of life lower than Britain in 1891 (see Figure 1.1); in Guinea-Bissau people at birth can expect to live only to the age of 40.

**Figure 1.1
Expectation of life: how
Britain compares.**

From: *The Daily Telegraph,*
5 July 1991

Note:
Text figures are based on
Social Trends (1992) or the
Geographical Digest
(1992–3). Consider some
reasons why these may differ
from the chart figures.

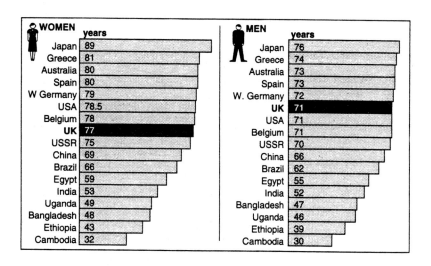

1. Two hundred and fifty years ago only 2.5 per cent of the population of the world lived in towns with populations of over 20,000. There were no cities with more than 1 million people. Now more than 30 per cent of the world's population live in towns consisting of more than 20,000 people and the number of cities with populations of more than 3 million are shown in Figure 1.2.

   a. How many cities are there with a population of over 3 million?

   b. 'Millionaire' cities are often poor and suffer from many problems including pollution, housing shortages and crime. Make a list of other problems which they may suffer from.

   c. Mexico City is expected to have a population of almost 30 million by the year 2000. What might it be like to live there then?

Figure 1.2
Millionaire cities.

From: *The New Geographical*
Digest (Philip, 1986)

Tokyo is one of the richer 'millionaire' cities.

2.   St Kilda is an island lying 110 miles west of the Scottish mainland. Until the beginning of this century it was inhabited by people who had been almost completely isolated from the rest of the world. In 1930 the island was evacuated because the few remaining islanders could no longer support themselves.

Rural isolation in the Hebrides. Would you like to live here?

The need for St Kilda to establish better communications with the mainland and other islands of the Hebrides did not arise until the community was already set on a downward course. As the islanders grew less able to support themselves and became habituated to outside assistance, as their health deteriorated and famine threatened, contact with the world came to be essential. In the past the remoteness of the island had been an important factor in the survival of the community, but when communications with the mainland improved enough to destroy its independence, though not sufficiently to bring St Kilda into the swim of things, isolation became the chief obstacle to its continued existence.

Charles MacLean, *Island on the Edge of the World*

a. Find St Kilda on a map.
b. In what ways might contact with the outside world have made St Kilda less independent?
c. What kind of things might people in an isolated community want once they had experienced them?
d. Do you think there are any places in the world today where the same kind of events may occur that took place on St Kilda at the beginning of this century?

3.   *The village*

The following extract describes the influence of urbanisation on life in three villages:

> One of them [the villages], on a main road, has accommodated itself. There is a small factory; there are hotels and petrol stations; it is no longer an agricultural village, it has changed its nature. The other two, off the beaten track, have declined in population, and, so we are led to understand, in vitality. In one of them where large-scale farming is typical, a number of villagers go off every day to work in a nearby town. There they – especially the women – acquire urban tastes, an uneasy sense of their not being quite up to them, and a competitive spirit which drives them to display increasing signs of sophistication. The children at eleven plus go off to the town for their schooling and misbehave when they get back. All this has led to a decline in village activities. The third village, composed of smallholders or small-scale farmers, has resisted all change. They are suspicious of education, as something imposed from outside, they are alleged to have refused a bus service, they are deficient in such amenities as water and electricity, in fact they have tried to resist all interference, and social activity is at a low ebb.
>
> W. Sprott, *Human Groups*

Consider which of these villages you would most like to live in and say why.

Sprott wrote *Human Groups* more than thirty years ago.

Table 1.1 *Rates of disorder by standard region per 100,000 population (excluding former Met. County areas and GLC)*

	Incidents	Rate per total population	Rate per population 15–24 years
Yorks and Humber	18	1.20	7.78
South-East	101	1.10	7.21
South-West	40	0.94	2.75
East Anglia	16	0.87	5.92
East Midlands	33	0.87	5.65
West Midlands	18	0.73	4.81
North-West	4	0.18	1.15
North	2	0.14	0.85
Wales	3	0.11	0.72

> Table 1.1 comes from the 1989 Home Office Research Study into the increasing level of disorder in rural areas. What factors during the last thirty years are likely to have increased the effect of 'urbanisation' on village life?
>
> 4. Countries vary in how they define a 'town'. In Denmark a population of 200 is required, in Ghana and Greece a total of 5,000 people is needed. What do you think are the differences between a village, a town and a city?

1.4   POPULATION IN BRITAIN

An explosion in the size of Britain's population took place between 1750 and 1850, when the population almost tripled (from 6.5 million to 18 million). During the next 100 years it more than doubled, but now it has levelled off. We cannot afford to wait 200 years for the population explosion in the Third World to stop, for in the last thirty years the number of people in it has doubled.

The reasons for the population explosion in Britain were:

1. a static birth rate
2. a reduction in infant mortality
3. falling death rate.

These were caused by:

1. improved hygiene (even simple things like using knives and forks)
2. better diet
3. the prevention of epidemics (such as typhoid)
4. preventive medicine (e.g. vaccination against smallpox)
5. increasing medical knowledge (e.g. pasteurisation)
6. the disappearance of plague (brown rats took over from the black rats that carried the plague flea).

The population boom continued in Britain for three main reasons:

1. People were used to the idea that they would have to have several children in order to guarantee support in their old age.
2. Children were an economic asset in agriculture as they could work in the fields. Even in industry they might earn marginally more than was needed for their keep.
3. Methods of birth control were not known, and even when they were publicised, the government opposed them as an expanding population was needed in the factories and for the armed forces.

The birth rate in Britain slowed down as welfare services removed the 'insurance' aspect of children. People got used to the idea that most children would survive and laws regarding education made children an economic liability rather than an asset. Birth control methods became widely known and new methods were introduced. Moreover, new industrial methods required fewer workers and colonial expansion ceased.

In developing countries today much the same process is being followed, but the first **expansion** stage has taken place much more quickly. (Why do you think this is so?) What remains to be seen is whether the **contraction** stage can be equally foreshortened if a catastrophe is to be averted.

---

1. Consider the information in Table 1.2:

Table 1.2 *Population of England and Wales*

Date	Total population	Increase over ten years
1600	4,812,000	
1700	6,045,000	
1750	6,517,000	
1801[1]	8,893,000	
1811	10,165,000	1,272,000
1821	12,000,000	1,835,000
1831	13,897,000	1,897,000
1841	15,914,000	2,017,000
1851	17,928,000	2,014,000
1861	20,066,000	2,138,000
1871	22,712,000	2,646,000
1881	25,974,000	3,262,000
1901	32,528,000	3,277,000 (average)
1961	46,105,000	2,262,800 (average)
1971	48,749,000	2,264,400
1981	49,011,000	262,000
1991	49,194,000[2]	

[1] Figures from 1801 to 1991 are from censuses enumerated in those years.
[2] Provisional figure.

a. Over which ten-year period was the percentage increase in population greatest?
b. Why did the population increase so rapidly between 1801 and 1851?
c. Why did the percentage increase in population decline in the 20th century?

2. Study the population statistics given in Table 1.3:
a. Which country in the table increased its population by the greatest percentage between 1971 and 1981?

Table 1.3 *Population and population structure: selected countries*

	Estimates of mid-year population (millions)			Projections (millions)		Birth rate[1] 1990	Death rate[2] 1990	Population density (per sq km)	
	1971	1981	1989	2000	2010	1990	1990	1960	1989
United Kingdom	55.9	56.4	57.2	59.0	60.0	13.9	11.2	213.7	234.1
Belgium	9.7	9.8	9.9	9.9	9.7	12.4	10.5	298.1	325.4
Denmark	4.9	5.1	5.1	5.2	5.1	12.4	11.9	106.0	119.1
France	51.3	54.2	56.2	57.9	58.8	13.5	9.3	82.8	101.6
Germany[3]	78.4	78.4	78.8			11.3	11.5	202.9	219.6
Greece	8.8	9.7	10.0			9.9	9.2	62.9	75.9
Irish Republic	3.0	3.4	3.5	3.5	3.4	15.1	9.1	40.3	50.1
Italy	54.1	56.5	57.5	57.6	56.4	9.8	9.3	166.0	190.9
Luxembourg	0.3	0.4	0.4	0.4	0.4	13.0	9.9	121.0	145.0
Netherlands	13.2	14.2	14.9	15.9	16.4	13.2	8.6	279.5	362.5
Portugal	8.6	9.9	10.3	10.6	10.8	11.2	9.9	97.4	111.5
Spain	34.2	37.8	38.9	39.4	39.1	10.2	8.6	60.1	77.0
European Community	322.4	335.8	342.7			11.9	10.1	124.8	144.3
China	787.2	1,007.8	1,104.0	1,285.9	1,382.5	21	7		115
India	550.4	683.8	796.6	1,042.5	1,225.3	33	11		242
USSR	245.1	267.7	283.7	307.7	326.4	20	10		13
USA	207.0	229.8	246.3	266.2	281.2	16	9		26
Japan	104.7	117.6	122.6	189.1	131.7	11	6		325

[1] Live births per 1,000 population.
[2] Deaths per 1,000 population.
[3] Figures shown include both the Federal Republic of Germany and the German Democratic Republic.
Source: Social Trends 12, 1982 and 21, 1991.

    b. Which countries in the table had the smallest percentage growth between 1971 and 1989?

    c. Which country/ies in the table is/are:

       i. the most densely populated?

       ii. the most sparsely populated?

    d. Overall, which three countries in the table would you expect to have the greatest problems in dealing with increasing populations?

    e. Is there any evidence that the rate of population increase is slowing down in the developing countries?

3. Select five countries from the table given in question 2, taking no more than two from Europe. Obtain up-to-date population figures for these countries and then draw a graph indicating population trends.

4. Consider the following information:

In 1798 at the start of Britain's population explosion Malthus wrote *An Essay on the Principle of Population*. His 'law of population' was that the human species 'when unchecked, goes on doubling itself every twenty-five years' until restrained by 'vice and misery'.

Some people used Malthus's theory as an excuse to do nothing for the poor as it was felt this would merely mean that more children would survive and make matters worse. Sometimes similar arguments are used today to justify not helping the Third World.

Malthus could not know in 1798 that contraception would reduce population increase; that new areas producing large quantities of food would be developed; that refrigeration and new methods of transport would make food accessible from far-off places. (Can similar new developments occur again?)

Britain supports a population of 229 per square kilometre; Canada only 2 and Brazil only 14.

Fish farming is just developing. New foods based on soya beans and plankton from the sea are being produced.

One pair of rats can have 20 million descendants in three years, while one swarm of locusts can number 1,000 million. Pest control could also greatly increase the world's food resources.

Use the information given above, other information in this book, plus any other information which you can obtain, to make two lists of notes for two different and opposing speeches:

    a. 'Mankind will bring the population explosion under control.'

    b. 'Malthus was right: the world will become over-populated and famine and misery will result.'

The last night of the Proms.

1.5   THE WORLD OUTSIDE – THE FUTURE

> Wider still and wider shall thy bounds be set,
> God who made thee mighty, make thee mightier yet.
>
> A. C. Benson, 1902

Those who sing these words of 'Land of Hope and Glory' on the last night of the Proms do not really expect them to come true; the people of Britain in 1902 certainly did.

The collapse of the mighty British Empire is one symptom of the vast changes that have taken place in the last 100 years. The balance of power has shifted violently several times. New countries have appeared, old ones have disappeared or come under foreign domination. Most of the new countries are former colonies of the Western European nations, and in order to understand some of the problems that we and they have today we need to know something of the background to **colonisation**.

The Industrial Revolution occurred in Europe first. The countries of Europe needed two things in order to develop:

1. raw materials to manufacture goods in the new factories
2. markets in which to sell the goods they made.

It was not in the interests of the colonising powers to manufacture goods in the new colonies as they wanted to maintain employment and circulate the resulting wages in their own countries. So, although rubber was produced in Malaya the tyres were made in the Midlands; chocolate was made not on the west coast of Africa but in York and Birmingham; sugar was refined in London rather than Jamaica.

Where manufacturing industry already existed in the colonies, it was discouraged by taxation. Before colonisation, Britain bought large quantities of cotton cloth from India; later the raw cotton was sent from India to the new mills in Lancashire to be woven. Some of the cloth produced was then sold back to the Indians.

Now the former colonies are developing their own industries and this has meant that some of ours have declined. We no longer have a captive market for our products and must compete with other industrialised nations. Perhaps one of the reasons that we have problems is that we had no real competition in some areas in the past. As the developing nations industrialise, we shall have an increasingly difficult time economically unless we adapt so that we can compete effectively. There are opportunities as well as dangers, for the developing nations will be markets themselves for goods.

A further problem for western nations is that coal is no longer the major fuel. The main oil-producing countries, previously all poor or unimportant (such as Saudi Arabia, Libya and Nigeria) have become increasingly important economically and politically. This major shift in 'the balance of power' occurred in 1973 when OPEC (the Organization of Petroleum Exporting Countries) doubled the price of oil and a few weeks later doubled it again. Fortunately, Britain is almost self-sufficient in oil because of discoveries in the North Sea, although the type of oil produced is not ideal for all purposes and some oil still has to be imported.

If crowding encourages crime, will increasing urbanisation lead to a violent, murderous society where no one can trust their neighbour? Will increased crime lead to harsh laws and a ruthless police force which will destroy our freedom in order to permit our survival? Will democracy prove too weak an instrument to prevent industrial anarchy as our resources are used up and automation replaces manpower in many jobs? Will the poor of the Third World rise and attempt to seize a fairer share of the world's resources as their populations continue to boom and ours remains static? Or will we realise that our welfare depends on other people? Will we then try and get along with 'them' as though they were part of 'us'?

---

1. All my people are lonely, crowds are the most lonely thing of all.

    L. S. Lowry, 1887–1976

    a. What do you think Lowry meant by this statement?
    b. About 30 years ago Sainsbury carried out a survey of suicides in London. He found that there was a much higher suicide rate in the 'bedsitter' areas than in the more settled parts. Why do you think this was so?
    c. The crime rate is much higher in urban areas. Make a list of the reasons why this may be so.

DISCUSSION

1 Between 1985 and the year 2000 it was estimated that the population of the Earth would increase as follows:

Asia	56%
Africa	25%
Latin America	11%
Developed nations	8%

Income ratios between the developed and developing countries were as follows:

1960	11.5 to 1
1980	11.8 to 1

Excluding oil these became:

1960	27.3 to 1
1980	40.6 to 1

Should there be greater equality of wealth and power among the nations of the world?

If so, how could the resources of the world be more fairly allocated?

Are people justified in using violence to improve the quality of their lives?

Might the rich countries share their wealth with the poorer ones?

Is there any possibility of the poorer countries forcing the rich ones to share – if so, how?

Should people aim to live a simpler life and use less resources?

2 Would a new housing estate on the outskirts of town provide a better environment than slum dwellings in a city centre?

Is town life today better than in the past?

3 The 3.5 billion people of the world are spaced very unevenly over the land. Some of the small island nations are the most tightly packed of all. Barbados, an island in the West Indies, has 1,470 people per square mile, and Mauritius, an island in the Indian Ocean, has 1,112 people per square mile. In Japan there are 708 people for every square mile of land. Some of the European countries are very densely populated too: Holland has 932 people per square mile; West Germany has a density of 606 people per square mile; Great Britain has 587 per square mile. The Asian nation of

Bangladesh has one of the highest population densities in the world – 1,300 people per square mile.

Just as population density varies from one country to another, so the density varies within each country. Rural areas have a low population density, while urban areas have a high density. Since the beginning of the Industrial Revolution, the world has seen a steady movement of people from the countryside towards the cities. This movement from country to city occurs when cities can provide jobs, high standards of living, and fine culture. But it also occurs where cities are desperately poor and offer new residents massive unemployment, shanty-town housing, and hardly any education or culture at all. It seems that cities the world over continuously draw people in from the countryside with the hope of jobs, a better life, and the promise of excitement that a city culture can provide.

Statisticians have discovered that densely populated cities produce disproportionately high numbers of divorces, suicides, child abuse cases, mental breakdowns, and violent crimes. Disorders caused by stress, such as ulcers, heart attacks, and high blood pressure, are more common in big cities.

Adapted from C. Jones, S. Gadler and P. Engstrom,
Pollution: The Population Explosion

a. What is meant by 'population density'?
b. Which three countries of those that are mentioned have the highest population density?
c. Why do people move from rural areas into cities despite poor living conditions?
d. What statistical evidence is there to indicate that people are influenced adversely, both physically and mentally, by urban living?

I

World faces old age boom

by GEOFFREY LEAN

B Y the end of the century there will be twice as many people over 60 alive as there were in 1970.

A report about to be published by the United Nations Fund for Population Activities says that numbers in rich countries will have grown by over 50 per cent and in poor countries by over 150 per cent. In both they will have increased by over half as much again as the population as a whole.

The number of over-80s will also double in this period.

The reasons are that people are living longer, and birth rates are falling as the pace of population growth slows down.

In rich countries, 11 of which have reached (or are close to) zero population growth, the rapid increase in the elderly will cause 'manifold social and economic consequences', reports Mr Rafael Salas, the UN joint executive director.

A dwindling proportion of wage-earners will have to look after increasing numbers of the aged. In the United States there are now six wage-earners for every retired person; in 50 years' time there will only be three.

In 1967 there were 10 workers at General Motors (USA) for every company pensioner; now there are only four, and in the 1990s there is only expected to be one.

The proportion of pensioners in Europe will almost double. This change could mean that four times as much will have to be taken from each pay packet to provide for old age.

Governments will need to shift resources from child welfare to caring for the elderly, as the old replace children as their societies' most numerous dependants. They are also likely to change their policies to encourage immigration to swell the workforce.

In the Third World, where life expectancy has been steadily growing and birth rates are now falling substantially, the growing number of the aged 'is likely to place intolerably heavy burdens on the working population'.

From: The Observer, 10 June 1979

a. How many people over the age of 60 will exist in the year 2000?
b. What is meant by the term 'birth rate'?
c. What is meant by 'zero population growth'?
   What are the 'manifold social and economic consequences' of a rapid rise in the elderly:
   i. in rich countries?
   ii. in the Third World?
d. See if you can find out any up-to-date evidence to prove or disprove the likelihood of the estimates given for the year 2000.

2 Here is some information prepared from the parish records of Wath-upon-Dearne, a small mining town in Yorkshire.

	1902	1971	1991	
Average age of death	38	70	70	

	1861	1941	1961	1991
Average age of marriage				
Men	25	27	24	27
Women	23	24	21	23

	1861	1941	1991
Most common occupation			
1.	miner	member of armed forces	No regular pattern. Very few miners.
2.	labourer	miner	Secretarial,
3.	mining deputy	railway worker	professional, service and technology (e.g. computing) jobs now predominate

a. Try and explain the reasons for the changes outlined above.

b. Ask your local vicar whether your group can study your parish records and if you are given permission, prepare a table similar to the one above.

3 If you can, visit a zoo and draw up a report of the ways that particular animals are behaving unnaturally (i.e. differently to the way that you think they would behave in the wild). It would be best in most cases to allocate a particular group of animals to a particular individual – try to make sure the animal allocated suits the temperament of the individual involved!

In your final report try to draw some comparison between the behaviour of your zoo animals and the behaviour of people in towns.

Would you prefer to be an animal in a zoo or the same animal in the wild? Consider the case for and against carefully.

To what extent are human and animal behaviour similar?

4 As the fungus sprouts chaotic from its bed,
so it spread—
Chance-directed, chance-erected, laid and built
On the silt—
Palace, byre, hovel—poverty and pride—
Side by side—
And above the packed and pestilential town
Death looked down.

Rudyard Kipling

This poem about the growth of Calcutta in the 19th century reflects the way that some towns and cities in the UK grew during the Industrial Revolution.

a. Using a particular town or city as an example show how each of the elements listed in the poem is, or is not, reflected in its composition.

b. Do you think that the poem could still reflect the growth of modern towns and cities? If so, in what ways is it still a true reflection? Mention any factors which you think have reduced the poem's validity.

c. From what you have read or seen on television about 'Second' and 'Third' World towns and cities such as Calcutta, say to what extent the poem still has relevance to those urban centres.

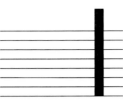

OUTLINE OF AN APPROPRIATE GCSE INVESTIGATION/PROJECT

(For guidance, see 'Coursework for GCSE' on pages ix–xiv.)

Title   An investigation into the existence of a sense of community within a local estate.

Hypothesis   (An assumption that you propose to test as impartially as you can.) There is little sense of community within the area where I live.

Secondary sources   These might include statistics from your local council's annual report; historical references or up-to-date reports from your local library. If you choose this type of project it may be because there has been local publicity and if this is the case references in the local newspapers may provide background material.

Primary sources   **Questionnaire** Postal questionnaires (costly and may not be returned) to prominent local people living on the estate or associated with it. These might include a local pub landlord; a headteacher; a vicar, priest, imam or rabbi.

Interviews   These might include ten people from each of a number of groups representing differing ages, for example 11–21 (youth club); 22–40 (mums and toddlers); 59+ (OAP dinner club).
  Questions might relate to such issues as: length of residence; number of contacts per week with relatives and/or neighbours; victimisation (crime or racial); vandalism; facilities (e.g. leisure); the extent to which people work outside the area; whether people enjoy living on the estate.

In analysing your results consider how **representative** your selection, or **sample**, was (i.e. did it represent as nearly as possible the general population of the area, i.e. the same proportion of males and females; young and old; ethnic groups; middle class and working class, etc.)? Did you feel your questions were answered honestly?

GCSE QUESTION

Note: GCSE questions often require answers using information from interrelated themes. This one is mainly, but not exclusively, concerned with population.

Village life

It isn't like it was here. When you've known a place to be bustling with people, it's sad to see it so lifeless. I remember when there was a blacksmith over there in the Square, and there were plenty of jobs on the farms. We all worked on the land then, but not any more. All this modern machinery has done away with a lot of the jobs, and people go off to the towns to look for work instead. You can't blame them either; there's nothing to keep them here any more.

Source: interview – old man

I don't know why people think it's difficult living in a village. I drive into town once a month and load up the freezer. If I do run out, there's always the village shop.

Source: interview – young mother

I love the village atmosphere, but I commute to Liverpool to work each day. I'd never find a job round here, and salaries are so low anyway, so I have to work in the city.

Source: interview – young father

(*i*)   Give *one* reason why people are moving to the towns from the village. (1)

(*ii*)   Give *two* reasons why people commute from the village to work. (2)

(*iii*) What is the role of the village shop, and why is it not the main shopping point for the new village dwellers? (3)

(*iv*)   How do you think that the village way of life differs from that of the town? (6)

(*v*)   How far do the interviews above provide reliable evidence of a decline in village life? (8)

SELF-TEST QUESTIONS

(Answers on page 287)

1. a. How many cities with a population of more than one million were there 250 years ago?
    b. Approximately how many such cities are there today?

2. Why did the population of the world only grow slowly until the 18th century?

3. What does 'gregarious' mean?

4. What is meant by the term 'peer group'?

5. Give three reasons why early man may have lived in tribes.

6. Give three examples of each of the following: a 'primary' industry; a 'secondary' industry; a 'tertiary' industry.

7. What is an 'urban community'?

8. Why did Desmond Morris suggest that it is wrong to call our cities 'concrete jungles'?

9. What is meant by the term 'expectation of life'?

10. What three linked factors cause a 'population explosion'?

UNIT 2 FAMILY LIFE

An extended family in Britain comes together for a 'rite of passage'.

2.1 WHAT A FAMILY IS

As far back as we can trace in our history the family has been the most important group in human society. It still is and probably always will be. The family group may not be one that we would immediately recognise – father, mother, two or three children and, perhaps, a grandparent or two – but it will usually consist of two or more adult people who have a steady relationship with each other that enables them to live together while their children are young.

There is a growing number of one-parent* families, however, in Britain today (estimated rising from 8 per cent of all families with dependent children in 1971 to 20 per cent in 1991). These may be the result of divorce, the death of one parent or births outside marriage. Can you see any advantages in one-parent families?

The family system will vary in some societies and usually only one kind of system is **sanctioned** (approved) in any particular society. The society makes rules stating which people are allowed to live together and if a man and woman wish to set up home together there is usually some sort of ceremony to show that they are obeying the rules. We call this marriage.

* Sometimes the alternative terms 'single-parent' or 'lone-parent' are used.

A one-parent family from south London.

Taboo

Marriage is the system by which a society recognises the right of a man and a woman to live together and have a stable sexual relationship. It is a system that tries to make sure that certain people do not mate. Prohibitions of this kind are called **taboos**. The crime committed if people who are forbidden to marry because of a close family relationship have sexual relations is **incest**.

Incest taboos have the following consequences:

1. They prevent competition for marriage partners among those closely related and help produce stability and harmony in the family.
2. In traditional society they encourage links with other groups, thus increasing the number of potential allies in time of trouble and also establishing trade links.
3. They prevent possible **genetic** damage that may result from inbreeding (whether primitive man realised this is debatable).

The rule that people must marry outside their own kinship group is called **exogamy**. Marriage to close relations (e.g. first cousins) is sometimes encouraged so as to restrict ownership or power. This kind of marriage is called **endogamy**.

---

1. The Marriage Act 1949 prevents a man from marrying his:
   mother, stepmother, mother-in-law
   mother's sister, father's sister
   adoptive mother

> sister, half-sister
> daughter
> sister's daughter, brother's daughter
> granddaughter, step-granddaughter,
> granddaughter-in-law
> a. Find out who else a man is forbidden to marry.
> b. Now work out whom a *woman* must not marry.
>
> 2. Look up 'households' in the index of a copy of *Regional Trends* (produced annually by the Central Statistical Office), which should be available in your school or college library.* You will see a reference to 'lone parent' and a table number; refer to this table and see which area has the largest percentage of 'lone-parent families' and which has the smallest. Compare this with the figure for your own area. Consider some reasons which might account for the statistics that you have obtained.

2.2 WHY FAMILIES?

A marriage by itself does not make a family. The essential feature of a family is children. The basic reason for having families is to enable children to grow up ready to play their parts in their community. **Socialisation** is the term used to describe the process by which we learn the values of the group to which we belong and the role that we are expected to play in that group. Most people think that it would be difficult to arrange for new members of a society to be reared without a family system, and governments usually do what they can to encourage stable family life.

The Israeli kibbutz, however, aims to restrict family life: meals are eaten in a common dining hall of the settlement and the children sleep together, separately from their parents. But even here arrangements are made for parents and children to have some social contact, and some kibbutz women are trying to re-establish the traditional pattern of motherhood.

Many experts think that young children need the continuous attention of their mother – or 'mother substitute', who could be a man – if they are to grow up to be normal members of the society. This view is contested by others who believe that the importance of this continuous relationship has been exaggerated. However, there is no doubt that children do benefit from a degree of stability in their early years and an opportunity to establish a close relationship with an adult person. The child's need for close personal attention means that it is usually better for children to be brought up in a family rather than in institutions with large numbers of other children. This means that

---

* If not, try your public library.

a sharing of responsibilities between father and mother has usually developed in most societies. It would be difficult and unfair for a woman to be expected to have the sole responsibility for caring for herself and her child, and most societies have thus made rules which involve the man in some kind of contract to keep both their children and the mother or mothers of their children.

The family is not mainly concerned with sexual relationships. This can be illustrated by one study which found that out of 250 societies, 65 allowed unmarried and unrelated people complete sexual freedom. It is unlikely that people who marry in societies where complete sexual freedom outside marriage is approved would marry mainly for sexual reasons. One writer, Malinowski, said: 'Marriage is the licensing not of sexual intercourse but of parenthood.'

1. Some animals and birds (for example the rhinoceros, white whale, orang-utan, eagle and swan) instinctively desire to stay with the same mate. Do you think this is also true of people?

2. Study the following passage:

It must never be forgotten that even the bad parent who neglects her [sic] child is nonetheless providing much for him [sic]. Except in the worst cases, she is giving him food and shelter, comforting him in distress, teaching him simple skills, and above all is providing him with that continuity of human care on which his sense of security rests. He may be ill-fed and ill-sheltered, he may be very dirty and suffering from disease, he may be ill-treated, but, unless his parents have wholly rejected him, he is secure in the knowledge that there is someone to whom he is of value and who will strive, even though inadequately, to provide for him until such time as he can fend for himself. It is against this background that the reason why children thrive better in bad homes than in good institutions, and why children with bad parents are, apparently unreasonably, so attached to them, can be understood. Those responsible for institutions have sometimes been unwilling to acknowledge that children are often better off in even quite bad homes, which is the conclusion of most experienced social workers with mental health training and is borne out by evidence already quoted. It will be remembered that when a group of children, aged between one and four years, who had spent their lives in institutions were compared with a similar group who lived in their, often very unsatisfactory, homes and spent the day in day-nurseries because their mothers were working, the difference in development was much in favour of the children living at home and attending day-nursery. In another follow-up study, comparing the social adjustment in adult life of children who spent five years or more of their childhood in institutions with others who had spent the same years at home (in 80 per cent of cases in bad homes), the results were clearly in favour of the bad homes, those growing up to be socially incapable (this included a greater tendency towards crime, lower intelligence and poorer speech) being only about half (18 per cent) of those from institutions (34.5 per cent).

John Bowlby, *Child Care and the Growth of Love*

   a. Why do you think institutions may be less desirable than bad homes?

   b. Many children who grew up in institutions do not suffer the consequences stated. Why do you think this is so?

3. *Social Trends* is produced by the Central Statistical Office each year, although the content sometimes varies. You should be able to discover the answer to either (a) or (b) below from a copy in your school or college library.

   a. Look up 'cohabitation' in the index (this is defined as living together as husband and wife without having legally married). In 1981 the proportion of women aged between 18 and 49 who were cohabiting was 3.3 per cent.

     (i) Is cohabitation increasing or decreasing?

     (ii) Which age group is most likely to cohabit?

     (iii) Consider some reasons for the statistics and trends you have discovered.

   b. The number of children cared for in 'institutions' has altered considerably since the extract by John Bowlby was written in 1951. Look up 'children in local authority care' in the index of *Social Trends*.

     (i) Are the numbers of children 'in care' increasing or decreasing?

     (ii) Roughly how many children were in an institutional setting (e.g. a community home) compared with those in a family setting (e.g. with relatives or foster parents)?

     (iii) Give some reasons which you think may account for the trend you have indicated in (i) above.

2.3 DIFFERENT SORTS OF FAMILY

About 75 per cent of all the people in the world live in societies where it is regarded as right that a man or a woman should have only one marriage partner at a time. This practice is called **monogamy**. However, in other societies it is acceptable for more than two people to enter into a marriage; this is called **polygamy** (do not confuse this with **bigamy**, which is when a man marries more than one woman or a woman more than one man and the law prohibits such behaviour).

Polygamy can take two forms:

1. **Polygyny**:   one man married to more than one woman.
2. **Polyandry**:   one woman married to more than one man.

Polygyny is much more common than polyandry and exists in many countries of the Middle East and Africa, particularly in Muslim countries. It is often a privilege of the wealthy, as a payment (dowry) must often be made to the father of each bride. Polygyny assists a man to become richer because his wives themselves become his workforce. Marriage to more than one woman also allows alliances to be formed between families so that they gain power and influence.

Polyandry may also assist the economy of a country. For example, in Tibet, among the Sherpas and other groups in the high Himalayas where brothers marry a single wife, it limits the number of children who have to share limited resources.

Polyandry was common among some Innuit groups.

Economic circumstances are probably most important in the development of a particular family system, but there are sexual and social reasons as well.

The family system might have difficulty in surviving if there were large numbers of unmarried women or men, and the sort of family system that exists may be influenced by whether there are more men or women in the society. Generally more boys are born than girls, but boys are weaker at birth (and in many ways remain so). In a community where standards of hygiene are low and a lot of babies die, one finds that more male babies die; this outweighs the greater male birth rate and increases the number of females. In the past this female surplus was increased because more men than women were killed in war, hunting and accidents.

As countries become 'westernised' and industry develops, polygamy tends to disappear, not because of sudden changes in morality, but because improved hygiene lowers the infant mortality rate. At the same time it is no longer an economic advantage to have lots of wives.

1. In 1650 the city of Nuremberg in Germany decreed that every man should marry two women in order to increase the population which had been greatly reduced by the Thirty Years War.

   Would you be prepared to accept polyandry if the proportion of men in our society continues to increase (in 1991 there were about 6,200,000 males and 5,900,000 females between the ages of 16 and 29)?

2. Do you think there are advantages in having marriages arranged by parents as happens in some countries?

3. The General Household Survey is carried out by the Office of Population, Censuses and Surveys and is based on a representative sample of 20,000 people across the country. It is produced every year and is a good source of **unbiased** facts, that is facts which have not been selected to prove a particular point. These may provide a comparison for your own more localised survey. When you carry out your survey you will need to:

   • make a list of questions (the questionnaire). These may be **closed** (asking respondents to tick the appropriate box) or **open** (asking respondents to write answers using their own words). (See pages 86 and 121 for more details on open and closed questions.)
   • test the questionnaire by using a pilot survey. Ask a few people to answer your questions to make sure they are easy to understand and to reply to. Then rewrite the questions if necessary.
   • select the people to be questioned. These need to be as representative of your target as possible. Usually you would use a **sampling frame**, that is, a group from which you propose to select your sample. A major sociological study might use the electoral roll, or doctors' lists of patients. You might use college or school registers or youth club membership lists. You select people at random, which does not mean haphazardly: **random sampling** means that you do not choose individuals, but take every fifth, tenth, etc., person on the list regardless of who they are.

Look at Figure 2.1, which has information from the General Household* Surveys of 1991 and 1961.

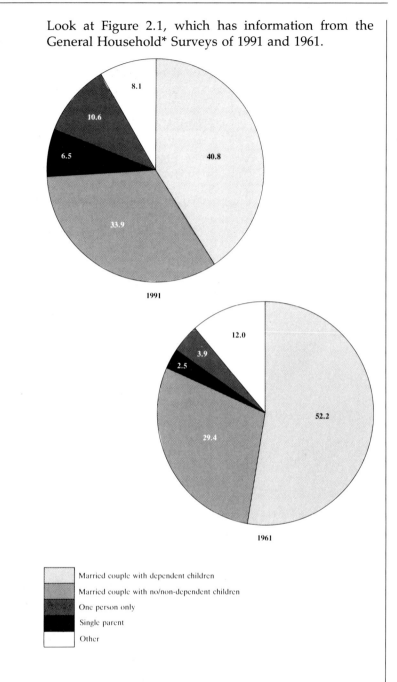

Figure 2.1
People in Britain by type of household, 1991 and 1961 (%).

This type of chart is called a **pie chart** because it is round and broken into slices like a pie.

a. Compare the information given for 1961 with that given for 1991.
b. Suggest some reasons for the changes that you identify.

* A *household* is a single person or a group of people who have the address as their only or main residence and who either share one meal a day or share the living accommodation.

2.4   THE CHANGING FAMILY PATTERN

The family pattern has been changing in Great Britain. In the past people did not tend to move from their birthplace and tended to go into the same sort of occupation as their parents. They had to look after relations if they were old or ill and they needed relations themselves who would be near by to help them out if they became sick or unemployed. Mothers needed help from their own mothers or sisters in looking after large families. In a hostile world people felt safest with their own relations near them. This large family unit of parents, children, grandparents, uncles, aunts and cousins is called the **extended family**.

Everyone has an extended family, but they may not keep in touch with the members of it, or may only meet some of its members occasionally. However, the extended family is still an important feature of life in many long-established communities, particularly in the North of England and among ethnic groups that have settled in Britain recently, especially Indian and Pakistani families. There is a growing tendency, however, for the more usual family type to consist of just a husband, wife and their own children living together with no relations near by. This family type is called the **nuclear family**.

The reasons for the gradual disappearance of the extended family as the operating family unit and its replacement by the nuclear family are:

1. Improved educational opportunities which mean that new job prospects exist and these often require a move to a new area.

A nuclear family today.

2. Transport is simple and greater travel opportunities make a move less frightening.
3. New housing estates often attract young families away from traditional areas.
4. Improved welfare facilities mean we have to depend less on our relatives.
5. Family planning and other factors listed below have resulted in smaller, more manageable families.

The modern 'model' family of television advertising is a husband, a wife and two children. There are several reasons why this is now the typical family:

1. People can regulate the size of their family easily if they wish.
2. The size of available housing (modern homes are on average larger than the average of a century ago, but people no longer expect to share bedrooms – or even beds – to the same extent).
3. Many women wish to continue in employment.
4. As the school-leaving age rises children cannot be sent out to work early to add to the family income.
5. The rising expectations of a good standard of living, which includes such things as living space and holidays.
6. The influence of some religious objections to birth control has declined.
7. Married couples now often live away from their extended family and so there is no one available to 'baby-sit' and generally help out.
8. Improved standards of health mean that it is no longer necessary to have many children in order that a few may survive.

There are advantages in the change from the extended family to the nuclear, but try and think of the disadvantages too. For the old? For the young?

Since we now expect more from marriage and because of what some people consider is the increased stress of modern family life, marriages fail more often than they did in the past. People are also living a great deal longer, so they have to be able to put up with each other for a longer period. Shorter working hours and longer holidays also increase the amount of time married couples spend together and increase the possibility of friction.

Certainly divorce has become increasingly easy. In 1857 a divorce was only possible by means of a private Act of Parliament; by 1971, following the Divorce Reform Act 1969, in England and Wales (1977 in Scotland) anyone could obtain a divorce providing they could prove that their marriage had broken down to a point at which it would be impossible to rebuild the relationship. It was thus no longer necessary to prove desertion, or cruelty, or adultery, although these could be used as evidence of marriage breakdown. Increasingly generous legal aid and now the availability of 'divorce by post' without any need to appear in court have both contributed to a rising divorce rate.

Some see more divorce as a sign of the breakdown of our present family system, but between two-thirds and three-quarters of all divorcees remarry, so there does not appear to be a general movement away from the idea of marriage and family.

1. The divorce rate is usually stated 'per 1,000 existing marriages' as in Table 2.1. However, different methods of calculation are sometimes used, for example the proportion of divorces to marriages in a given year.

Table 2.1 *Marriage and divorce: EC comparison*

	Marriages per 1,000 eligible population		Divorces per 1,000 existing marriages			
	1981	1989	1961	1971	1981	1989
United Kingdom	7.1	6.8	2.1	5.8	11.9	12.6
Belgium	6.5	6.4	2.0	2.8	6.1	8.6
Denmark	5.0	6.0	5.7	10.8	12.1	13.6
France	5.8	5.0	2.9	3.5	6.8	8.4
Germany (Fed. Rep.)	5.8	6.4	3.6	5.2	7.2	8.7
Greece	7.3	6.4	1.5	1.7	2.5	
Irish Republic	6.0	5.0	0.0	0.0	0.0	0.0
Italy	5.6	5.4		2.5	0.9	2.1
Luxembourg	5.5	5.8	2.0	2.6	5.9	10.0
Netherlands	6.0	6.1	2.2	3.7	8.3	8.1
Portugal	7.7	7.1	0.4	0.3	2.8	–
Spain	5.4	5.6	–	–	1.1	–

Source: Social Trends 22, HMSO, 1992; Social Trends 18, HMSO, 1988.

a. Which country had the greatest proportionate increase in divorce between 1961 and 1981?
b. Why did the number of divorces increase so much in the UK between 1961 and 1971?
c. Why do you think the divorce rate is so low in Italy, Portugal, Spain and Greece?

2. Consider the following source material:

Table 2.2 *Percentage of women cohabiting: by age*

Great Britain	Percentages			
	1979	1981	1986	1988
Age group (*percentage*)				
18–24 years	4.5	5.6	9.0	12.4
25–49 years	2.2	2.6	4.6	6.3
18–49 years	2.7	3.3	5.5	7.7

Source: Social Trends 21, HMSO, 1991.

'Cohabitation' is defined as living together as husband and wife without having married legally. Cohabitation has increased in Great Britain in recent years; ... Cohabitation is more prevalent at ages 25–29 years for men than at other ages (13 per cent were cohabiting in 1988) and 20–24 years for women (15 per cent).

ibid.

Table 2.3 *Marriages: by type*

United Kingdom	Thousands and percentages			
	1961	1971	1981	1989
Marriages (*thousands*)				
First marriage for both partners	340	369	263	252
First marriage for one partner only				
Bachelor/divorced woman	11	21	32	35
Bachelor/widow	5	4	3	2
Spinster/divorced man	12	24	36	38
Spinster/widower	8	5	3	2
Second (or subsequent) marriage for both partners				
Both divorced	5	17	44	50
Both widowed	10	10	7	5
Divorced man/widow	3	4	5	4
Divorced woman/widower	3	5	5	5
Total marriages	397	459	398	392
Remarriages[1] as a percentage of all marriages	14	20	34	36
Remarriages[1] of those divorced as a percentage of all marriages	9	15	31	34

[1] Remarriage for one or both partners.
Source: Social Trends 22, HMSO, 1992.

Marriages where one or both partners have been divorced previously are more likely to end in divorce than those of people of similar ages who are marrying for the first time; at 1980–1981 divorce rates, the estimated chance that the marriage of a divorced man would again end in divorce is one and a half times that of a single man who marries at the same age. Similarly, a divorced woman who remarries is approximately twice as likely to divorce as a single woman who marries at the same age.

Combined results from the 1984 and 1985 GHS indicate that 15 per cent of all non-married women between the ages of 18 and 49 were cohabiting. Divorced and separated women were the most likely to be cohabiting amongst the non-married, and widows were the least likely. Over a third of single mothers with dependent children were cohabiting, compared to a tenth of single women with no dependent children.

Social Trends 15, HMSO, 1985

a. Using only the source material provided:
  (i) What kind of woman is likely to represent a substantial proportion of those co-habiting in the 18–24 age range?
  (ii) Which category of woman is most unlikely to be co-habiting?
b. Using the same source material:
  (i) Which category of marriage increased by the greatest proportion between 1961 and 1989?
  (ii) As a result of the information in (i) what would you expect to happen to the divorce rates?

3. Look at Table 2.4.

Table 2.4 *First marriages: by sex and age at marriage*

Great Britain	Marriages per 1,000 eligible population (i.e. per 1,000 women aged between 16 and 19, etc.)			
	1961	1971	1981	1989
Spinsters aged				
16–19 years	77	92	42	18
20–24 years	259	247	142	92
25–29 years	166	168	120	111
30–34 years	72	75	66	77
35–44 years	29	30	28	31
Bachelors aged				
16–19 years	17	27	12	5
20–24 years	159	169	96	55
25–29 years	185	169	121	98
30–34 years	91	85	70	80
35–44 years	39	34	31	33

Source: adapted from *Social Trends 21*, HMSO, 1991.

a. In 1989, what percentage of spinsters married before they were 25? What is the comparative figure for men?
b. Try and explain why women, on average, marry earlier than men.

4. Consider again the information contained in Figure 2.1.
a. What kind of people might be included in the 'one person only' category?
b. Give some reasons why the 'one person only' category has increased most since 1961.
c. Why has the percentage of households consisting of a married couple with dependent children fallen during the period shown?

2.5   FAMILY ROLES

We use the term **sex** to denote physical differences between males and females; **gender** is used to describe differences in behaviour, attitudes or roles. There appears to have been marked changes in gender behaviour over the last 100 years.

Although the mother of the modern nuclear family rears her family in a far shorter time than was usually the case in her grandmother's day, many pressures on her have increased. Families which in the past may have had a maid, a cook, a chauffeur and a governess now may have the mother taking on all these functions or roles. In working-class families the mother may be cut off from the companionship and help of her own mother and her other relatives. Both kinds of mother are often marooned at home with their babies while their husband is at work. The modern mum will probably be spending some time at work once the children are old enough to go to school. Indeed, in 1978, for the first time, more than 50 per cent of all married women in Great Britain had a job outside the home; this figure rose to 59 per cent by 1985 (27 per cent full-time and 32 per cent part-time). Increasingly, even women with children under five are working (27 per cent in 1984, 40 per cent in 1989).

The father's role has also changed dramatically as he is becoming much more home-centred. The fierce Victorian father of popular imagination is becoming a thing of the past, and the modern dad is more likely to be in the kitchen or changing the babies' nappies than wielding his belt at his children or dominating his cowering wife. The father in a family has an important part to play in the rearing of the children and a recent study shows that in the United States the father

Relationships between fathers and children are changing.

on average takes part in more activities with his sons than his wife does. The increasing importance of the father in the home, as hours of work lessen and factors like television encourage men to stay at home more, is just one change that is taking place in British families.

In the modern family both husband and wife are much more important to each other as individuals than before and this increases the stress on them. They are more likely to spend most of their leisure time together, take an equal part in disciplining the children, deciding family finances and looking after the home. Children, too, are more likely to be involved in decision making, but are more likely to be dependent on their parents for a longer period.

Some terms used by sociologists to describe families are:

- **Patriarchy**: a group (e.g. a family or society) which is ruled by a man, for example the father of a family.
- **Matriarchy**: a group ruled by a woman.
- **Egalitarian, companionate** and **symmetrical** are terms used to denote a family pattern in which husband and wife appear to be more equal, to be companions as well as spouses, and to have similar roles.
- **Segregated** is used to describe a pattern in which husband and wife have clearly separate roles, perhaps spending most of their leisure time with friends or relatives of the same sex.

---

1. *The Victorian family*

Read this extract and then answer the questions that follow.

There is a persistent image of Victorian family life as stable, moral and responsible, as all the things which today's families are supposed not to be. There is also a long tradition of believing that things would be much better if only we could go back to the past.

But what was Victorian family life really like? How different was it in reality from today's? Could we return to it, and if so would we really be better off? What lessons in understanding our own society can the Victorian family offer us?

We live today in an age where more than one couple in four can expect their marriages to be broken by divorce within 20 years of marriage. During the 1970s well over one million dependent children were affected by the divorce of their parents. But the Victorians, too, had problems of marital disruption and of single-parent families. In the 1851 census, 18 per cent of all households containing children and a household head who was aged less than 65, were single-parent households. This compares with 9 per cent in 1981.

We do not know how many marriages were broken by desertion or separation in the past, though contemporary comment suggests that the numbers were not small. What we do know is that, of couples who married at the average age in the 1860s, around one in three had their marriage broken by death within 20 years. Their figure is remarkably close to the death-plus-divorce expectations of couples marrying today. The chances that a child would experience a broken home were higher right up to the end of the 19th century than they were during the 1970s. Broken families on our present scale are not new. But what we do lack today for people divorcing are the socially supportive rituals and institutions which relieved at least some of the tensions and misery of family break-up in the past.

Victorian sexual morality was rather different from the image which seems to be held by some of the moralists in our own society. Prostitution was widespread, some of it highly organised (including a flourishing trade in children), much of it a source of supplementary income for ill-paid or out-of-work milliners, dressmakers and domestic servants. Their clients came from all classes, but they included many superficially respectable heads of upper middle-class families. Stories even persisted throughout the 19th century that the Edinburgh brothels were at their busiest during the week that Church of Scotland gathered in Edinburgh for its annual general assembly.

The 'double standard' of Victorian sexual morality was notorious, and it was reinforced by the sexual frustrations imposed upon so many marriage beds by the ignorance and prudery in which most middle-class girls were brought up. Those who wish to return to Victorian standards of 'ignorance' in the upbringing of girls would do well to read some autobiographies first.

Among the mass of the population, however, such inhibitions were less present. Illegitimacy was by no means rare. In the early 19th century, more than half of all first births were conceived out of wedlock, a figure which fell only slowly over the early part of the century. In the 1850s, on average, more than 6 per cent of all births in England, and more than 8 per cent in Scotland, were illegitimate (compare this with 8.4 per cent for England and Wales in 1971, and 11.8 per cent in 1980) ... Whatever the problems of sexual morality in our own society, we should not fool ourselves that the Victorians had the question solved.

What about the control exercised by the family over its members, and care and affection between generations? The first thing to bear in mind is the early ages at which many children used to leave home. Half of all adolescents left by the age of 16 to go into service, lodgings or apprenticeships....

Many Victorian parents clearly loved their children and did everything they could to ease the suffering that was often their lot in life. But you get a strong impression from contemporary accounts that wife-beating, family neglect and brutality towards children were more frequent in Victorian Britain than they are today. One factor must have been the enormous quantities of alcohol drunk, especially by men (peaking in the 1870s at an *average* of something like eleven pints of beer and one-third of a pint of spirits per adult male per week). Among the middle classes there is strong autobiographical evidence to suggest that many felt a remoteness and fear of their fathers which inhibited any real affection for the whole of their lives.

Nor should we think that the Victorians had any workable family-based answer as to how to care for the elderly. Despite the popular image of Victorian children listening to stories at their grandmother's knee, three-generation households were surprisingly rare in the past. In 1851, 20 per cent of Scots aged 65 and over lived apart from any relative (the same percentage as in Britain in 1962); only 16 per cent lived with a married child, again the same as in Britain in 1962. In spite of all the attempts by late Victorian administrators to pass the support of the aged onto the family, the Poor Law continued to provide the normal source of financial support for the aged (as it had right back into the 18th century).

Michael Andersen, *New Society*, 1983

a. According to the source material were there more one-parent families in 1851 or 1981?
b. In the early 1800s what percentage of first births were conceived outside marriage?
c. What percentage of Scots aged over 65 lived with a married child in 1851?
d. What evidence does the author present which suggests that the family in Victorian days was not superior to the family of today?
e. Now obtain up-to-date statistics to compare with those given, for example the corresponding figure for single-parent families in the 1991 census; the illegitimacy rate (look up 'Births – outside marriage' in the index of *Social Trends*).

2.   *Group exercise*

The questionnaire on pages 44–5 is intended to try to establish whether a change is occurring in traditional gender attitudes.

First discuss the questions and make any alterations you think appropriate.

Try to identify 100 people of differing ages, gender and occupation. If each member of your group is allocated a different specific target, for example five women between the ages of 20 and 30 divided roughly into working-class and middle-class occupations, you will between you have the beginning of a crude **stratified sample**. This is a sample which is drawn in correct proportion from each identifiable section within the group being studied. For example, if 13 per cent of the group being studied were from ethnic minorities and 20 per cent were under 18, the same percentage figure for each stratum would apply in the sample group as well.

Collect all your answers and try to express them in percentage terms to see whether different views are held by men and women, middle-class and working-class people, young and older people.

Note: You are trying to find out what people *really* think, not what they think will please or shock you. Good interviewers will:

- introduce themselves and what they are trying to do but will express no opinion themselves
- be sensitive in handling their interviewees but be prepared to probe deeply as necessary
- be careful of non-verbal communication that might suggest a particular response, for example badges, extreme forms of dress
- not express approval or disapproval of responses, that is be 'non-judgemental'.

Although GCSE examination groups encourage group projects, those for assessment must be written up individually.

Questionnaire to establish whether a change is occurring in traditional gender attitudes

Age .... Sex .... Occupation ....

1. Do you think the saying 'a woman's place is in the home' still stands?

    YES   NO

2. In your family do the male members help with everyday household chores automatically or do they need to be told/asked to do so?

    YES   NO   DON'T DO THEM

3. If you have had children did you have a preference for a girl or a boy before the birth of your first child? (If you have not had a child would you prefer a girl or boy?)

    GIRL   BOY   NO PREFERENCES

4. In a partnership would/do you expect the male partner to take an active role in looking after the baby (e.g. cleaning/changing nappies)?

    YES   NO

5. In a partnership would you expect a male or female member to stay in if you both wanted to go out and could not get a babysitter?

    MALE   FEMALE   NEITHER

6. If both husband and wife go out to work should both share all the housework?

        YES   NO

7. If the female member of a partnership could earn more than the male member should they swap roles (e.g. the male to be the househusband)?

        YES   NO

8. Do you think the 'do-it-yourself' tasks in the home (e.g. decorating) should be mainly the job of the male or female or either?

        MALE   FEMALE   EITHER

9. Do you think that women should be compelled or encouraged not to work after the birth of a child?

        YES   NO

10. Do you prefer to have a man or woman in positions of authority (e.g. Prime Minister, regardless of politics)?

        MALE   FEMALE   NO PREFERENCES

2.6   YOUNG PEOPLE IN THE FAMILY

Although parents may seem to have less power than in the past they may in fact have greater influence than ever before over their children.

Children are less likely to play outdoors as the danger from traffic increases; trips in the family car or caravan are becoming common; high-rise flats make coming in and out of the home tiresome; examination pressure on more and more young people increases the amount of time many have to spend on homework; and television encourages children to stay at home.

The home, and therefore the parents, seem to be becoming more and more important to the child. Certainly parents now have more time to talk to their children, show affection and take them out. Argument in many homes seems to be replacing physical punishment as a way of solving problems. The differences in outlook between parents and children are often stressed and there is said to be a 'generation gap'; however, parents and children may well have more in common than such views would suppose.

In 1988 the views and approach to life (**attitudes**) of young people in Manchester were studied by Murray and Thompson (81-item questionnaire, 2,061 respondents). This survey found that the attitudes of most young people to their parents, leaders and police was a positive one.

This survey confirmed the findings of earlier reports such as the 1984 survey of family life carried out by the National Council for

Voluntary Organisations, 'Ask the Family', which found that children were better behaved than ever before. In the same year a report *Young People in the Eighties* (Department of Education) found the majority of teenagers to be friendly, responsible, happy and helpful – most spent the majority of their spare time at home or in friends' homes, listening to music or watching TV.

Group project

As a group, carry out a survey similar to the one outlined below. This survey was published in 1976 and was carried out when the respondents were 16 years old. It found that:

- one-third smoked (only 6 per cent up to ten cigarettes a day)
- half had had an alcoholic drink in the week prior to interview (only 20 per cent of these in a public house)
- half had occasionally played truant from school (only 8 per cent were hard-core truants)
- two-thirds gave watching TV as their main spare-time activity (many claimed they would like more opportunity of doing voluntary work out of school hours)
- half would have liked to have a job that helped others
- most got on well with their parents
- only 3 per cent were opposed to marriage
- most would like to marry when between 20 and 25 years old
- most would like to have two children
- 90 per cent lived in a house or bungalow (50 per cent owner-occupied)
- two-thirds had a family car
- half had a telephone
- two-fifths had colour television
- 2 per cent had no bathroom
- 3 per cent had no lavatory
- 2 per cent had no hot water supply
- 39 per cent did not have their own bedroom
- 8 per cent had to share a bed
- the main reason for rows with parents were:
  1. dress or hairstyle (11 per cent often, 36 per cent occasionally)
  2. time of coming in at night (8 per cent)
  3. not doing homework
- slightly more got on best with their mother
- two-thirds of those with a brother or sister quarrelled frequently with them.

This survey was based on 14,000 young people born between 3 and 9 March 1958, and is part of a **longitudinal** survey – one carried out over a period of time, useful for tracing development or change. It was a nationwide survey organised by the National Children's

Bureau and it surveyed the same group of people at various ages. It is more likely to be **representative** of 16-year-olds then than the much smaller selection or **sample** of young people that you and your group will be able to interview. However, it will be interesting to compare your findings with these much earlier ones.

Draw up a questionnaire to get similar information to that obtained in the NCB survey. Most of the factual questions are straightforward and require 'Yes'/'No' answers. However, in phrasing your questions on 'reason for rows' and 'who you get on best with' be careful not to suggest an answer by the way you phrase your question.

Try to ask as many people as possible but ask multiples of 10, 20, 50, 100, etc. in total so that you can convert your group's responses to percentages (so many out of every hundred) easily.

2 DISCUSSION

1

i. The proportion of children born to an unmarried mother increased from 6 per cent in 1961 to 28 per cent in 1990.

ii. As a percentage of all births, the number of illegitimate births registered by both parents was 3.8 per cent in 1971 rising to 20 per cent in 1990. There was an increase in the proportion of illegitimate births registered by both parents.

iii. Wives of non-manual workers tend to wait longer after marriage before having their first baby than wives of manual workers do, although the interval between marriage and first live births has increased for both.

iv. The total number of legal abortions increased from 53,000 in 1969 to 154,000 in 1990. The percentage of those involving married women decreased from 47 per cent to 25 per cent.

    a. Discuss the reasons that might account for the facts given in items (i) to (iv) above.

    b. Draw a bar chart to illustrate (i) above.

    c. Draw two pie charts to illustrate (ii) above.

2 In 1960 5 per cent of all births in the United Kingdom were to an unmarried mother. In 1990 28 per cent of all births were outside marriage. In Sweden the comparable figure is over 50 per cent and in Greece only 2 per cent.

    a. Do you think people should have children before they get married?

    b. Do you support the idea of trial marriages?

2 ADDITIONAL ASSIGNMENTS AND INVESTIGATIONS

1 Try and establish what proportion of your group belongs to a family that operates mainly as an extended family and what proportion is normally only in contact with their nuclear family. Clearly the dividing line is indistinct, but a suggested criterion is to regard members of an operating extended family as those that see two relatives other than mother, father and siblings on average once a week or more, *or* as those that have a close relative other than the above living with them. You may, of course, disagree with this criterion and establish your own for your own group.

2 Carry out a simple survey of your own group and calculate what proportion of the television programmes they have watched in the past week have been about families. Why do you think many people enjoy watching programmes that have family life as a major part of their theme?

3 Describe the advantages and disadvantages gained or suffered by a family where the mother goes out to work. (Check what the textbooks say and then discover the actual views of some families with working mothers.)

4 Find out what you can about the following organisations:

- Gingerbread, 35 Wellington Street, London WC2E 7BN
- National Children's Bureau, 8 Wakely Street, London EC1V 7QE
- National Council for One-Parent Families, 255 Kentish Town Road, London NW5 2LX
- NSPCC, 67 Saffron Hill, London EC1N 8RS
- Child Poverty Action Group, 1 Macklin Street, Drury Lane, London WC2B 5NH
- Equal Opportunities Commission, Overseas House, Quay Street, Manchester M3 3HN.

OUTLINE OF AN APPROPRIATE GCSE INVESTIGATION/PROJECT

(For guidance, see 'Coursework for GCSE' on pages ix–xiv.)

Title An investigation into whether conjugal roles* within the family are becoming more symmetrical.

Hypothesis Husbands both do and expect to do less domestic work than their wives.

Secondary sources *The Symmetrical Family*, M. Young and P. Willmott (1973).

Housewife, Ann Oakley (1976).

These sources may be used for **comparative** purposes, that is to compare the situation today with those of 15–20 years ago. You need to point out that your study has to be limited to a small group, unlike the major studies that you are comparing your results with: this means that the comparison has limited validity. If you are to compare your study with others you need to base your sample as closely as possible on those of the earlier studies, for example were ethnic groups represented?

If you wished to make a comparison even further back in the past you could use *Coal is Our Life*, Dennis, Henriques and Slaughter (1956) or *Family and Kinship in East London*, Young and Willmott (1957).

Primary sources **Questionnaire** Keep your questions simple – use some of the same questions as those used by Oakley, and Young and Willmott, if comparing with these studies.

Use an appropriate sampling frame, such as college or school registers or youth club membership lists. It is important that you demonstrate that you know how to obtain a representative sample although your numbers may be too small for your sample to be really representative.

Your sample should be kept manageable: it is better to use small numbers and carry out the investigation thoroughly than to be too ambitious and fail to complete it properly. Perhaps 10 or 20 people – use numbers that you can easily convert into percentages.

---

* 'Conjugal' means to do with marriage. However, increasingly it may also refer to unmarried couples living together.

In this study, you will wish to compare males and females so you will require equal numbers of each.

Your questions might include those relating to cleaning, shopping, cooking, ironing, childcare, etc.

You may wish to develop your investigation by interviewing or observing.

Presentation   Try and use a variety of modes of presentation.

You might show the housework done by males and females in terms of hours for each day of the week – this could be in the form of a bar chart (see example on page 101). You may use a pie chart (see page 34) to show the proportion of childcare performed by men as compared with women.

Analysis   In analysing your study use the information you have actually collected, rather than selecting that which fits your hypothesis. Remember you can get a Grade A just as easily by proving your hypothesis wrong as by proving it right, or by showing how it was proven in part.

Criticise your study by pointing out the difficulties you experienced (the failure of people to return questionnaires; people trying to impress, or shock you in interview situations; the difficulty of obtaining a representative sample). These are the same difficulties that all sociologists experience and you will be credited for observing them.

2 GCSE QUESTION

Note: GCSE questions often require answers using information from interrelated themes. This one is mainly, but not exclusively, concerned with family.

Read the two newspaper reports and then answer the questions which follow.

A   **British still favour marriage – survey finds**

A1   Despite Britain's rising divorce rate, most people still want to get married and want to make marriage work, according to a major new survey.

A2   'Marriage cannot be written off,' says anthropology graduate, Miss Catherine Guy, author of 'Asking about Marriage' – the collected results of the survey, which was carried out for the British National Marriage Guidance Council.

A3   'People still hold to ideas which are associated with the first half of the century rather than the sixties and seventies. Great emphasis is put on love, understanding, loyalty, trust and faithfulness,' she says.

A4   Some 4,280 people were involved in the survey, which took the form of more than 50 projects carried out by marriage guidance councils throughout Britain.

A5   In the projects, ordinary people were asked about their expectations and experience of marriage. They ranged from school and college students to older people, and included the married, divorced, and couples who were living together. A minority were marriage guidance clients, but most projects took the form of questionnaires to 'non-client' couples.

A6   Miss Guy said: 'It leaves an impression not of gloom, but of people with high hopes and the best intentions about marriage.'

A7   'Despite the pressures of modern life, marriage is still a secure, loving, confiding relationship,' she says. Miss Guy points out, however, that patterns of marriage are changing. 'It is adapting, and will have to go on adapting as the social environment changes.'

These are among the main findings of the projects:

A8   *Divorce:* 'Despite the current high level [it] is not seen as an escape clause. People still marry in the hope and expectations of life-long marriage,' says Miss Guy. Divorce is socially acceptable, but many people are personally unhappy about this, and condemn the ease of obtaining a divorce. However, they remain sympathetic to the individuals involved.

A9   But divorced and remarried couples often feel 'different, marked out, or stigmatised,' she says, and suggests that they may be less likely to think of their new relationship as 'stable' compared with once-married couples.

A10   *Living together:* About one-third of adults in two studies had lived together before marriage, and many school and college students think they will, too.

A11   But 'the vast majority do not see cohabitation as a permanent alternative to marriage,' she says. Most people see cohabitation as a 'trial run' for marriage, and while it may express uncertainty about marriage, it may also demonstrate people's 'seriousness about committed relationships'.

A12   *Happy marriage:* There is virtual universal agreement about what makes a happy marriage – communication, tolerance and sharing. Lack of these factors – plus external factors such as unemployment and in-law problems – are thought to be prime marriage-wreckers. Material factors, such as having a home of one's own, the husband having a job, and the ability to manage money, are rated highly for happy marriages.

A13   *Children:* About 90 per cent of couples in their first marriage want, or have, children. But among couples with first babies questioned in one survey (in Jersey), there were calls for more help, advice and discussion before and after a birth – particularly for fathers. One survey suggested that the small number of couples who are childless by choice believe they are closer in their relationship, and have more freedom, as a result.

The Irish Times, 15 August 1985

B   **Wedded bliss: Parveen Verma with Ranjena, the wife he picked from 20 candidates – by Paul Nathanson**

Between 1970 and 1977 divorces doubled in England and Wales to 140,000 a year. Now a third of all marriages end in divorce. However, the figure is believed to be a fraction of this in the Hindu and orthodox Jewish communities where a system of arranged marriages still operates.

What are arranged marriages and how is it that they are more resistant to the disruption of divorce?

Parveen Verma, 32, is a lawyer living in Harrow-on-the-Hill with his wife, Ranjena, 25, a radiographer.

Parveen was born in Kenya but educated in Britain from the age of 14. Ranjena was born in India but brought up in Newcastle.

Their marriage, like almost all other Hindu marriages, was arranged. Both sets of parents sought suitable partners for their children in London, the north-east and even India. Meetings took place and they had to choose from the chosen.

With his liberal English education, Parveen felt uneasy about arranged marriages . . . until he was 29.

Then he agreed to meet girls suggested by his parents since he wanted to marry an Indian and retain the culture of the extended family. This means a man's house is not only home for his wife and children but also for his parents and unmarried brothers and sisters. Parveen detests old people's homes.

Choice

In ten months he met about 20 prospective brides before finding the right one.

'At least I had the choice,' he says. 'The whole concept of arranged marriages is really no different to computer dating or the old-fashioned English society balls.'

Ranjena was 22 when her parents started looking for a suitable husband. To their chagrin she refused five. 'When I was introduced to them, I was expected to say yes or no the next day. It didn't seem right to me, but my parents couldn't understand.'

She met Parveen in London in 1980 and they exasperated their parents by waiting six months before getting engaged. It is not uncommon for Hindu couples to marry within ten weeks of meeting.

Indeed, Parveen's father agreed to his own marriage within a day of seeing Parveen's mother, who herself had no say in the matter.

By contrast, Ranjena believed in a love marriage rather than a reasonable arrangement with love perhaps coming later. Yet she agrees that arranged marriages are positive since parents check carefully that partners come from similar backgrounds.

Disgrace

Centuries of tradition have preserved arranged marriages even in modern Britain, though there are signs of stress in families where parents give their children no say in the choice.

Divorce is by no means unknown among Hindus, Sikhs and Muslims but, says Dr Sushil Soni, chairman of the Indian Association of Ipswich in Suffolk, they try to avoid it. 'It is regarded as a disgrace and the divorce rate in the Hindu community in the UK is perhaps one in 100.'

Naomi and Michael Lewin are an orthodox Jewish couple, whose eight-year-old marriage was arranged. Yet, like the Vermas, only the initial introduction was arranged: the final decision was left entirely to them.

Naomi, 29, had already turned down one suitor, while Michael, 32, hadn't even agreed to see two girls suggested by his parents. 'The most important things were ideas on life and religion and how to bring up children,' he says. 'I believe that arranged marriages are a better and safer way of marriage and of avoiding divorce.'

Unlike her Hindu counterparts, Naomi did not look for a romantic love match. She did not want to break away from the tradition of arranged marriage but she did have very definite ideas on the kind of man and life she was looking for.

'He had to be kind and caring and we had to be able to grow within the marriage, without getting restricted. And in fact we're very, very happy.'

Yet, as with the Hindus, arranged marriages among Jews are by no means a guarantee against divorce. The Lewins are aware of more divorces in the orthodox community than before, though they cannot pinpoint reasons.

Mrs Chody suggests communication difficulties and impatience. 'We have instant coffee and we want instant happiness,' she says. 'Couples are not willing to work their conflicts through. But divorce in the traditional Jewish community is seen as the very last resort. There's so much investment in the value of a secure, happy, stable family life.'

Sunday Express, 20 November 1983

(i) Which of the two newspaper reports uses *most* personal opinion as a basis for its statements about marriage and divorce? (1)

(ii) In extract A what do you think is the personal opinion of Miss Catherine Guy about the state of marriage? (1)

(iii) In extract A it is said that a minority of those surveyed were marriage guidance clients. Give *two* reasons why researchers should pay attention to such information about the sample. (4)

(iv) Give *one* piece of evidence from the passage in *The Irish Times* (extract A) which suggests the importance to marriage of having children. (2)

(v) Explain and illustrate the difference between evidence and personal opinion with reference to the two paragraphs (A10, A11) on living together in *The Irish Times* account. (4)

(vi) In which particular communities does the *Sunday Express* report (extract B) claim that the divorce rate is much less than for the whole of England and Wales? (2)

(vii) What explanation would you give for the fact that where marriages are arranged divorce seems to be less common? (2)

(viii) According to the two extracts give one of the problems faced by divorcees. (1)

(*ix*)   Give *one* reason why a reader of the two extracts should be careful in drawing conclusions about marriage and divorce.   (2)

(*x*)   Contrast the reasons for entering an arranged marriage with the normal reasons given for entering a non-arranged marriage.   (6)

SELF-TEST QUESTIONS

(Answers on pages 288–89)

1. Give the term which is used to denote each of the following:
   a. one man legally married to more than one woman
   b. one woman legally married to more than one man
   c. one man married to one woman
   d. more than two people legally married to each other
   e. two people illegally married to each other as one is already married

2. Give three reasons why it has been useful for one man to marry several women in some societies.

3. List four functions that the family performs.

4. In which communities within the United Kingdom is the 'extended family' most likely to be the norm?

5. Give four reasons why the nuclear family is becoming more common as the normal operating unit.

6. Why is divorce becoming more common?

7. What changes have taken place in recent years in the 'role' of (a) mothers and (b) fathers in Great Britain?

8. What is the 'generation gap'?

9. Give three reasons why parents and children may spend more time together today than in the past.

10. Single-parent families often result from divorce. What other factors may cause them?

UNIT 3 LEARNING FOR LIFE

3.1   INFORMAL EDUCATION

From the moment that we are born we start to learn, and only a fraction of what we know is gained in schools and colleges. A great deal of what we know or believe is learnt in the family, in play with our friends, watching and imitating neighbours and strangers, reading, watching television, listening to the radio.

This is the way that children have always learnt the values and skills of a society; in fact even today probably three out of every four adults in the world have never been to school. However, as societies became more complicated – and particularly once writing was invented – parents and neighbours could not teach all the skills necessary and schools began to develop, although they were only needed for a small proportion of the population at first. Although nearly everyone in Britain goes to school today, it is still in our early years that we absorb the basic ideas that will influence our behaviour in the future. It is then that we learn the **norms** and **values** of our society and the **role** that we are expected to play in it.

Norms	The *normal* behaviour expected in a particular situation. This behaviour is acceptable to the rest of our group.	As babies we dribble into our food and nobody minds. If you spat into your food as an adult you would probably find yourself eating alone.
Values	These are the general principles accepted by a group as the standards by which the conduct of individuals is judged.	One value in our society is a respect for life. Nearly everyone would be horrified in our society if one of us killed people in order to shrink their heads and hang them up in our homes. Most would be shocked if one of us went around killing dogs. Many are

upset if birds are shot. Some object to cows being killed for meat.

Roles In each society a particular pattern of behaviour is expected of a person. The part we play in a particular situation is our **role**. (We have **ascribed** roles that we are given, for example woman, mother. We have **achieved** roles that we choose, for example doctor, comedian.)

Different behaviour is expected of us in different situations. If we went to see our doctor in her surgery and she was wearing a red nose and a funny hat, while singing at the top of her voice, we might have little confidence in her treatment. However, if we were at her Christmas party and she was behaving in this way, we would probably not be worried.

3.2 LEARNING OUR ROLES

Probably the most important role that we learn is that appropriate to our sex, that is what is considered the correct dress, behaviour and personality for someone who is masculine or someone who is feminine – our **gender**.

What gender roles are these children learning?

Children learn the behaviour that is expected from boys and girls – they are dressed in a particular way, given different toys to play with and encouraged to engage in activities that are regarded as appropriate to a male or female. They learn the approved way to behave by watching their mother or father.

In some societies it is regarded as appropriate for men to show sorrow easily by crying, in others boys are supposed to have a 'stiff upper lip'. In our society boys are generally expected to be adventurous, tough and assertive; girls are expected to be sympathetic, soft and submissive.

> Only men wear flowers in their hair and scented leaves tucked into their belts or arm bands. At formal dances it is the man who dresses in the most elegant finery and ... when these young men are fully made up and costumed for the dance they are considered so irresistible to women that they are not allowed to be alone, even for a moment, for fear some women will seduce them.
>
> W. Davenport, 'Sexual patterns and their regulation in a society of the Southwest Pacific',
> in F. A. Beach (ed.), *Sex and Behaviour*

1. It has been suggested that most young people have far more in common with their parents in terms of attitudes and behaviour than they have with any other young person chosen at random.

   As a group draw up a short questionnaire to see whether this is true. Suggestions for this questionnaire are:
   - Restrict your questionnaire to ten key, or important, questions.
   - Divide these into five questions on attitudes (e.g. view of trade unions or religious belief) and five questions on behaviour (e.g. holiday activities, smoking, etc.).
   - Obtain a sampling frame (e.g. the registers from other classes in your age group or 'cohort').
   - Take a random sample from this list, for example every third person. Allocate an **interviewer** from your group to each **interviewee** identified. (Allocate at random: for example, the first person in your group to the third person on your sampling frame, the second to the sixth person, etc.)
   - Interview the parents of the young people you have interviewed, or ask them to complete your questionnaire themselves.
   - Compare the responses of the young people with those of their parents.

2. Try and arrange to attend a children's playgroup as a participant observer (i.e. someone who appears part of the situation), or as an observer (i.e. someone who is obviously

just watching). You may note such things as girls' and boys' preferred activities; any differences in preferences (e.g. toys) between different ethnic groups; whether the playgroup leaders spent more time with some children than others, and if so, whether these groups of children had any characteristics in common.

    a. What difference did your presence have on the behaviour of the children?

    b. In what ways do you think a good playgroup might benefit a child?

    c. In what ways might a playgroup benefit the mother/ guardian of a child?

3.   Consider the following toys and give them a rating from 10 for strongly masculine to 90 for strongly feminine. (A rating of 50 would mean that the toy is appropriate for either sex.)

plane	tool set
teddy bear	cosmetics
rocking-horse	telephone
doll's wardrobe	racing car
tractor	skipping rope
football	

If other members of your group have completed this exercise compare the results and discuss the reason for any similarities or differences between you; if not, carry out a survey of your family or friends to see to what extent you agree.

4.   We learn other roles too. We may be regarded as the tough nut in the group or the funny one, and we will tend to act out the expectations other people have of us.

    Suggest dress and behaviour which you would consider odd in the following:

        a teacher in the classroom

        a nurse in a hospital ward

        a dentist playing with his children

        a coal miner at the workface

        a teenager in a disco

        the same teenager working in a solicitor's office

        the Prime Minister in the House of Commons

3.3   INTELLIGENCE

Some people think that our ability to absorb and use knowledge or to perceive and solve problems – our intelligence – is based mainly on what contacts with our surroundings we have made in the early years of our life. They believe that this **environment** moulds our mind.

Other people think that we are born with the intelligence that we have – that we gain it from the genes that we have inherited with our blue eyes or fat nose from our parents. One extreme writer has actually suggested that people of low intelligence should be paid not to breed. However, he is an exception and most experts think intelligence is the result of a mixture of inheritance and environment.

In 1937 some American psychologists studied 69 sets of identical twins and found that such twins, when brought up together, were likely to have a very similar intelligence (the chances were 90 in 100). When reared separately the chances of them having similar intelligence fell to 80 in 100, showing the influence of environment, but the importance of heredity. However, many extremely intelligent people have had apparently dull parents. It is most likely that our genetic inheritances are so mixed that we cannot be certain what a person's intelligence is going to be, and environment is certainly a most important factor in deciding how a child will develop.

Intelligence Quotient (IQ)

This is the name given to the result of tests which place the person being tested on a scale based on an average result of 100. Generally speaking, a person would require an IQ of 120 to cope with university studies; below 70 a person would have difficulty in learning nearly anything.

The measurement, however, is only a guide to performance. It cannot be exact in any particular instance and the person tested may be unwell or nervous, bored or tired.

People may have special abilities, a marvellous memory, a genius for music, outstanding skill at sport, or brilliance at handling figures – but be quite ordinary in other ways.

---

1. In the United States intelligence tests given to army recruits during the Vietnam War have shown that in each State black people scored lower than white, but that black people from the northern States had a higher average score than whites from the southern States.

   Think of some reasons to account for these results that have nothing to do with inherited intelligence.

2. Intelligence is only one quality that we must have in order to be successful in life. List five qualities in addition to intelligence in order to succeed in the following occupations:
   - bank manager
   - mother
   - nurse
   - bus driver
   - teacher
   - bricklayer

3.4   ENVIRONMENT

The influences which surround us as part of our environment include our home, our room, our friends, even the food we eat. For example, a child's mental development may be influenced by the food it is given as an infant. The human brain develops earlier than the rest of the body (by five years old the brain is almost full size), and if the child has a very bad diet the brain may not develop fully.

Whatever the main origin of our individual abilities to absorb and use knowledge it is certainly true that what we learn is influenced by our surroundings. Deaf children brought up without hearing a human voice do not naturally learn to speak; children have been found who have apparently been reared by animals and these children have had animal rather than human patterns of behaviour.

How a child performs at school is greatly influenced by home background. In 1991 a detailed study of school exam results in 71 Nottinghamshire schools carried out by Sheffield University showed that the new league tables of school exam results are highly misleading if they fail to take into account social disadvantage. There was a clear link between deprivation and school success. For example, the higher the number of pupils with free school meals the lower the pupil attendance and stay-on rates.

The 1991 survey was evidence that the early study by Jackson and Marsden, *Education and the Working Class*, 30 years before, still appears valid. This study of working-class children in Huddersfield found that the children of manual workers (social classes IIIM, IV and V in the Registrar-General's classification for the census) suffered a number of disadvantages compared with children from non-manual backgrounds (social classes I, II and IIIN). These included the following facts:

1.   The middle-class parents valued education because they had been successful in it and were more likely than working-class parents to encourage their children in their education.
2.   There were more books in the middle-class home which encouraged the child to read and improve his or her vocabulary.
3.   Teachers are middle class and therefore the speech and expected behaviour in school are middle class.
4.   There was more likely to be room to study in peace in the middle-class home. Richer parents could afford educational visits, private lessons and additional books; they could also afford to keep their children in education longer.
5.   Middle-class people were more likely to encourage **deferred gratification** with regard to education, that is the idea that study now will lead to more money and satisfaction in the long term.

Later studies up to that of 1991 confirmed the findings of Jackson and

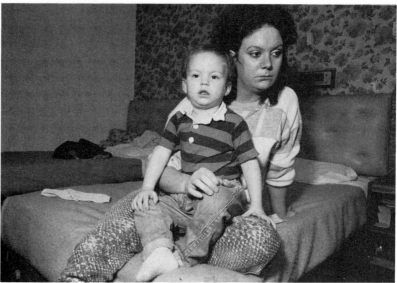

A teenager with his own bedroom and a toddler in bed-and-breakfast accommodation. Are they likely to have the same chances in life?

Marsden and Basil Bernstein, who in 1961 suggested that working-class people speak a 'different language' from that of the middle class – a **restricted code**. Middle-class people speak a more formal language – an **elaborated code**. As this is also the language of the school, middle-class pupils understand their teachers better and are less likely to be **labelled** (identified permanently) as non-academic and put in a lower **stream** (a group of pupils of similar ability who are taught together). Other research findings have indicated that children put in high streams tend to improve and those put in the lower streams deteriorate, regardless of their original level of ability.

It is important to realise that home backgrounds vary enormously and some working-class children receive a great deal of help and encouragement at home. Research findings only indicate general trends.

1. Examine the five 'facts' established by Jackson and Marsden in their 1962 study *Education and the Working Class*. Try to establish whether the situation in Huddersfield 30 years ago is similar to that in your own area today.

   You may draw up a short questionnaire and ask a sample of children whose father* is a manual worker (working class) to answer questions on parental encouragement, the number of books in their home, the existence of a quiet room to study, etc. (working-class families are much smaller today). Then ask a similar number of children whose father* is a white-collar worker (middle class) to complete the same questionnaire.

   Similarly, you might interview teachers to see to what extent the statement 'teachers are middle class' is true. They are factually, so far as the census is concerned, but do they have middle-class accents, attitudes and backgrounds?

2. Because sociologists look at what is likely to happen in certain situations there is a danger that students may wrongly assume that because identified factors exist particular behaviour is certain to occur; for example, on pages 63 and 64 those factors which make it *less likely* that a child from a working-class background will succeed at school are given – but we know that some children from a working-class background will succeed brilliantly.

   This question identifies some factors, such as role models, which make it *probable* that the child in question will behave in a particular way; you are being asked to suggest reasons why this may *not* occur.

   a. 'I am seven.

   'My Dad is in prison for pulling a job. My Mum is usually out at the pub with her boyfriend at night.

   'My big brother Joe is a great guy – he lifted a load of stuff from the scrapyard last week without being caught. The twins keep me awake crying at night as they sleep in my room. I don't – much!

   'All the chances may be against me, but what might happen to stop me following in my family's footsteps?'

* The Registrar-General classifies the population in the census by social class and this is determined by the 'head of the household' who is defined as the husband. You may not agree! If there is no male head, the occupation of the mother is the basis for classification.

b. 'I am seven.

'My Dad works hard but spends some time with me most nights. Mum has a part-time job, but gets home before I arrive back from school.

'My sister Sara is doing her A Levels; she thinks she will go into nursing. Our house is not very big, but Dad has put up a partition so that I have a little room to myself.

'I sound like a future success, so what might happen to make me a criminal?'

3.

Black pupils beat white in classroom tests

by Charles Hymas
Education Correspondent

SHE is one of the most able black children of her generation. Natalie Wint scored top marks in English, mathematics and science in the government's controversial new classroom tests.

Her remarkable success, rivalled by fewer than one in 17 pupils, has been revealed in results that have astonished Britain's leading educationists.

For the first time, researchers have discovered evidence that the brightest young Afro-Caribbean children outshine their white classmates in Britain's primary schools.

A new study commissioned by the School Examinations and Assess-ment Council, the official watchdog on school standards, challenges traditional views that Afro-Caribbean pupils are "trapped" by under-achievement and low expectations almost from birth. It found 10% of black seven-year-olds gained the top grade in mathematics and 19% in science, compared with 6% and 18% for whites.

Natalie, who lives in central Birmingham, is proof that being black and living in an inner city does not inevitably spell failure. St George's Church of England primary, where she was one of several black high-flyers, serves estates where one in four people are unemployed.

Yesterday, education spokesmen welcomed the findings, which contrast with studies of exam performance by Afro-Caribbean children who lag behind their white classmates and other ethnic groups.

Desmond Nuttall, director of the centre for educational research at the London School of Economics, described the results as "very encouraging" and said the gap in achievement was narrowing. "It may be useful evidence to remind teachers in secondary schools that they are receiving Afro-Caribbean pupils as well-equipped as white children and that they should not let them drop back."

Motivation was the key to academic success, particularly for children from ethnic minorities, John Eggleston, professor of education at Warwick University, said. Eggleston, who in the 1980s conducted pioneering research revealing how much better white children did in exams, said: "The driving force is sheer ambition and determination reinforced by huge parental support. It's quite breathtaking. These results at seven will enable parents to challenge assumptions of low capability that some teachers still carry around in their minds."

From: *The Sunday Times*, 12 January 1992

a. How did the results of black children in mathematics compare with those of white children in the tests for seven-year-olds described in the source material?
b. What *two* reasons are suggested for the growing success of black children in the British education system?
c. Why do you think the performance of black children in British schools might be improving?

4.

Girl pupils put the boys to shame

GIRLS were the undisputed winners in the tests for seven-year-olds, beating the boys at reading, writing, spelling, science and mathematics.

The results showed 84 per cent of girls reached or bettered the expected standard at writing— 11 per cent ahead of their classroom rivals.

At spelling the gap was even wider.

At least 78 per cent of girls could spell words like "car" and "sun"—with many doing better —compared to 66 per cent of boys.

The gap was narrower in maths, with three per cent more girls achieving the expected standard. At science one per cent more girls than boys reached the highest level.

The findings are further evidence that girls, already ahead at GCSE, are on the march through the education system.

For the first time, more girls than boys applied to enter university this year.

Prof Desmond Nuttall, director of the Centre for Educational Research at the London School of Economics, said the findings blew a hole in older theories of why girls were often ahead at 16.

These argued girls were more diligent and mature, reaching puberty earlier than boys, but this was obviously not true at seven.

"Clearly we need to do more research as to why girls are ahead, then we can help boys catch up," Prof Nuttall said.

Sir Wyn Roberts, Welsh Minister, put forward his own theory last month after similar results in Wales.

"Girls are possibly more attentive in class than boys, with a greater interest in their schooling and what they are being taught," he said.

From: *The Daily Telegraph*, 20 December 1991

a. In the new national achievement tests introduced in 1991 for seven-year-olds did the boys or the girls do best?

b. See if you can find out whether more boys or more girls were actually accepted for university in 1991.

c. Why do you think girls are now doing better than boys in the education system?

5. 'Pupils who fail to learn have no one to blame but themselves.' Comment on this statement using the following notes as a guide:

teachers	home influences
curriculum	career opportunities
friends	health

3.5   THE BRITISH EDUCATION SYSTEM

Education in special groups away from home developed as societies became more complex. One necessary factor was that the society produced a surplus of food and so could afford to keep people who were not actually producing anything themselves – like teachers!

In China, Confucius stressed the importance of schools 500 years before Christ and in 124 BC state examinations were introduced there. The Greeks and Romans had schools and universities; choir schools, and later grammar schools and the first 'public schools', served the needs of the church and new merchant class in medieval Europe.

The United States and Germany both developed state systems of education before the British (the State of Massachusetts as early as 1647). The education which people received in these schools helped them to challenge British economic supremacy, forcing the British government to produce the Education Acts of 1870 and 1902. The former introduced a national system of elementary education, and the latter set up local education authorities to provide public secondary education. Education only became compulsory in 1880 when school boards were required by law to make sure that all children aged between five and thirteen attended school.

In the 19th century, the public school flourished as it was needed to produce administrators for the far-flung British Empire, and charity schools, later financed partly by the government, helped to produce skilled workers for the factories as the Industrial Revolution got under way.

Although some grammar schools had existed for hundreds of years, they grew in number in the late 1890s and early 1920s. They were modelled on the public schools, and were to provide the clerical and professional workers the modern world needed. Meanwhile, elementary schools provided education from five to fourteen years of age for the new skilled manual workers who needed a basic formal education so that the factories and workshops could operate efficiently.

After the Second World War, more people demanded greater

Nature study in an elementary school in the early 1900s.

A south London primary school today.

opportunities and in 1944 a coalition government, representing all three main political parties, brought in an Education Act which raised the school-leaving age to 15 and reformed the educational system in other ways. This is sometimes called the 'Butler Act' after the Minister responsible. This Act did not create secondary modern, grammar and technical schools, but they developed from it.

The idea was that those children who were best able to cope with an 'academic' education would go to grammar schools (about 20 per cent of the population), and those who would be best suited to a more general education would go to the secondary modern schools. The secondary technical schools were for those who showed a particular aptitude for skilled craft work, but these did not catch on in most parts of the country. (If two sorts of schools were involved, this system of education became known as the 'bipartite' system; if three, it was called the 'tripartite'.)

However, the best-paid and often the most interesting jobs were seen to go to those who had received a grammar school education, and very quickly the selection of children at 11 years of age (the 11 plus) for the sort of school that would suit their abilities best became a question of 'passing' or 'failing'.

With more books and other opportunities for development at home, more children from richer backgrounds 'passed' the 11 plus. Some people wanted to end the division of the population into two distinct groups requiring differing kinds of education because they thought it split people up into two distinct classes: it was **socially divisive**.

Some people came to believe that in an all-ability, or 'comprehensive', school opportunities for all could be increased, academic standards improved for most, a wider syllabus offered and more specialised equipment for minority interests provided. Other people took the view that the most intelligent children would be held back and would not achieve their full potential in such a mixed-ability school. Again, some parents were worried that their children would pick up what they regarded as bad manners and would also hide their ability because less academic pupils would be in the majority.

1. The following is an extract from a book written by Professor Michael Rutter and his colleagues at the University of London, entitled *Fifteen Thousand Hours: Secondary Schools and their Effects on Children*. The title refers to the number of hours spent in school by a child between the ages of five and sixteen.

   One of the common responses of practitioners to any piece of research is that it seems to be a tremendous amount of hard work just to demonstrate what we knew already on the basis of experience or common sense. Was the effort really worthwhile? It might be felt that the same applies to this study. After all, it is scarcely surprising that children benefit from attending schools which set good standards, where the teachers provide good models of behaviour, where they are praised and given responsibility, where the general conditions are good and where the lessons are well conducted.

   Indeed this is obvious but, of course, it might have been equally obvious if we had found that the most important factors were attending a small school in modern purpose-built premises on one site, with a particularly favourable teacher–child ratio, a year-based system of pastoral care, continuity of individual teachers, and firm discipline in which unacceptable behaviours were severely punished. In fact *none* of these items was significantly associated with good outcomes, however measured.

   M. Rutter *et al.*, *Fifteen Thousand Hours*

   a. List what the authors regard as important in obtaining high achievement.
   b. List what they regard as unimportant.
   c. What do *you* think?
   d. *Fifteen Thousand Hours* was written in 1979. Can you identify any changes that have taken place in schools since then?

2. The national debate on what is the most effective kind of school continues. Find out, for example, what a City Technology College is and what people think of the idea.
   a. In 1990 some 86 per cent of all state pupils in England

were taught in comprehensive schools. What were the respective figures for Scotland, Wales and Northern Ireland? (Try *Social Trends.*)

   b. Do you think a selective or a comprehensive system is preferable? Why?

3.   a. Find out the current cost of educating a child at a 'public school'. (Try looking up 'public school' in the index of *Whitaker's Almanack.*)

   b. Find out what proportion of children go to public schools.

   c. Why do you think some parents wish to send their children to public schools?

   d. If you had a child, would you wish to send him or her to public school?

   e. Do you think public schools should be abolished?

4.   Use a copy of *Social Trends* from your school, college or public library to find the following:

   a. Education is the most expensive service provided by local authorities in the UK. Find out how much was spent on education in the most recent year available.

   b. The pupil–teacher ratio is the average number of pupils per teacher. Find the most recent pupil–teacher ratio for primary schools and for secondary schools in the UK. (Try and find out the figure for your own area – your local education authority will have this.)

3.6   THE FUTURE OF EDUCATION

A political battle has been waged for the past 20 years to decide the future structure of British secondary education, but by 1984 most areas had a comprehensive system, although some grammar schools remained. In 1988 the Education Reform Act made a return to more selective education likely, as a result of schools being allowed to 'opt out' of the state sector; and because of the introduction of 'City Technology Colleges'.

There are dangers in comprehensive education. For example, in densely populated areas, the pupils in any one school may be from only one area where there is bad housing, or where many of them may not be supported in their educational efforts by their parents. If this is so, the opportunities for the more able children in these 'neighbourhood' comprehensives may indeed be fewer than under the old system.

Another development that is under way in British education is the development of more courses for adults who wish to continue their education, either to increase their academic qualifications or to learn new and creative ways to use their leisure. This may become particularly important as we develop longer holidays and a shorter working week.

More manual and routine clerical work is becoming organised and performed by machines and computers. This could mean that more people will have greater opportunities to use their time in a more satisfying way, but the mere withdrawal of work without any compensating activities will lead to boredom and chaos. One important job for formal education to perform in the future may be the preparation of people for the world of leisure, as well as – or even instead of – the world of work.

Although many people do have more leisure there is an increasing need for British industry to keep up with rapid improvements in technology worldwide. The need for vocational education and training, that is, education directly related to preparing people for work or retraining those already in work, led to the setting up in 1991 of small groups of employers in each area with a responsibility to ensure that appropriate education and training is available; these groups are called Training Education Councils (TECs).

The importance of vocational education is also reflected in the setting up of tertiary colleges in many parts of the UK, which combine academic and vocational studies for those over 16.

In the 1970s and 1980s it was the young, particularly, who were at risk as job opportunities contracted. Many of the routine jobs for which young people were often used had disappeared, while many employers found older and more experienced people more reliable and easier to train.

However, the decline in the birth rate in the 1970s led to a considerable reduction in the 16–18-year-old 'cohort' in the late 1980s and through most of the 1990s young people will be in short supply. In some regions youth unemployment will disappear, while employers and colleges will have to compete in order to attract sufficient trainees and students.

1. Check Figure 3.1 and find what the percentage reduction in young people aged 15–24 in Europe will have been between 1987 and 2000. What effect do you think this reduction is likely to have?

**Figure 3.1
Europe's shrinking youth
population.**

From: *European Lifestyles
1989*, Mintel (reproduced in
The Daily Telegraph, 10 May
1989)

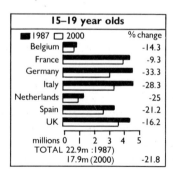

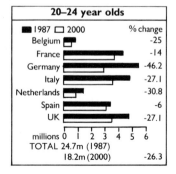

2. Even in comprehensive schools, many teachers feel that at
    least for some subjects they need to 'stream' or 'set' so that
    the children who are best or worst at a particular subject
    can be taught together. What do you think about this?

3.7   YOUTH CULTURE

The concept of 'youth culture' in Britain has only developed
during the last 40 years. In all societies there is a distinction between
the young and the adult, fully mature members of the society; but few
have a distinctive culture which implies a different life-style with different values.

To suggest that the youth of Britain in general really do have a
different 'culture' from their parents is probably an exaggeration. Suc-
cessive surveys indicate that the majority of each generation carries
forward most of their parents' attitudes and values.

1988   Murray and Thompson found that most young people
       accepted authority and had good relations with their
       parents.

1984   *Young People in the Eighties* (DES) found that 67 per cent
       completely rejected drugs and were 'responsible' and
       'helpful'.

1984   'Ask the Family' (National Council for Voluntary
       Organisations) found a high overall standard of
       behaviour.

1976   The National Children's Bureau found that most
       teenagers got on well with their parents: 'Britain's
       future, in fact, appears to be in the hands of a remark-
       ably conventional generation of young men and
       women, not markedly different from the parents who
       worry about them.'

There is probably more evidence for a distinctive youth culture if
one examines life-styles. The youth of today have been more affluent
than that of previous generations, particularly in the interlude
between leaving school and getting married, although the increase in
unemployment among young people and the consequent decrease in
income may lead to changes. Young people often have a larger **dis-
posable income** than adults who have commitments to pay mort-
gages, car loans, fuel bills and the like.

Commercial organisations have naturally developed to meet the
needs and wishes of young people, particularly in dress, appearance
and entertainment. Most young people are probably aware that they
are being manipulated to provide profits for commercial undertakings, but they are prepared to accept this providing their desire to
'belong' is met.

Some distinction in dress is common for young people in many societies. Early explorers, starting with Captain Cook in 1774, found that adolescents in the Marquesas Islands had a great deal of freedom, dressed in special yellow clothes, dyed themselves yellow with saffron and spent nearly all their time in enjoyment.

It is natural that young people in the Marquesas, as in Britain, should want to establish their own **identity**, otherwise they would tend to grow up as carbon copies of their parents and there would be little chance of change and progress. Youth is the time to explore new experiences and ideas, and it might be true to say that though there is no distinctive youth culture, there is a youth **sub-culture**. While young people in general accept many of the basic values of the adult world to a greater or lesser extent depending on the individual, many like to have a distinctive dress, life-style and ideals – they have a culture within a culture.

'Teenagers are news, but only certain kinds of teenagers'. Are these teenagers 'news'?

Some young people are affected by this sub-culture only to a very limited extent – the length of skirt, width of trouser leg, hairstyle or make-up. Since the 1950s a proportion of teenagers have immersed themselves rather more completely in the sub-culture, adopting very distinctive dress styles and surface attitudes: first the 'Teddy Boys', then the 'Rockers', followed by the Mods, Hippies, Skinheads

(Bovver Boys), Hell's Angels and Punk Rockers. Perhaps only the Hippies and Hell's Angels came near to being a distinctive culture, often cutting themselves off entirely from their families and backgrounds. Ironically the two groups were entirely opposite to each other, one putting over a doctrine of love and the other of hate.

We saw in Unit 1 that almost everyone desires to be fully integrated into a group. Modern adult society effectively prevents young adults from integrating into the adult community in the way that would occur in non-advanced societies. They are discouraged from early marriage and home ownership and encouraged to extend their education as long as possible for career reasons. At the same time improved nutrition causes young people to develop physically more quickly, reaching puberty (often a sign of adulthood in non-advanced societies) three to five years earlier than young people did at the beginning of the century. Not unnaturally, many teenagers tend to form themselves into gangs of 'peers', that is groups of about the same age with the same interests, shortly after most of their age group reach puberty, although the incidence of gang formation is often overemphasised and tends to be restricted to particular areas.

At the same time young people who work are often doing so with adults as equals and with near-adult wages (and often greater spending power). Those who are extending their education are often aware of their greater knowledge in some areas than their parents. In these circumstances, it is not surprising that the traditional respect which adults expect may sometimes be lacking.

However, even this distinction can be exaggerated. In 1964, in his book, *The Sexual Behaviour of Young People*, Michael Schofield commented:

> The newspapers are still run by adults and still reflect the views of the adults who respond to the new economic power of the teenagers with a strange mixture of bewilderment, scorn and envy. So teenagers are news, but only certain kinds of teenagers – those who are in trouble, those who are defying convention, those who are good copy.

1. The ESRC (Economic and Social Research Council) reported on a major research programme, 'Young People Today', in 1988. Tables 3.1 and 3.2 summarise a few of the findings:

Table 3.1 *Weekly spending money remaining after payment of board*

	15–16-year-old 'cohort' (%)	17–18-year-old 'cohort' (%)
Less than £17	90	30
£17 to less than £26	7	17
£26 to less than £40	2	21
£40 to less than £60	1	20
More	–	10

Table 3.2 *Percentage taking part in the activity below at least once a month*

	Younger cohort (15–16-year-olds)	Older cohort (17–18-year-olds)
Religious meeting	17	14
Cinema	35	31
Watching sport	59	52
Youth club or group	36	16
Pub*	32	79
Drinking alcohol*	40	77
Dances/discos	43	62
Cigarette smoking	21	29

*Generally illegal, even for most of the older cohort.

a. Prepare a simple questionnaire and carry out a survey of your own group to see to what extent you compare with the relevant cohort shown here.
b. Why do the figures for 'pub' and 'drinking alcohol' differ?
c. What effect might the high spending pattern of some individuals in the groups shown have on other individuals?
d. Find out under what circumstances the age groups shown can

   i. visit pubs,
   ii. drink alcohol legally.

2. Below is a list of some of the things that you can or must do legally at a particular age. The ages at which most additional activities become legal are 16 and 18.
   a. i. Add at least ten activities to those which are shown which may be engaged in at 16 without breaking the law.
      ii. Add a similar list to that shown for 18-year-olds.
   b. At 16 we may be physically mature, but we are not fully socially mature. In what ways are we not fully adult at 16?
   c. How has this contributed to the development of a 'youth culture'?

When you reach this age	Right or responsibility
5	Go to school.
7	Take money from Post Office Book.
10	Be convicted of a criminal offence (but not fined).

12	Make a will in Scotland if you are a girl (boys wait until 14).
	Buy a pet.
14	Pawn something.
	Be fully responsible for crimes.
	Own an air rifle.
	Perform in public without a licence.
15	Possess a shotgun if supervised by someone over 21.
	Allowed in knackers' yard.
	Open a National Giro Account.
	Enter into some contracts (e.g. apprenticeships).
16	Join a trade union.
	Leave school.
	Consent to sexual intercourse if you are a girl.
	Own a passport.
17	Drive a car.
	Have a firearm licence.
	Go into a betting shop.
	Fly a private aircraft.
18 (Age of majority since January 1970)	Marry without parents' consent.
	Leave home without parents' consent.
	Get a mortgage.
	Be tattooed.
19	Join the police.
21	Sit on your local council.
	Be a Member of Parliament.
	Sell alcohol with a licence.

3. 'Youthscan' is directed by Professor Neville Butler, of the International Centre for Child Studies, London.

Imagine a whole generation of people whose lives have been charted from the cradle to the grave, who have been measured and examined in the most minute detail from the moment of birth. Imagine a generation which is repeatedly monitored so that we know almost everything there is to know about it from facts about its health, education and social situation to its opinions and attitudes on almost any subject you care to name.

It may sound like the sort of impossible situation science fiction is so fond of dreaming up, but it's actually happening here and now.

The project, which is assisted by American Express and major national companies, is called Youthscan and is the brainchild of Professor Neville Butler. He began it in 1970. All 15,000 children born in England, Scotland and Wales in one week of that year,

April 5–11, were examined at birth with finer attention to detail than even the most doting of mothers could manage.

'We got a lot of information at birth,' says Professor Butler. 'Whether they were born too small, too big, too early, too late, pushed out, pulled out, how they got on with their mother when they saw her the first time and so on.'

The aim of the project is to re-examine those same children at various stages of their lives and it looks back at the circumstances of their birth – 'from the sperm to the worm, from the womb to the tomb', as the professor puts it – and so build up a complete picture of their generation.

The children were looked at again at five and 10 years, and have just been surveyed for the fourth time at 16, an age at which they are becoming very interesting indeed.

Youthscan has already revealed facts previously undreamed of. It found that a quarter of children wearing glasses did not need them. It discovered that women who smoked had smaller babies, and it will now follow those same babies through life to discover how it affects them later on. It also uncovered the alarming and totally unsuspected statistic that some 18 per cent of teenagers have a literacy problem – a fact that is food for thought when you consider, for example, that this is the generation most at risk from AIDS and that the Government opted for a written leaflet through the letterbox to inform them of how the disease is spread.

Information about smoking, drinking, education and how their television-watching habits influence their lives are of obvious interest to both government and sociologists.

Equally interesting are the uses to which commerce and business can put the results of the study.

Expressions (The American Express Magazine),
September 1988

a. What is the term used to describe a study over an extended period of time?
b. In what ways might commerce and industry use this study?
c. Make a list of what benefits may result from this study or ones similar to it.

3.8   YOUTH ACTIVITIES

The youth sub-culture creates many of its own activities, whether it be standing at the corner watching all the girls or boys go by, going to discos, riding motorcycles, choosing clothes or listening to pop music – in these areas the adult is an intruder. Some adults try to remain part of the youth culture, but unless they are a pop star or personality, they are subject to ridicule, just as a teenager would be if he or she continued to act as a child. Why are we so severe in insisting that people act out their appropriate roles?

However, there are many youth activities where adult involvement is welcomed and five million young people belong to these more formal **youth organisations**. Youth clubs take many forms: some are school based with a 'youth tutor' in charge, although school leavers can also usually join; others are connected with a church. Some are run directly by the local authority as part of its **youth service** with a youth leader in charge. In many, the members take a major part in fund-raising, organising activities and deciding policy.

The National Association of Youth Clubs is now the largest youth organisation with more than half a million members in affiliated clubs. This organisation is not connected with any religious groups or political movement, though there are other large youth groups connected with the Methodist, Catholic, Anglican and Salvation Army churches.

What advantages and disadvantages do formal youth organisations have over informal activities?

In recent years there has been a growing realisation that young people crave adventure – they want to test their own endurance and courage in a world where natural dangers are few. Perhaps the motives of the boy who dies in a motorcycle pile-up on a motorway or who breaks into a house are not so different from those who climb mountains and descend pot-holes. Two major organisations now encourage young people to accept the challenge of exploring new activities and reaching high standards:

1. **The Duke of Edinburgh Award Scheme** is aimed at people between 14 and 25 and most towns have a local committee. If there is no scheme in your college, school or club, write to your local education authority. You will be able to compete for the bronze, silver and gold awards in four out of five sections:
    a. Service
    b. Interests
    c. Expeditions
    d. Physical activity
    e. Design for living
    Many employers are keen to employ Gold Award holders. They know that these young people have determination and energy.

2. The **Outward Bound Trust** operates six centres in Britain where you can join a 26-day course. The courses are deliberately tough and give people a real opportunity to experience adventure.

    Those who wish to spend a period helping others, unpaid but with board and pocket money, can join the **Community Service Volunteers**.

There are a great many other youth organisations not listed here and there is no reason why any young people should allow themselves to become bored. Most people find that doing something constructive is more satisfying than just hanging around with their friends.

1. Find the current numbers involved in the two activities listed below:

	1971	1981	Today
Community Service Volunteers	5,000	35,000	?
Duke of Edinburgh Award Scheme	122,000	170,000	?

The Community Service Volunteers organisation places young people in full-time community service for periods of 4–12 months. The figures given are the total number (in thousands) of months of full-time service undertaken by volunteers.

The numbers for the Duke of Edinburgh Award Scheme are for participants.

2. Find out which of the following has had a decrease in membership during the last ten years (or nearest available dates):
    *   Girl Guides
    *   Army Cadet Force
    *   National Association of Youth Clubs

3. Draw up a questionnaire which seeks answers to the following:

    'Would you prefer to belong to an organisation that catered for just boys or girls, or would you prefer to belong to a mixed group? Why? What organisations, if any, do you belong to? Do you prefer adult involvement in your leisure activities or not?'

4. Try to interview someone who clearly belongs to a specific current youth sub-culture, for example who will admit to being a 'football hooligan'. Try to determine their motives for being associated with the group. Try to find out the real truth – remember the person concerned may seek to shock you or disguise their real motives.

3 DISCUSSION

1. 'Give me a child until he is seven and I will give you the man.' To what extent is this statement, credited to the Jesuits, likely to be true?

2. The author was teaching 'environment versus heredity' to a group of adult students in Somerset; he observed that most of what we regarded as natural behaviour for males and females was the result of our socialisation. There was a pause and then a middle-aged farmer in the group said, 'I wish you would come and tell that to my bloody bull.' To what extent do you think physical differences account for differing male and female behaviour?

3. Is the function of the education system in this country mainly to train people for future employment? Or is the main purpose of education to pass on certain values to a new generation? Or is there a different purpose?

4. Until 1986 state schools in Britain were permitted to beat children; and private schools still can. Do you think children can be disciplined without the threat of violence? How?

5. There has been surprisingly little systematic research into the effects of different patterns of discipline. However, the few studies that have been undertaken both point to its importance and emphasise that discipline and punishment should not be seen as synonymous. As already mentioned, Reynolds observed that the combination of good discipline (in terms of rule enforcement), the involvement of pupils in discipline (as shown by the use of a prefect system), and a low use of corporal punishment was most likely to be associated with good attendance. Heal (1978) found that misbehaviour was worst in schools with formal punishment systems; and Clegg and Megson (1968) noted that delinquency rates tended to be highest in schools with a great deal of corporal punishment. They also describe the improvement in one school where a new head reduced the number of rules and reduced the use of corporal punishment but also increased the monitoring and enforcement of the rules that remained and insisted on higher standards of staff behaviour. Other studies have found that firm, quiet reprimands are more effective than angry, punitive responses.

   M. Rutter *et al.*, *Fifteen Thousand Hours: Secondary Schools and their Effects on Children*

   a. What is the difference between discipline and punishment?

b. Is there any evidence in this extract that corporal punishment improves discipline?

c. What factors does the writer believe will improve discipline?

d. What do the following words mean in the context of the passage above:
    i.   synonymous
    ii. delinquency
    iii. monitoring
    iv. reprimands
    v.   punitive

ADDITIONAL ASSIGNMENTS AND INVESTIGATIONS

1. This question is based on the lists of men and women's different abilities which follow.

Some of the differences appear to be the result of 'environment conditioning' but some seem to result from actual differences in the body chemistry and structure, for example early castration of males results in less aggression. The right hemisphere of the brain (perceptual abilities) is more active in men; the left (linguistic abilities) more active in women.

How do you think social conditioning or environmental conditions might help to encourage the apparent differences listed?

Note: The qualities listed have been found by some researchers to be more evident in men or in women as listed. You do *not* have to agree!

Warning: As a social scientist you are trying to study society in a scientific manner. In your project/coursework key factors in determining your grade will be:

- your ability to collect evidence in an *unbiased* and *accurate* manner
- your ability to present evidence in a *clear* and *logical* way
- your ability to make *reasoned* and *impartial* conclusions from your evidence.

Always examine information *critically*. How was it obtained? Who collected it? Why did they collect it? How do you know it is correct? Remember these points as you consider the claims made in the table which come from a variety of research studies. Some can be checked fairly easily (e.g. the number of males and females sent to prison each year) but qualities such as 'creativity' are much more difficult to measure.

    a. To what extent do you agree with each statement?

    b. Try to check the accuracy of each statement by reference to secondary sources (e.g. *Social Trends*). How many have you managed to check?

    c. If you have to find out whether the remaining statements are true using primary research (i.e. doing the research yourself) consider in each case how you would tackle the problem. Now select three statements and carry out your own research to try and prove them true or false.

I am a woman. Am I superior to a man?

I am more likely:
- to have a better short-term memory
- to be quieter and more deft with my fingers
- to be less curious
- to be more sensitive to pain
- to be more sensitive to touch
- to have a better sense of smell (except during menstruation)
- to be worse at aiming at a target
- to be able to spell better
- to be able to read better
- to be able to write better
- to be able to use language better
- to be able to endure long periods of discomfort
- to be more responsive to sound
- to be less prone to disease and accident

I am a man. Am I superior to a woman?

I am more likely:
- to be a genius
- to be a mental defective
- to be a criminal
- to be better at arithmetic
- to stutter
- to reason better
- to be colour-blind
- to commit suicide
- to tolerate pain
- to understand machines
- to be more imaginative
- to be more aggressive
- to be creative
- to be more responsive to sight

2 If you are at a state school contact your nearest public or other private secondary school (and vice versa if you are at a public/private school).

Try and arrange a visit to the school to interview some of the pupils of your own age there. Either use a **structured** interview technique with definite questions in a clear sequence, or an **unstructured** technique which has the advantage of gaining answers to matters of fact or opinions quickly. In this form of interviewing you should have a list of questions but can ask them in any order or rephrase them to encourage the person being interviewed. This type of interview is particularly useful in determining qualitative aspects such as depth of feeling. You may find a tape-recorder useful, as you can have a greater and freer flow of information without taking notes.

You may seek to determine differing attitudes to education; differences in life-style or career aspirations (the jobs people hope to do).

Start with a **hypothesis** to test. This is a guess or 'hunch' that you wish to prove or disprove, for example 'Public school boys and girls all expect to go to university and get professional jobs; state school boys and girls have lower aspirations'. Your hypothesis may be proved wrong. As a social scientist this is *not* a defeat for you; it indicates that you have approached your research in an appropriately unbiased manner.

OUTLINE OF AN APPROPRIATE GCSE INVESTIGATION/PROJECT

(For guidance, see 'Coursework for GCSE' on pages ix–xiv.)

Title   An investigation into the influence of the home on the future behaviour of young children.

Hypothesis   The most important influence in the socialisation process of early school-aged children remains the home.

Secondary sources   Two possible sources are:

Sue Sharpe, *Just Like a Girl: How Girls Learn to be Women* (1981).

D. Gittins, *The Family in Question: Changing Households and Familiar Ideologies* (1985).

Primary sources   **Observation** An in-depth study of two children, one male, one female (if a mature student observing your own children, try to counteract any **bias** by getting another student to carry out interviews with them).

Questionnaire Issue perhaps 20 to parents with children in the same age group (perhaps four to eight years). Try to make your sample as representative as possible.

- Your questionnaire may be **closed** (i.e. only a limited response is possible – yes/no/don't know). This is easy to analyse but may limit responses.
  An example of a closed question might be:

  > What books does your child choose to read?
  > a. Own choice from home?
  > b. Own choice from library?
  > c. School books?
  > d. Your choice?

  Note that other possibilities are excluded (e.g. Friends' books or 'It varies...').

- Your questionnaire may be **open** (i.e. any answer is possible). This is difficult to analyse but may provide a greater variety of responses which more accurately reflect the true position.
  Examples of open questions might be:

  > What does your child like doing most?
  > Where did he/she learn to do that?

Interviews   Interviews might be conducted with four to ten children. You will have to consider:

> Where should the interview take place?
> Should the parents be present?
> What bias may result from the child's desire to please?

Your questions might seek to determine to what extent the child's *attitudes* have been influenced by the home (e.g. parents, brothers and sisters, grandparents) or other 'agencies' (e.g. television; friends (peer groups); school; books).

As you have used the word 'remains' in your hypothesis you need to test out what the situation was in the past. You might do this by using 'secondary' sources or by interviewing older people (e.g. teachers who were teaching or training 30 years ago).

State whether you have proved or disproved your hypothesis. Remember to question the *validity* of your findings – to what extent are they likely to be accurate?

Assessors do not expect you to be able to carry out a truly scientific piece of research, you have neither the time nor the resources. What is expected is that you follow a *scientific method* and are aware of *why* your findings may not be valid. For example, your sample may not be large enough or it may not be representative (say why you could not make it so).

Appendices   e.g.

> Sample of your questionnaire
> Questions used in your interview.

Do *not* pad out your research. State clearly what you did and why. Illustrate with appropriate diagrams, graphs, photographs, etc., but do *not* make it into a scrapbook (no marks are given for repetitive illustrations or long extracts from books).

3 GCSE QUESTION

Note: GCSE questions often require answers using information from interrelated themes. This one is mainly, but not exclusively, concerned with education.

Item A

Item B

> Boys and Girls can do
> woodwork or needlework
> ... In needlework you can
> make a doll, skirt or night
> dress case ... In
> woodwork you can make
> a model of a plane, car or
> boat ...

Of course it is not just school subjects which keep up traditional gender divisions. The family, neighbourhood and peer group place equally strong, if not greater, pressures on young people to be 'typical' girls and boys.

It seems to me that very little has changed during the growth of comprehensive education. Girls still rarely take the subjects which have been done traditionally by boys. Even at a school which prides itself on offering equal chances and choices to both sexes traditional gender differences remain. What hope is there then for young people in schools which have more narrow-minded practices?

Item C

Subject choices, by sex: 4th and 5th year (1985/86)			
Year	Subject	Boys doing subject	Girls doing subject
4th	craft design technology	80	8
4th	home economics needlework	—	70
5th	metalwork woodwork	70	—
5th	home economics needlework	10	50

Items B and C adapted from Frances Pinney, 'Sugar and Spice',
The Social Science Teacher, Summer 1986

(**a**) Study the cartoon, Item A, and then describe how children are socialised into becoming 'typical' girls and boys. (2)

(**b**) Study Item B. Identify and explain briefly any *one* form of pressure which is placed upon young people to keep to their traditional gender roles. (2)

(**c**) i) Explain the expression 'traditional gender divisions'. (2)
ii) How does the information presented in Item C show 'traditional gender divisions'? (2)

(**d**) Items B and C show that girls and boys often choose different subjects in schools. Identify and explain *three* reasons for their subject choices. (6)

(**e**) How have both legal and social changes helped to improve the status of women in our society during this century? (6)

SEG, Sociology Paper 2, 1988

SELF-TEST QUESTIONS

(Answers on page 289)

1. What is meant by each of the following terms:
    a. norm
    b. value
    c. role

2. Give an example of a society where the behaviour of a young man is or was expected to be quite different from that in Great Britain today.

3. Give an example of an experiment that seems to show that intelligence may be inherited, at least in part.

4. What is an 'Intelligence Quotient'?

5. What is our 'environment'?

6. What sort of schools developed from the 1944 Education Act?

7. List three arguments in favour of comprehensive schools and three against them.

8. What is meant by pupil–teacher ratio?

9. Why are middle-class children more likely to succeed in the education system than working-class children?

10. What is a tertiary college?

4 US AND THEM

4.1 MINORITIES

Some people are rich, some are poor; some are black, some are white; some are men, some are women. None is superior or inferior to others, but people often think they are.

People expect particular groups to behave in a particular way, based on what they have been told or what they have observed; although this information may only be based on a few individuals, they expect all similar people to behave in the same way. It is as if they have hung a label round the other people's necks saying 'troublemaker' or 'stingy'. This is called **stereotyping**. People often tend to live up to the 'label' that has been attached to them. Sometimes the stereotyped group behaves in the expected way and the stereotyped image is reinforced.

To a limited extent we are all influenced by the stereotyped image of ourselves; the doctor will act out the role of a doctor, behaving quite differently from the way in which he or she behaved as a medical student. Young people may tend to behave as young people are expected to behave, and if the media concentrates on the more sensa-

A street scene in Southall. It is easy to stereotype an easily identifiable minority.

tional aspects of the minority, this may in time influence the behaviour of the majority towards them.

When minority groups are easily identifiable stereotyping is easier. Those with the expected appearance or pattern of behaviour are readily picked out and all members of the target group are identified with these particular 'traits'. Minority groups themselves are often conscious of this tendency to label and are more careful in their behaviour as a consequence. For example, in a study of Jews in Leeds in 1964 it was found that drunkenness and juvenile delinquency was less common among Jews than among other members of the community; a major reason for this was the desire of the Jewish community to protect its good name.

Some groups may benefit from being a minority and may cultivate the differences between themselves and the majority. For example, former public schoolboys may adopt particular mannerisms, dress and expressions in the knowledge that these are likely to lead to advancement in careers where other former public schoolboys are in positions of authority. However, few minority groups are in this position: their characteristics are much more likely to lead to **discrimination** against them.

Discrimination is when people are treated in a particular way because of their group membership. Discrimination may take many forms: it may be open (**overt**), in signs such as 'No Irish need apply', or 'Whites only'. More difficult to counter is hidden (**covert**) discrimination: a name like Goldstein may be sufficient to bar someone from a golf club which does not wish to admit Jews; someone with an Indian or Pakistani name may be invited for a job interview although there is no intention of employing him or her; the flat may suddenly have ceased to be available when a black person comes to view it. The working-class person who 'made it' may be discouraged from the West End club by condescending smiles and whispered comments. The middle-class child may be made equally uncomfortable at the working-class neighbourhood comprehensive school.

Such hostility will often persuade the minority group to turn inward upon itself. The sub-culture is more secure; one is accepted within it – although all its members may not be regarded as equal, jeers at one's accent, dress style and food are missing. There are also other factors which encourage minority groups to avoid being fully **assimilated*** (absorbed) into the general community:

- *Religion* Different religions may: discourage marriage to people who are not members of the religion (e.g. Catholics); having fasting or praying periods which make working with non-believers difficult (Muslims); have particular rules

---

* **assimilation** is the process by which something becomes fully part of something else. There is argument as to whether full assimilation is desirable or not. Many people, including many members of ethnic minority groups, would prefer ethnic minority cultures to remain distinct.

regarding what may be eaten (Jews); and have a general view, common to many religious groups, that the beliefs and morals of their members will be corrupted by close contact with the prevailing culture.

- *Dress* The turbans of Sikhs used to make it difficult for them to be employed in jobs where a particular type of hat is part of the uniform, for example police, traffic warden, bus driver, although this rule is now usually relaxed. The trousers (*chalwar*) worn by Pakistani girls may make it difficult for them to attend schools where a skirt is part of the uniform (insistence on this is now rare).
- *Values* Strict rules of behaviour between the sexes deter many Asian women from leaving their immediate neighbourhood.
- *Language* The sheer difficulty of communication will reduce the chances of mixing.

In the face of external hostility and internal social pressure many members of minority groups will remain in the areas where there are shops and restaurants catering for their needs, schools with provision for their children and places where they can worship. The sacrifice of the possibility of greater job satisfaction, better housing and more financial security may be regarded as better than a constant struggle in an unequal battle.

1.

**Figure 4.1
An ape-like Irish man argues with a noble Britannia in a *Punch* cartoon of 1881.**

a. Look at this representation of an Irishman in Figure 4.1 (note, for example, the word in his hat band). What image is being presented of the Irish as a group?
b. Collect examples of stereotyped representations of people from differing ethnic or national groups, for

example Scottish, West Indian, French. (You may find bound collections of old editions of *Punch* in your public library, which you may photocopy.)

2. Read the passage below and answer the questions which follow:

    It is common to regard minorities as creating problems for the society in which they live, but this is more likely to be a consequence of certain attitudes and practices by the majority. The process is not a simple one: stereotyped opinions about the minority are widely held, and distinctions between 'our people' and 'them' are made. The feelings developed in the minority may lead to a strong sense of grievance against the majority and an increased determination to retain their identity.

    E. Butterworth and D. Weir (eds.),
    Social Problems in Modern Britain

    a. What is meant by 'stereotyped opinions'?
    b. Who are 'more likely' to create problems associated with minorities?
    c. Why do many minorities seek to keep their separate identity, according to the author?
    d. Which 'minority groups' have increased in number since this passage was written in 1972? (Many libraries keep copies of *Social Trends* from previous years.)

4.2   RACE AND ETHNIC GROUPS

Physical differences make it easy to recognise other groups, to stereotype them and discriminate against them.

People often use the term 'race' when they are referring to an **ethnic group**; that is, a group with a particular **culture**, a particular way of life, based perhaps on a common ancestry, customs, dress, religion and language. For example, there is, in fact, no separate Jewish or Irish 'race'; when people refer to these groups, they are referring to ethnic groups.

Race is merely a division of humankind into different biological groups based on physical differences. These differences between races are small and are based on types of hair, skin colour, facial features and height. In addition, the physical characteristics of people within one racial group can vary a great deal. For example, the tallest and smallest people in the world are both Negroid. Some groups are sometimes classified as being a mixture of the major racial groups, such as Australian Aborigines, who have 'Caucasoid' hair but 'Negroid' noses.

The three racial groups that people are usually divided into are (in order of numbers):

Mongoloid	Some general characteristics of this group are straight black hair, medium width noses, yellowish or brownish skin, little body or facial hair, slight stature (little difference in stature between men and women). Examples are Eskimos, Chinese, Native Americans.
Caucasoid	Some general characteristics of this group are wavy blond to dark brown hair, narrow noses, pinkish or brownish skin, thin lips, a lot of body hair on males, variable height but many tall. Examples are Arabs, Europeans, Jews, Indians, Pakistanis.
Negroid	Some characteristics are wiry, tightly curled hair, broad noses, little body or facial hair, thick lips, blackish, brownish or yellowish skin. Examples are most Africans south of the Sahara, Melanesians.

Racial classification is not just based on appearance: the type of blood and the form of the skull are also taken into account.

The physical characteristics that different racial groups possess have come about as a result of **adaptation to the environment**. This means the development in animals of those characteristics that help them survive. For example, in the animal world the slowest antelope are those that are killed first by predators. Because only the swiftest survive and mate the next generation of antelope are usually born with the same ability.

Here are some of the reasons why differing types of people have developed:

1. The pigment 'melanin' is present in everyone except albinos. It protects the sweat glands from damage in hot climates. Those with the most melanin are most suited to these climates. If a white person tans quickly in hot weather they have more melanin than someone who burns easily. (Hair colour is also governed by melanin.)
2. The pigment in the iris of the eye protects it from sunlight, therefore brown eyes tend to predominate in hot countries and lighter colours in cold lands.
3. Long noses warm air before it enters the lungs and are helpful in cold climates.

Sometimes all the appropriate characteristics do not develop (e.g. the noses of Eskimos); sometimes recent migration (and this can be thousands of years ago in terms of evolution) means that the appropriate characteristics have not yet had a chance to develop. Both whites and Bantus live in South Africa, but both have only been there for about 300 years.

Racial differences develop in the same way as height or any other physical characteristic. If we are small it is unlikely that we would expect someone taller to be less intelligent or otherwise inferior just because of their height; yet many people do make this assumption about others who have a different skin pigmentation from their own!

> 1.   Within each racial group there are sub-groups; for example, in Western Europe there are people belonging to the Nordic, Alpine and Mediterranean sub-groups. How would you expect people who belong to each of these sub-groups to look?

4.3   RACISM

When people are biased for or against something or somebody without a sensible reason, we say that they are **prejudiced**. One of the most common forms of prejudice is that directed against people we see as physically different from ourselves – racial prejudice.

Prejudice usually stems from fear. The stranger is seen as a threat because his pattern of conduct is unknown; the immigrant usually competes for work against the least skilled who are least secure themselves and who have the greatest social difficulties, for example in finding accommodation. Because single men are often the first to arrive in any wave of immigration, it is likely that immigrants initially become associated with anti-social behaviour, fighting and general lawlessness, just as soldiers garrisoned abroad tend to be.

'Racial' hostility can be directed at groups within the larger society who can in no way be described as belonging to a different 'race'. In Germany in the 1930s the Jews were an easy target at which to direct blame for economic problems because they tended to live in communities, retained some physical features reminiscent of their Mediterranean origin and had a distinct life-style based on their religion. This kind of prejudice is really **ethnic** prejudice.

Sometimes prejudice is directed against those who really have few distinguishing physical characteristics and in such cases a physical difference is often invented. In the 19th century, a fear of the economic effects of the arrival of thousands of Irish immigrants resulted in considerable prejudice against the Irish in Britain:

> [The Irishman is] the sorest evil this country has to strive with. In his rags and laughing savagery, he is there to undertake all work that can be done by mere strength of hand and back. He abides in this squalor and unreason, in his falsity and drunken violence, as the ready-made nucleus of degradation and disorder.
>
> Thomas Carlyle, 1839

As prejudice increased, the Irish were drawn in cartoons as similar to monkeys (see the example on page 93) and it was believed that the English were racially superior to the Irish. After Charles Darwin published his Theory of Evolution, many people used his theories to support their own view that Celts were nearer to the apes in the evolutionary process than were the Anglo-Saxons!

In Britain prejudice against the Irish as the cause of poor housing, lack of jobs, bad education and crime has declined although it still exists. The arrival of thousands of West Indians and then Asians in the 1960s presented an even more easily identifiable target for blame.

Racism can be found in many societies, white, black, brown or yellow, but the most common form today is that directed by whites against blacks.

How 'fair' such racialist attacks are, may be easily judged:

1. *Housing.* Some of the worst housing conditions in Britain until recently were in Glasgow; very few blacks or Asians live there. However, because immigrants have little money on arrival, they tend to concentrate in the poorer areas of cities where housing and other facilities (including school buildings) are likely to be worst.

2. *Employment.* Owing to the higher proportion of the black and Asian population of working age, it is usual for a higher proportion of black people to be at work. However, when employment becomes scarce black people may suffer discrimination by white employers. Between 1986 and 1988, 12 per cent of 'white' ethnic origin men were unemployed. This compared with 15 per cent of West Indian men and 17 per cent of men of Indian origin, and 24 per cent of Pakistani or Bangladeshi men (*Social Trends 20*, 1990).

3. *Social services.* Taking all expenditure on health and welfare, education, housing, national insurance and assistance into account, the average immigrant in 1981 received about 90 per cent of that received by an average member of the settled population. Immigrants, therefore, appear to take up less than their 'fair' share of social service expenditure.

4. *Overcrowding.* Immigration is not causing Britain to become more overcrowded since more people usually leave this country to settle abroad than arrive each year.

Fortunately, racist parties in Britain have received a derisory share of the votes in general elections. In some other countries racism takes on a much deeper, more sinister and evil aspect, or political parties with a racist message gain much more support. In America the Ku-Klux-Klan have been responsible for the most terrible crimes against black people. In South Africa a policy of **apartheid** was fostered by its government until 1991. Apartheid in theory meant that black and white people should develop quite separately in their own areas. However, the need for cheap black labour meant that black people

Ian Stuart, lead singer of the rock group Screwdriver, in his bedsit. The walls are adorned with racist posters.

were tolerated in white areas, but were educated in separate schools, ate in separate restaurants, sat separately in cafés and theatres and generally received inferior treatment. The 'homelands' set apart for black people are in the poorest, most infertile areas with few facilities or services.

Legislation against racism

As a result of government investigations into discrimination against immigrants in the fields of hotel and boarding-house accommodation, insurance, finance and entertainment, a Race Relations Act was passed in 1965. This outlawed discrimination 'on the ground of colour, race, ethnic or national origins' in 'places of public resort'. 'Incitement to racial hatred' was also made illegal. The Race Relations Board was established to investigate complaints of racial discrimination.

Following further evidence of discrimination (Political and Economic Planning Report 1967) another Race Relations Act was passed in 1968. This extended the areas in which discrimination was illegal to the provision of goods, facilities and services, employment, sale of property and advertising. The Act also established the Community Relations Commission which co-ordinates some 80 local community relations councils and makes grants to help with the salaries of community relations officers.

In 1976 a further Race Relations Bill became law. This tightened up the definition of discrimination and improved the treatment of ethnic minorities in the areas of employment, housing, clubs and advertising.

1. Find out to what extent the position in South Africa today
    has changed compared with that of the 1980s.

2. Study the information in Table 4.1 on page 100.
    a. Which groups are included within the term 'other' in the
        table?
    b. Excluding 'other', which ethnic group had the greatest
        proportion of managers and professional people?
    c. In order to obtain a more accurate picture of employ-
        ment opportunities, either by ethnic group or gender,
        what additional information would you need?

3. Look up 'migration' in *Social Trends* and find out the
    following:
    a. What was the net migration for the most recent years
        quoted? ('Net' means the total obtained by subtracting
        the number of emigrants from the number of
        immigrants. A + sign shows that more people entered
        than left the country for settlement.)
    b. Are more people expected to enter or leave the country
        for settlement in the first quarter of the next century?
    c. How does the Office of Population forecast future
        migration?

4.4   ETHNIC MINORITIES IN BRITAIN

Britain has absorbed people from different cultures for centuries and has gained a great deal by doing so.

1. In 1685 80,000 French Protestants (Huguenots) who were
    fleeing from persecution in France settled in England. They
    were mainly responsible for establishing the weaving
    industry that helped to industrialise the country.
2. From the middle of the 19th century onwards thousands of
    Irish people came to Britain to escape famine and low living
    standards. They provided much of the labour that Britain's
    industrial revolution needed. Many of their descendants
    have reached prominent positions today, particularly in
    medicine, education and politics.
3. Persecution in Central Europe drove many Jewish people to
    take refuge in Britain at the end of the 19th century. They
    established a flourishing clothes manufacturing industry and
    their descendants, and others that have arrived since, are
    among the leaders of the retail trade, banking and entertain-
    ment industry.

Each of these groups tended to concentrate into particular areas. In

Table 4.1 *People in employment: by sex, ethnic group and occupation, 1984–86*

Percentages and thousands

	Males					Females				
	Ethnic group					Ethnic group				
	White	West Indian or Guyanese	Indian/ Pakistani/ Bangladeshi	Other[1]	All males[2]	White	West Indian or Guyanese	Indian/ Pakistani/ Bangladeshi	Other[1]	All females[2]
Occupation (*percentages*)										
Non-manual										
Managerial and professional	34	10	38	42	34	25	27	26	30	25
Clerical and related	5		6	8	5	30	27	23	25	30
Other	6		5		6	10		9		10
Total	46	21	48	57	46	65	58	58	63	65
Manual										
Craft and similar	26	34	19	13	26	4		16		4
General labourers	2				2	0				0
Other	26	40	30	29	26	31	38	24	30	31
Total	54	78	51	43	54	35	42	42	36	35
All occupations[3] (= 100%) (thousands)	12,911	107	253	133	13,552	9,293	113	122	83	9,731

Notes:
[1] Includes African, Arab, Chinese, other stated and mixed.
[2] Includes ethnic origin not stated.
[3] Excludes occupation inadequately described or not stated.

Source: Social Trends 18, HMSO, 1988

London the Huguenots settled in Spitalfields, the Irish in Kilburn, Camden Town and Hammersmith, the Jews in Stepney. For a period they tended to marry and mix mainly within their own group, but then they gradually became absorbed in the general culture.

During the last 25 years there have been two main new waves of immigrants: those from the West Indies, and Asians from the Indian sub-continent.

An **ethnic group** is a group with a common national or racial background – everybody belongs to an ethnic group. In Britain the term 'ethnic minority' is often used only to describe non-white minorities; this is incorrect (e.g. people of Polish ancestry are also an ethnic minority), but it is the non-white ethnic minority population that is indicated in Figure 4.2.

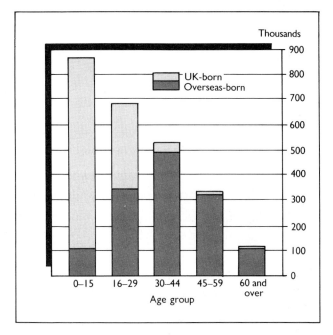

**Figure 4.2
Ethnic minority population: by age and whether UK-born or overseas-born, 1987–89.**

From: *Social Trends 22*, HMSO, 1992

The non-white population of Great Britain is small – in 1988 2 per cent were of Indian, Pakistani or Bangladeshi ethnic origin; 1 per cent were of West Indian or African ethnic origin. However, the proportion of those belonging to different ethnic minority groups is much higher in some areas than in others – for example, one in twelve of the population of the South-East.

Asian immigration

The Asian communities in Britain consist of people from Pakistan, Bangladesh and India. Those from Pakistan and Bangladesh are mainly Muslim and generally keep more closely to their traditions than do those from India.

Table 4.2 *Population: 1986–1988*

Great Britain	Percentages and thousands					
	West Indian or Guyanese	Indian	Pakistani	Bangladeshi	Chinese	African
Total (= 100%) (thousands)	482	779	433	112	132	127
	Arab	Mixed	Other	White	Not stated	All ethnic groups[1]
	72	284	149	51,600	498	54,666

[1] Including 'White' and 'Not stated' ethnic groups.

Source: adapted from *Social Trends 22*, HMSO, 1992

These 'Asians' had been settling in Britain in small numbers for many years, but in the late 1950s former British Army officers who had taken up jobs in industries with labour shortages returned to those areas in the Indian sub-continent that they had known during the war to recruit workers. Many of these immigrants came from communities with very low incomes and so they sent money from their earnings in Britain to support their families at home. Many still

Asian immigrants arriving at Heathrow in the late 1960s.

hope to save money and return to buy farms. Other immigrants have followed since the 1950s.

Although most 'Asians' are from agricultural backgrounds, many (particularly those expelled from Uganda) are businessmen, particularly shopkeepers. The Asian community also contains many professional people such as doctors.

Main areas of settlement are London (particularly Southall), Bradford, Wolverhampton, Slough, Blackburn, Leicester and Birmingham.

Some things that may help Asians to settle in Britain

1. Their attitudes are similar to those of the British 'middle class', regarding education, money, etc.

Some things that may not

1. *Language*
   English is not their first language.
2. *Values*
   Some Asian women are not encouraged to mix outside the community, or to wear Western dress, etc.
3. Culture, particularly entertainment, is more distinctive than the West Indian and, in the case of entertainment, may not attract white Britons.

Do not accept these statements as true – carry out your own survey to test their validity. (See 'Questioning evidence' on pages viii and xiv.)

Because of their distinctive physical characteristics and because of the Asian communities' desire to retain their culture, it is probable that it will take longer for Britain's new immigrants to become absorbed than it did for previous groups. Do you think it desirable that they should, or would you wish the ethnic minorities in Britain to keep their distinctive features?

A considerable proportion of all ethnic minority groups are now not immigrants at all but people born and brought up in Britain. It is inaccurate to refer to such native-born British people as second-generation immigrants. They are simply black and Asian British people.

West Indian immigration

In the early 1950s the British economy expanded after the war and there was a shortage of labour. London Transport set up a recruitment office in Barbados and nurses were also actively

*Immigrants from the West
Indies disembarking at
Southampton in 1962.*

recruited. News of the job opportunities in Britain were sent home by
the new arrivals and increasing numbers of West Indians, particularly
from Jamaica and Barbados, arrived between 1953 and 1962.

The main area of settlement was London, particularly the Brixton
and Notting Hill areas, but there are fairly large communities
elsewhere, particularly in Birmingham.

*Some things that may help West Indians
to settle in Britain*

1. *Language*
   English is their first language.
2. *Values*
   They held some of the same values
   as others living in the areas in
   which they wished to settle.
3. *Dress*
   There is no distinctive national
   dress (although individuals may
   seek a separate identity through
   dress, e.g. Rastas).
4. *Culture*
   Their social activities, music, etc.,
   are attractive to many white Britons.
5. *Religion*
   Although West Indians may be

particularly identified with the Pentecostal churches, their religious beliefs are substantially the same as those of the majority (except for a small minority of Rastafarians).

Some things that may not

1. West Indian parents may be stricter with their children at home; children may react by being wilder at school and elsewhere.
2. Many fathers are shift workers and mothers also work. This leads to lack of contact with schools and children out of school.
3. Prejudice may hurt West Indians most, as they have always regarded England as somewhere where they belong.

> **Do not accept these statements as true – carry out your own survey to test their validity.**

> **Do not accept these statements as true – carry out your own survey to test their validity.**

Immigration legislation

1905   *Aliens Act.* This was mainly intended to restrict entry of Jews from Poland and Russia. Only Commonwealth and Empire citizens could enter freely.

1962   *Commonwealth Immigrants Act.* This restricted entry to students, dependants of those already in the UK and those with 'labour vouchers'. British citizenship was available after five years' residence, not one year as before.

1968   *Commonwealth Immigrants Act.* In this, medical inspections were introduced for dependants. British citizens not born in the UK no longer had unconditional right of entry but had to wait in a 'queue' for entry vouchers.

1971   *Immigrants Act.* This introduced the test of 'patriality'. The Act entitles UK citizens to enter only if they acquired their citizenship in this country (not in Hong Kong, for example) or if they have a parent or grandparent who acquired citizenship or if they have been settled in the UK for five years.

1981   *British Nationality Act.* This legislation has effectively restricted immigration into Britain to those who have a special skill in short supply in Britain; to some dependants of people already settled in Britain; and to those who have already acquired citizenship or have a parent or grandparent who was a British citizen.

'Primary' immigration* from the New Commonwealth† and Pakistan
has now virtually ceased.

Emigration

In 1986 213,000 people left Britain to settle elsewhere. Numbers of emigrants have declined since the 1960s as other countries
experience unemployment. Now a person must either have a job to
go to or a skill or profession in demand to be accepted by another
country. Since Britain's entry into the Common Market it is relatively
easy to work in a member state, but numbers doing so are not yet
very high because of language problems and a lack of suitable
employment. Traditional countries for British settlement are:
Australia, New Zealand, Canada, the United States and South Africa.
Reasons given for emigration include:

- better career prospects
- more opportunities for children
- better climate
- higher standard of living
- more freedom
- less class consciousness

1. a.   i. Would you be prepared to emigrate?
         ii. Where to?
         iii. What would be the advantages and disadvantages of
              emigrating to the country of your choice?
         or Why would you not be prepared to emigrate?
    b. Most people now living in Great Britain originated from
       somewhere other than where they are now living.
       Maybe their parents have just moved from somewhere
       else in Great Britain to seek work, perhaps their grand-
       parents came from Ireland, perhaps one of their
       ancestors came from Africa 200 years ago and became
       part of the black communities that then existed in ports
       such as Cardiff or Liverpool.
         Obtain a map of the world and using a red marker let
       every member of your group enter the place of origin of
       their mother and father (i.e. two dots). Use a green
       marker and enter your grandparents' place of origin (i.e.
       four dots). Then use a blue marker to enter your great-
       grandparents' place of origin or that of earlier ancestors
       if you know!

* People coming to settle in Britain for the first time, as opposed to relatives coming
   to join people already here.
† Those members of the Commonwealth that were later parts of the British Empire,
   such as India and several African states, as opposed to the old Commonwealth
   (predominantly white) countries, such as Canada and Australia.

2. Consider the factors on pages 103 to 105 which make the assimilation of particular ethnic groups easy or difficult. Alter and/or add to these suggestions after discussing them with members of the ethnic minority groups concerned. (Obviously if you are a member of a particular ethnic minority group you will be able to make an informed statement in respect of your own group.)

4.5 SOCIAL CLASS

In any group some individuals are regarded as more worthy of respect than others. When we say someone is 'more important' than someone else, we are saying that they have a higher **status** so far as we are concerned. Status can be obtained in two ways. It can be:

1. **Ascribed.** This means that our status is given to us with no effort on our part; we may have inherited our status from our parents (e.g. we may have inherited a title).

2. **Achieved.** This means we have earned our status. Perhaps we have become an MP or a brain surgeon.

Sometimes we may have a high status in one group and a low status in another. The daredevil leader of a motorcycle gang may be held in high regard by the gang, but most people may have a very poor opinion of him. A black lawyer in Carolina may have high status in the black community, but be regarded as inferior by a white man with a much humbler job.

Sometimes the status system is very rigid. In India until recently (and still to some degree) people were born into a position in society from which they could not move except downwards by marrying someone 'beneath' them, or becoming polluted by certain actions. This **caste** system, with the priests (Brahmins) at the top and the 'Untouchables' (such as leather workers) at the bottom, existed for centuries in Hindu society, which taught that contentment with one's position in society was a holy principle. The caste system was officially abolished in 1947.

The same sort of system existed in medieval Europe with the serf at the bottom, the freeman in the middle and the lord at the top. This 'feudal system' was based on land ownership but was not quite so rigid as the 'caste' system. It was possible for a serf to become 'free', for example by running away and living in a city for a year and a day.

Today in Britain, the way we talk, the way we live and the sort of job we do still label us as belonging to a particular position in society – to a **social class**. How rigid the British class system is can be debated. In the sixties many people believed that we were becoming a 'classless society', and that power and high status within the general society could be achieved by effort alone. That this is still to be achieved is shown by the declaration in 1990 by the British Prime Minister, John Major, that he intended to create a 'classless society'.

The most powerful group within a society – the people with considerable control and influence – is called an **elite**. The name given to the group of people who reach the top by their own efforts is the **meritocracy**.

Although the concept of social class existed before Karl Marx, he was the person who put forward the idea of a class as a group of people sharing common interests. These interests depended on whether or not they owned **capital**, the finance which controls industry and commerce (*Das Kapital*, 1867). Marx thought that the middle class of teachers, lawyers and clerical workers would die out as they would identify with the industrial workers who did not own 'capital' either. This middle group has actually grown enormously and has tended to try and adopt the life-styles of the upper class rather than the lower. On the other hand, there is evidence that as more people enter clerical work the status of office work has declined (see Lockwood, *The Black Coated Worker: A Study in Class Consciousness*, 1958) and more 'white-collar' workers are joining trade unions.

Class in Britain (Is there any?)

Certain types of dress may appear to identify people as belonging to a particular class. However, all evidence needs to be questioned. For example, the photograph on page 123 may have been

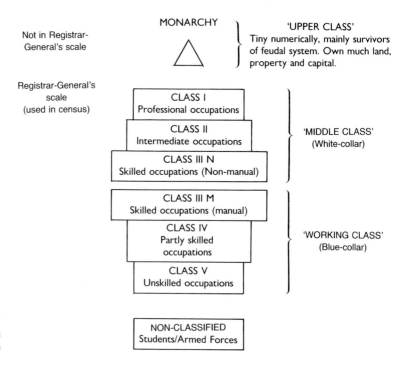

Figure 4.3
The British class system

have been taken in The Mall in London; this could mean that the people in formal dress are on their way to a Royal Garden Party. Many people attending such a party will be in Class I or II, but other guests could be from any social class, for example important local councillors. In any case the morning dress may be hired. An outline of the British class system is given in Figure 4.3.

1. Check the numbers in each of these class groupings in, for example, *Social Trends,* and then draw the diagram to scale.

2. Answer the following questions and list your reasons.

Figure 4.4
'One day, my son, all these freeholds will be yours!'

From: *Evening Standard,*
31 January 1991

a. Do you think people should be able to buy a private education?
b. Do you think people should be able to buy their own home?
c. Do you think people should be able to buy an army commission?
d. Do you think people should be able to buy private medicine and health care?
e. Do you think people should be able to buy holiday cottages?
f. Do you think people should be able to buy a holiday caravan?
g. Do you think people should be able to inherit wealth?

3. The official census lists people by social class, based on their jobs. This definition is really too simple, for in order to belong to a social class you must be accepted by the other members as having a common identity with them, so your class may depend on many other factors apart from occupation: where you were educated, what sort of accent you have, how you dress, how much you own. Can you add anything else to this list?

4. It has been suggested that only a working-class man holds his cigarette by cupping the lighted end in his palm. Can you suggest any behaviour that identifies someone with a particular class but has nothing to do with income?

5. Which of these leisure activities do you associate with: (a) upper-class people, (b) middle-class people and (c) working-class people:

horse racing	golf	football pools
greyhound	polo	orchestral
racing	stock car racing	concerts
bingo	ballet	pigeon racing
football	wrestling	tennis
rugby	bridge	snooker
dominoes	live theatre	

6. People who wish others to know what their status in society is often buy things which they do not need and may even not particularly want for any other reason. These things are called **status symbols**. From the list below choose items that you think are often status symbols:

a garden gnome	a Bentley car	a car telephone
a mink coat	a gold watch	
a detached house	a goat	
an automatic	a colour	
washing	television	
machine	an Alsatian dog	

7. Status symbols are not just part of modern Western society. **Conspicuous consumption** is common in many societies as a way of indicating status. The Kwakiutt Indians of Canada held 'potlatchs' which were ceremonial feasts where status was gained by destroying possessions. In the reign of Henry VIII a woman was not allowed to wear gold chains unless her husband could afford to provide a horse for the King's service. In New England she could not wear a silk scarf unless her husband was worth a thousand dollars.

   'Keeping up with the Joneses' is often used to describe the attempt to gain higher status, or at least look as though one has attained it. Can you gain higher status by acquiring the objects associated with it?

4.6   SOCIAL DIFFERENCES IN BRITAIN

We saw earlier in this unit that people in Britain are not equal. Some people regard this as normal and right, while others would wish to change the situation. But what is the situation?

Personally owned wealth is still concentrated in the hands of very few people. (If houses are excluded, the top 1 per cent of the population own 27 per cent of all the wealth.) The changes that have taken place are mainly the result of more people owning their own home, having more household goods and larger insurance policies. However, the 'privatisation' of former nationalised industries in recent years has also resulted in an increase in share ownership. By 1991 25 per cent of the adult population owned shares. Large fortunes, however, still belong only to the few. They include large houses, big estates, paintings, etc., as well as shareholding and money.

Some people say that sharing out wealth would merely give the state more power, but perhaps there is some way that wealth could be redistributed without this happening. What do you think?

The wealthiest people in Britain may be listed as follows:

1. *The hereditary peerage.* This consists of about 1,500 people, some of whose titles only date back to the beginning of this century when the Prime Minister, Lloyd George, sold them. But people who joined the aristocracy had to be wealthy, even if it was only to buy their way in. The Duke of Westminster, with more than £300 million, is probably the most wealthy person in Britain, although the Queen has an estimated private fortune of about £50 million (some say it is more than this).

2. *The gentry.* The old landed gentry are those who have owned their estates for generations. Much of their wealth is tied up in their land, but this is potentially very valuable. (Look at a copy of *Country Life* from your library – it will give you some idea of the gentry's life-style.)

3. *The City.* This group involves many of the families of the landed gentry, plus leading banking families like the Rothschilds. Large personal fortunes have been made in the City in recent years, mainly from property dealing. Some new 'whiz-kids' from the lower middle class have managed to accumulate fortunes.

4. *Commerce.* A few notable fortunes have been built up by men like Isaac Wolfson and Hugh Fraser in the retail trade, now mostly into the second or third generation, from those who started at the bottom. Robert Maxwell was a first-generation newspaper 'tycoon'.

5. *Entertainment and media.* This group includes pop stars, actors and writers who have made it to the top and who have large fortunes, often only temporarily.

Derby Day at Epsom. How might these people have made their money?

The other end of the scale.

At the other end of the scale are the poor. The welfare state will not allow anyone to starve, but living standards can often be very low.

1. Study the information given in Table 4.3.

    Table 4.3 *Distribution of wealth*

United Kingdom	Percentages and £ billion			
	1976	1981	1986	1989
Marketable wealth*				
Percentage of wealth owned by:				
Most wealthy 1%	21	18	18	18
Most wealthy 5%	38	36	36	38
Most wealthy 10%	50	50	50	53
Most wealthy 25%	71	73	73	75
Most wealthy 50%	92	92	90	94
Total marketable wealth (£ billion)	280	565	955	1,578
Marketable wealth less value of dwellings				
Percentage of wealth owned by:				
Most wealthy 1%	29	26	25	28
Most wealthy 5%	47	45	46	53
Most wealthy 10%	57	56	58	66
Most wealthy 25%	73	74	75	81
Most wealthy 50%	88	87	89	94

    * **Marketable wealth** is wealth that can readily be changed into cash if required (e.g. stocks and shares, bank deposits, houses and 'consumer durables' such as cars and washing machines). As it excludes trust funds, the wealth of the richest groups, who invest in these funds, is underestimated.
       The most wealthy tend to have their marketable wealth in the form of shares, etc. which tend to gain in value; the poorer groups tend to have theirs in the form of consumer durables which lose value.

    Source: Social Trends 22, HMSO, 1992

    a. Make a pie chart showing the distribution of wealth in 1989.
    b. What percentage of wealth was owned by the least wealthy 50 per cent of the population in 1989?
    c. When the value of homes is deducted from the total wealth, how much of the remaining wealth is owned by the most wealthy 5 per cent of the population?
    d. Which group has increased its share of wealth most during the period shown?

2. a. Do any of the following 'deserve' to be poor?
        i. *Mrs Hunt.* Deserted by husband when he found another woman. Six children all under fourteen.
        ii. *Mr Manley.* Demolition worker: good worker and

earns well. Heavy drinker and loses frequently on horses. Two children.

iii. *Mr Matthews.* Former regular soldier, lost an arm and partially sighted as a result of accident. Has not worked for five years.

iv. *Mrs Thomas.* Former bank clerk. Served three years in prison for fraud. Now says she finds it impossible to get employment. Five-year-old child by previous marriage.

b. Do any of the following 'deserve' to be rich?

i. *Mr Goole.* Managing director of large engineering works. Started as apprentice, bought small, run-down business with win on the pools.

ii. *Miss Cholmley.* Inherited large fortune from her father. Spends most of her time doing voluntary social work.

iii. *Sir Henry Pooles.* Cabinet minister. Father owned plantations in India and Ceylon. Freedom from financial worries has allowed him to devote all his time to politics.

iv. *Mr Southwark.* Large fortune based on property. Started with one large house in London on a mortgage and made it into rented bed-sits.

4 DISCUSSION

I Read the following poem carefully:

The Oxford Voice

When you hear it languishing
and hooing and cooing and sidling through the
    front teeth,
        the Oxford voice
         or worse still
      the would-be Oxford voice
you don't even laugh any more, you can't.

For every blooming bird is an Oxford cuckoo nowadays,
you can't sit on a bus nor in the tube
but it breathes gently and languishingly in
    the back of your neck

And oh, so seductively superior, so seductively
      self-effacingly
      deprecatingly
        superior.—
We wouldn't insist on it for a moment
      but we are
      we are
    you admit we are
      superior.—

                        D. H. Lawrence (1885–1930)

a. What do the following words mean in the context of the poem?
   i. sidling
   ii. languishingly
   iii. seductively
   iv. self-effacingly
   v. deprecatingly
b. Do you think some accents are superior to others? If so, in what ways?
c. Would you like to see accents disappear in Britain? Why/Why not?
d. Do you feel that accent can influence a person's chances in life? Identify ten well-known people (from politics, sport, entertainment, etc.) and identify their accents. How typical are these people of successful people generally in Britain?

2 Racism is not just black versus white

The simple notion of black-versus-white has finally been proved to belong to the history books.

What has being going on in a long hot summer of turbulence in New York has pitted black against Hasidic Jew in one area of Brooklyn, black against assimilated Jew and blue-collar Italian in another, and immigrant black against Korean shopkeepers in a third.

It has also revealed a split between West Indian and Hispanic blacks, many fresh off the boat, and American blacks with roots going back to Old South plantations.

In lower Manhattan, meanwhile, the Chinese and Asians from the Indian sub-continent are beginning to clash in competition for commercial opportunities, including heroin dealing.

Charles Laurence reports on new tensions

In Florida, Hispanics and blacks, who once considered themselves allies against the white power structure, have been feuding over jobs and politics, while in Washington DC there was a black/Hispanic riot last year.

Los Angeles has reported a sharp increase in violence between Mexican Hispanics—Latinos—and blacks, and between Latinos and Asians.

All the New York conflicts have surfaced in areas known to race-relations experts as "zones of transition", areas where the new are rubbing shoulders with the established. Differing cultural habits focus tribal prejudices, but the bottom line remains the old classic—economic competition.

From: *The Daily Telegraph*, 23 September 1991

a. Which groups in New York are in conflict with each other according to the source material above?

b. What reasons does the writer suggest are responsible for racism?

c. What do you think are the causes of racism?

3 Read the following extract carefully.

There's another problem. I remember black people and distinguish between them a lot quicker than between white people. It's the same with white people and their own kind. I don't begrudge them this but seeing as they run everything and they run the thing whereby if you get identified you can get messed up, then black people are at a disadvantage. Last Friday I got stopped by the police to be identified by some really drunk old white man who had been assaulted by a black youth. The drunk was staring at me for a long time from the back of the car. I kept praying, 'Say it's not me 'cause I know it's not me.'

All these community relations guys the police have is a waste of time. The police don't need any community relations because anybody in society will realise the need for police. The police should stick to their job, strictly, what they're supposed to be doing and not try pushing people over the limit. If I'm doing a good job I don't need to run around telling everybody what a good job I'm doing.

Until the police stop what they're doing to blacks, any black that joins the police force is going to be ostracised by his own community.

There's a lot of black kids that hate white people and especially the police. I wouldn't call it prejudice because prejudice – I looked it up in the dictionary once – means *prae judicum*, it's Latin. It's judging someone before evidence. Listen, if you're kicked around by people and that and you end up hating them, how can you call that prejudice? It's discrimination but it's not prejudice. It's experience.

Nance Lui Fyson and Sally Greenhill,
People Talking Series: Investigating Society

a. Why does the writer say that black people are at a disadvantage?
b. What do 'ostracised' and 'prejudice' mean?
c. Would you agree that 'anybody in society will realise the need for police'?
d. How does the writer distinguish between 'prejudice' and 'discrimination'?
e. From your experience would you say that the police treat black people unfairly?

4   Read the following material carefully.

Race and class prejudice

We asked a series of questions to establish measures of perceived race and class prejudice and discrimination in Britain.

The findings show a striking degree of unanimity that Britain is a racially prejudiced society, with 90 per cent of people saying there is prejudice against Asians and blacks, and the majority saying there is a *lot* of prejudice. The younger a person is the more likely he or she is to see Britain as a prejudiced country. Moreover, people are relatively pessimistic about trends.

Trends in race and class prejudice

Great Britain	Percentages and numbers	
	Race prejudice	Class discrimination
Percentages thinking race/class inequality in Britain		
Is greater now than in past	45	22
Is less now than in past	16	30
Is same as in past	36	45
Other/don't know/not answered	3	3
Will be greater in future than now	42	16
Will be less in future than now	17	32
Will be same in future	36	49
Other/don't know/not answered	4	3
Weighted sample size (= 100%) (numbers)	1,719	1,719

Similarly in respect of social class, a majority of the sample took the view that class prejudice is still an important feature of British life. Not only did over 70 per cent believe that British people are aware of social class differences nowadays, but a similar proportion believed that a person's social class still affects his or her opportunities. Pessimism about trends in class prejudice is, however, less marked than pessimism about racial prejudice.

Social Trends 15, HMSO, 1985

Although the 'British Attitudes' survey (1984) above showed a perception of continued prejudice against non-whites in Britain, an Audience Selection Poll (1985) asked: 'Would Britain be a better place to live in if only whites lived here?' The overwhelming majority – 80 per cent – said 'No'; only 15 per cent said 'Yes'.

Carry out a local limited survey using the question about racial prejudice in the extract above (and the Audience Selection Poll question quoted above). Have equal numbers of males and females and equal numbers in two age groups: 15–20 and 40+ so that you can test the accuracy of the statement in *Social Trends 15* that 'the younger a person is the more likely he or she is to see Britain as a prejudiced country'.

When you have completed your questionnaire present your findings in percentages divided by gender and age. Write a report of your findings comparing these, where appropriate, to the two national polls.

5 In 1990 the Prime Minister, John Major, stated that he wished to see a 'classless society'.

According to the Labour MP Harriet Harman, 'If John Major believes in a classless society, he should recognise that how long you live and how healthy you are depends on class.' *Until he does, talk of a classless society must remain a joke.*

Daily Mirror, 5 December 1990

Would you like to live in a completely classless society? Is such a society possible?

4 ADDITIONAL ASSIGNMENTS AND INVESTIGATIONS

1. Carry out a survey of immigrants in your school or college (including yourself where appropriate). Try and establish the major problems that immigrants face: language, food, hostility, accommodation, etc. Prepare a table (or pie chart or histogram) to show which of these problems are regarded as most severe.

2. Make a sheet plan of your area and try to divide it up to indicate areas of 'lower'-, 'middle'- and 'upper'-class housing. Then write a short report on each, outlining the major characteristics that you have observed.

3. Draw up a list of all business premises such as shops and restaurants owned by members of ethnic minority groups in your area. Arrange for members of your group to visit each (having a meal, making a purchase, etc., as the case may be) and to report back on what they have observed. Note both the differences and the similarities between this and similar premises not owned by members of ethnic minority groups. (Make a particular note of anything which you feel will help to enrich British culture.)

4 OUTLINE OF AN APPROPRIATE GCSE INVESTIGATION/PROJECT

(For guidance, see 'Coursework for GCSE' on pages ix–xiv.)

Title   An investigation into the influence of parents on the choice of marital partner in differing ethnic groups.

Hypothesis   In Britain Asian parents are more likely than white parents to try and influence their children's choice of marital partner.

Secondary sources   Asian newspapers in Britain; newspapers read by the majority (find out which these are in *Social Trends*).

Objectives – e.g. references to marriage partners per column inch ('quantitative'); prominence given to adverts for marriage partners ('qualitative measure').

Problems – e.g. language (may require translation).

Limitations – e.g. the proportion of Asians who read Asian newspapers as compared with those who read the same newspapers as those of the majority population.

Any books or reference works such as *British Social Attitudes*, Gower Publishing Co. Ltd, 1988.

Primary sources   **Questionnaire** Directed at:

1. Asian young people, 14–18
   a. Male
   b. Female
2. Asian parents
   a. Male
   b. Female
3. White young people, 14–18
   a. Male
   b. Female
4. White parents
   a. Male
   b. Female

In drawing up your questionnaire:

- Make sure your questions do not suggest answers.
- Limit your questions to those relevant to the hypothesis. About ten might be enough.
- Try and suggest a limited number of responses to each question. This will clarify and make your analysis of them easier.

Questions where you make a list of all, or most, possible answers and ask people to tick a box, are called **coded-choice questions**, or **closed** questions, because the responses you receive are limited to those you offer. The advantages of these questions are that you can establish patterns and use these to draw up graphs and other tables; the disadvantage is that you may not find out what people really think. **Open** questions allow any response, but may be difficult to analyse because all your respondents may give differing answers.

Pilot your questionnaire to ensure it is understood and 'works' on a few people before launching your main questionnaire, which you should alter in line with your pilot results.

Sampling Although you will have to limit the numbers in your sample try and make it as *representative* as possible (e.g. try and get the correct proportion of ages, sexes and 'class' backgrounds as exists in the general population).

Use a *sampling frame* if you can (such as your school/college roll for 14–18-year-olds or your local electoral roll for adults). Select *randomly* from it (e.g. every tenth person in the correct category).

Interviews A smaller selection of people should be selected for interviews (but again some attempt should be made to make it representative). You might limit your interviews to those currently getting married and their parents. Your interview should be an opportunity to get answers in more depth than is possible in a questionnaire.

Observation Perhaps difficult for this project; if you cannot think of a way of incorporating it say *why*. Remember the investigation or project is examining your knowledge of research methods and your practical ability rather than your actual results.

Analyse your findings in detail. Give your results clearly relating these to the evidence you have found. Use graphs, pie charts, etc., wherever possible, to illustrate your findings.

Say whether your findings have proved or disproved your hypothesis, stating why as briefly as possible.

Appendices e.g.

Sample of your questionnaire.

Questions used in your interviews.

Some sample extracts from newspapers or other secondary source.

Bibliography.

4 GCSE QUESTION

Note: GCSE questions often require answers using information from interrelated themes. This one is mainly, but not exclusively, concerned with inequality.

Consider the photograph and the passage which follows:

Source A

Photo: Sheila Grey/Format

Source B

Although most people talk of belonging to the 'upper', 'middle' or 'working' class and have a pretty good idea of what they mean by these terms we find on closer examination that the concept of 'class' is a rather vague one, and different people mean different things when they use the term.

G. O'Donnell, *The Human Web*,
John Murray, 1978

(**a**) One way of determining an individual's social class is to find the occupational group to which he or she belongs. Give *four* examples of different jobs and the classes with which they are associated. (4)

(**b**) The occupational group to which a person belongs is not the only way of determining social class; what other factors can be taken into account? (6)

(c) Do you agree with the writer of Source B that 'the concept of class is a rather vague one'? Give reasons for your answer.   (6)

(d) The photograph can be taken to indicate the extent of class divisions in our society, yet some social scientists claim that these divisions are less important nowadays. Giving reasons for your opinions say whether or not you agree that class differences are less important.   (8)

4 SELF-TEST QUESTIONS

(Answers on page 290)

1. What do we call the situation in which people are treated in a particular way because of their group membership?

2. Name four factors that may inhibit the absorption of minority groups into the general community.

3. What is the name given to a group identifiable by a common culture based on a common ancestry?

4. What are the most commonly accepted names for the three racial groups into which people are sometimes divided?

5. What were the major areas of discrimination controlled by the Race Relations Acts of 1965, 1968 and 1976?

6. Which group of immigrants concentrated their settlement in these areas of London?
   a. Stepney
   b. Spitalfields
   c. Hammersmith
   d. Brixton
   e. Southall

7. a. What do we call status which is given?
   b. What do we call status that is earned?

8. What is a 'meritocracy'?

9. Name three forms of 'marketable wealth'.

10. State four differences between social classes in Britain.

A BETTER LIFE?

Are these people really poor?

5.1 POVERTY

Some people deny that poverty exists in Britain today just as Charles Booth, a rich Liverpool merchant, did in the 1870s when he carried out a survey to prove that a quarter of the population did not live in poverty as the Social Democratic Federation claimed.

Charles Booth was shocked to disprove his own hypothesis and to find poverty was even more widespread than had been claimed. Booth published his first survey in *Life and Labour of the People* (1889–90) and went on to help with the passing of the Old Age Pensions Act of 1908.

One of the problems about discussing poverty is that people mean different things when they say someone is 'poor': sometimes they mean that the person is starving, sometimes that the person cannot afford a car. Both these definitions may be correct; the first person might be in **absolute poverty**, the second in **relative poverty**.

Absolute poverty

Booth defined poverty as a state below which it was impossible to live a healthy life; he called the boundary of this state 'the poverty line'.

In 1899 Seebohm Rowntree developed Booth's work with the first of his three studies of poverty in York (such a study conducted over time is called a 'longitudinal study'). Rowntree divided poverty into:

- *primary poverty*, in which earnings were insufficient to maintain physical efficiency.
- *secondary poverty*, in which earnings could have been sufficient if they had not been used *wastefully* (Rowntree did not allow for luxuries such as cigarettes, alcohol and meat).

In his first study Rowntree found that 15 per cent of the population of York was in primary poverty; in his last study in 1950 he found that the proportion had dropped to 1.5 per cent.

Theoretically the development of the welfare state should mean that no one in Britain is in absolute poverty but if one considers the main categories of those in poverty listed by Rowntree – the old, the mentally and physically disabled, the ill, single-parent families, the unemployed, and those with large families but low incomes – it is easy to see why some people may be. For example, some people will have difficulty managing the little money they do have; elderly people may need more heat than others; some people may not know what benefits they can claim. In fact, very substantial sums of benefit remain unclaimed.

Relative poverty

This was defined by Townsend in *Poverty, Inequality and Class Structure* (ed. Wedderburn, 1973) as having 'resources so seriously below those commanded by the average individual or family that they are, in effect, excluded from ordinary living patterns, customs and activities'. (Relative poverty has also been called **relative deprivation** by both Robert Merton and Peter Townsend.)

Relative poverty is not simply a statistical comparison, it is a *feeling* of being deprived. People do not usually compare themselves to the monarchy and feel deprived because they do not have a palace and a yacht. It is by comparison with our **reference group** – the people with whom we think we should be compared – that we feel deprived or not.

Relative poverty is difficult to measure; Townsend and Abel-Smith in 1960 (*The Poor and the Poorest*) took anyone at or below the total amount that would be received by a person on supplementary benefits, which the Government considers the basic level of need. The problem is that if a government increased the benefit levels this would appear to increase the number of people in relative poverty.

Reasons for poverty

Structural poverty

Some people such as Westergaard and Resley (*Class in a Capitalist Society*, 1976) have claimed that the same process that keeps the rich rich keeps the poor poor. They believed that society was operated by and for the benefit of the wealthy and this required that some people should be poor. Gans (*More Equality*, 1973) took a similar view: the poor served a function in society by being available to do the dirty, dangerous and menial jobs and in providing jobs for those who 'serve the poor, or shield the rest of the population from them'.

Cycle of deprivation

The cycle of poverty shown in Figure 5.1 has been described by many researchers; Rutter and Madge (*Cycle of Disadvantage*, 1976) found the cycle occurring if three out of a number of factors were present. These factors included poor education, inadequate housing, family instability and large family. Large families are no longer a major cause of poverty – unskilled workers now usually have smaller families than do the middle class.

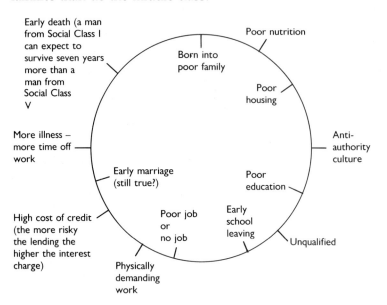

Figure 5.1

Culture of poverty

Oscar Lewis in his book *The Children of Sanchez* (1962) first used the term 'the culture of poverty' to describe how the poor Mexicans of his study had developed an attitude to life which made them able to cope with poverty but which in doing so made it inevitable that their poverty would continue. It has been suggested that, like these Mexicans, many poor people are hostile to authority such as social workers and that this example is followed by their children in hostility towards teachers and the police. The poor reject the norms of society because they cannot succeed within it; they therefore do not try to compete or they choose illegal means of obtaining the objectives set by society because they cannot achieve these objectives legally.

Poverty trap

This is the situation in which someone who has fallen into poverty finds it difficult to climb out again because of the way the benefits system operates: any increase in earnings results in the loss of means-tested benefit such as Family Credit or Housing Benefit. The effects of the poverty trap were reduced by the reform of benefits in 1988.

However, although some people are born into poverty and never rise from it and others fall into poverty and remain poor, many others experience periods of poverty – perhaps through temporary unemployment, child-rearing as a single parent or old age.

1. These people are given labels which act as convenient shorthand ways for the affluent to explain the existence of the poor; labels such as Unemployed, Disabled, Old Age Pensioner, Unsupported Mother, Ex-Prisoner. Recently other categories have been added to the list, Low Wage Earner, Large Family, Problem Family, Homeless Family. In some parts of the country the categories of Coloured Person, Foreigner or Catholic have similar implications.

    The rediscovery of poverty came briefly as a shock to the many people who believed that it was one of the giants of the 1930s which had perished in the post-war era, when the Welfare State made us One Nation.

    Bill Jordan, *Paupers*

    See how many of the categories of 'the poor' defined by Bill Jordan you can find in *Social Trends*. See what increase or decrease there has been in these categories over recent years.

2.

Britain is **STILL** a country where the rich live longer and the poor die sooner. And the gap has grown. Poverty is a killer, while the wealthy are able to buy health, the survey concludes.

"The evidence is overwhelming," says Toby Harris, director of the Association of Community Health Councils for England and Wales, which carried out the study.

"Social inequalities increased during the 1980s. And so has the health gap between rich and poor."

Today all the major and minor killers – notably lung cancer and coronary heart disease – hit the poor hardest.

Children, the report declares, are the main sufferers.

During the last ten years of Thatcherism, the numbers of youngsters living in poverty has doubled. At the same time, homelessness, housing conditions, childhood sickness, drug abuse and children's diets have all grown worse.

S EVIDENCE, the report points to infant deaths. In 1987, the mortality rate among babies whose fathers had unskilled jobs was 70 per cent higher than among those whose fathers had a professional occupation.

These are among the report's key findings:

● MANUAL workers suffer more ill-health than white-collar workers and have less chance of surviving life-threatening disease.

● DEATH rates in the North are significantly higher than in the South.

● PREVENTIVE health services are used more frequently by people from higher social classes.

● BAD housing and homelessness have strong links with poor health. Unemployment, too, contributes significantly to mental illness.

● MORE smoking, poor diet and less exercise are more commonly associated with poorer social classes.

From: *Daily Mirror,*
5 December 1990

Death rate in Lothian linked to poverty

by SARAH WILSON

PEOPLE living in deprived areas of Lothian are twice as likely to die prematurely as those who live in more affluent communities, a report revealed yesterday.

A strong link between poverty and early death has been established by the Lothian Regional Council study, which also examined the connection between social deprivation and infant mortality, illegitimacy and child poverty.

"The European Commission has recognised Pilton as one of the 25 areas of major deprivation in Europe. When people are poor, they get sick more easily."

Child poverty in Lothian more than doubled between 1981 and 1987, according to the survey. The number of children living with unemployed parents rose by nearly 80 per cent compared to a 19 per cent rise in the rest of Scotland.

From: *The Scotsman,*
14 April 1990

Illnesses highlight difference in class

AS MR MAJOR strives to create a classless society, the survey reveals that differences in health between classes are at record levels.

Unskilled men were one and a half times as likely as professional people to have a long-standing illness (40 per cent compared with 26 per cent). While 33 per cent of skilled female workers had a long-standing illness, among the semi-skilled the figure rose to 40 per cent and among the unskilled to 47 per cent.

From: *The Daily Telegraph,*
5 December 1990

Examine the secondary sources shown above.

a. List each of the factors that are stated to be linked with
    both poverty and poor health.
b. How reliable are these sources?
c. Now conduct a limited survey of your own and see if
    you can find a link with any of the factors you have
    listed under (a) and the social class of individuals.

(You might limit yourself to three categories:

Class I to IIIN, i.e. all white-collar workers and their
children

Class IIIM, i.e. all skilled manual workers and their
children

Class IV and V, i.e. all semi-skilled and unskilled
manual workers and their children.)

5.2   THE WELFARE STATE

Large sums of money are collected through direct taxation
such as income tax, and indirect taxation such as VAT. Much of this is
used directly to help those who are most in need, such as the sick, the
disabled, the unemployed or the handicapped. Most of the remainder
is also used for general services that cater for everybody regardless of
income, for example education, the police, the armed forces and
roads.

Some people think we have gone too far in looking after people's
affairs for them, and it would be better to collect less tax and make
people pay for such things as health care or education themselves.
What do you think?

Until about 100 years ago, very few people would have considered
that it was the responsibility of the state to cater for the needs of the
normal working person. Most would have considered that most
people should not be allowed to starve or die of neglect, but that it
was not the job of the state to help them find work (by providing Job
Centres), pay for them to go to university, give them money in addition to their wages if they had larger families (Income Support) or
subsidise their travel (on 'nationalised' railways).

The state did not accept many of the functions that most people
today consider as natural to it. It was believed that it was the function
of the family to care for its members: children were an insurance
policy against poverty in old age; brothers would help out during
unemployment or illness; mothers and sisters should assist during
childbirth and when the children were young. It was not until the
election of the Liberal government of 1906 that the welfare state as we
know it today started to emerge with the following provisions:

1908   Old Age Pensions
1909   Labour Exchanges
1911   Illness and some unemployment insurance.

The man mainly responsible for working these reforms, Sir William Beveridge, produced the 'Beveridge Report' on social insurance in 1942. This firmly stated that benefits were a right, not a charity, and that the welfare state should be paid for by contributions from employers, employees and the Government.

The main Acts resulting from the Beveridge Report were:

1945   Family Allowances (an allowance paid to mothers for each child – now Child Benefit)
1946   National Health Service
1948   National Assistance Act (additional cash for those in most need – now Income Support)
1949   Housing Act (this extended the policy of subsidising council housing).

There were also reforms in prisons, childcare and legal aid.

In July 1948 the *Daily Mail* carried this report:

> On Monday morning you will wake in a new Britain, in a state which 'takes over' its citizens six months before they are born, providing care and free service for their birth, for their early years, their schooling, sickness, workless days, widowhood and retirement.

Many people in the Britain of 1948 would have been surprised, and probably disappointed, to read in a booklet produced by the Child Poverty Action Group in 1979 that the British are more hard-hearted towards the poor than are other Europeans. Only a third of the British people questioned in an EC survey in 1979 thought there was poverty in Britain. Nearly half those questioned thought that the main cause of poverty was laziness or lack of willpower, the view of only 25 per cent of those questioned in other Common Market countries. A fifth of British people thought that the Government was doing too much to help the poor.

1.   The number of people living in Britain at subsistence level, that is just managing to keep themselves alive, has over the years been as shown in Figure 5.2.

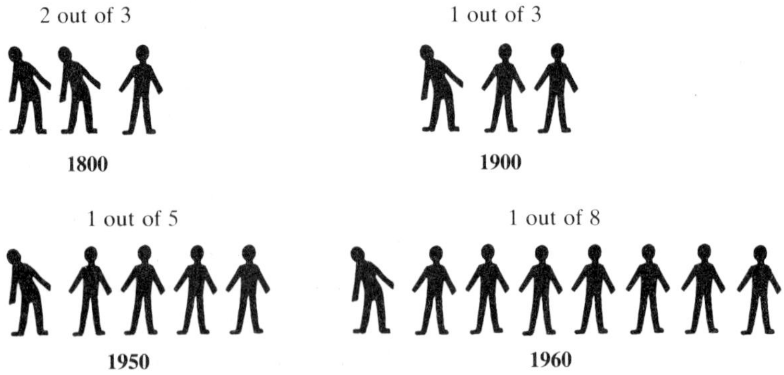

2 out of 3   1 out of 3

1800   1900

1 out of 5   1 out of 8

1950   1960

Find out how many are living at subsistence level today.

Figure 5.2
Number of people living in Britain at subsistence level.

5.3 BENEFITS AND SERVICES

The founders of our welfare state were pioneers of a system of welfare that has been adopted in many other countries. However, the UK is now by no means the leader in welfare provision.

The welfare state tries to ensure that everyone has a decent start in life and that real suffering and hardship are kept to a minimum from the cradle to the grave. As prices rise, benefit levels are also usually increased, although there is no automatic tying of benefit levels to the cost of living (**indexation**) as there is in some countries. In a book, it is impossible to give up-to-date benefit levels so you should find out for yourself the current rate of benefits.

Services and benefits provided in the UK include:

1. *Ante-natal clinics.* These are places where the development of the unborn baby is checked. In 1900, 5 out of every 1,000 births were likely to cause the death of the mother (**maternal mortality**) and 150 out of every 1,000 live-born children died in the first year (**infant mortality**). Now the respective figures are less than 1 and about 9.

2. a. *Child Benefit.* This is usually paid to the mother for each child. This is not means-tested and goes directly to all eligible mothers.

   b. *Income Support.* This was introduced in 1988, and is payable to low-income working families. This replaced Family Income Supplement, which was introduced in 1970 to help wage earners in full employment, particularly those with large families.

3. *National Health Service.* We can become ill at any time and the United Kingdom is unusual in meeting the full cost of hospital treatment and most of the cost of treatment by family doctors, opticians, dentists, etc.

4. *Sickness Benefit.* This is a cash allowance to those who are incapable of work through illness and have made enough National Insurance contributions.

5. *Schools* – and further and higher education (including subsistence awards and students' grants).

6. *Unemployment Benefit.* You must have made sufficient National Insurance contributions to qualify (these are partly paid for by yourself and partly by your employer). If you have not paid enough, or if your unemployment benefit is insufficient to meet your needs, you may receive Income Support. You can only receive this if no suitable work is available and it will be reduced or refused if you have brought unemployment on yourself or are responsible for prolonging it.

7. *Retirement Pension.* This is received by men at the age of 65 and women at 60. Even if you do not give up work it is paid automatically at 70 for a man and 65 for a woman. It is now divided into two parts: a basic flat-rate pension and a pension

based on how much the person concerned was earning before retirement. In addition you can obtain Income Support if the amount you receive altogether is regarded as insufficient to cover the official assessment of what a person needs to pay for food, heat, clothing, etc.

There are also a great many other social security benefits. For details of these look up 'National Insurance' and related cash benefits in an up-to-date *Whitaker's Almanack*.

To find out more about the help provided by the welfare state you should contact your local Citizens' Advice Bureau. You will find one of these in almost every town in Britain. They are part of a voluntary organisation, usually funded by a local authority grant and staffed mainly by volunteers. During a typical day in a bureau, workers will be helping people with many differing needs. Here are some examples:

> a family with young children facing eviction;
> a secretary in dispute with her firm over her holiday pay;
> a young couple in a muddle with HP commitments;
> a teenager wanting to leave home;
> a wife whose husband has left her without any money and wants to take the children;
> a pensioner enquiring about additional benefits;
> a woman wanting to complain about a faulty washing machine;
> a man wanting to know if he needs a vaccination to go to Hungary;
> an elderly woman needing help filling in a claims form or wanting a new regulation explained to her.

Such voluntary organisations are very important additions to the services provided by the welfare state. They:

- provide services to people who want to avoid contact with officials
- allow people to demonstrate their desire to help others
- bring in considerable additional money to welfare, which people would object to paying through taxes
- provide a huge army of unpaid workers with considerable skills whom the government could not afford to pay
- provide a social outlet for the members of the organisations
- may oppose official policies and seek to have them changed, which is difficult for government employees to do.

1.   Here are a few voluntary organisations. Find out more about them yourself and add some names of your own to the list.

Samaritans	Help would-be suicides and others in emotional distress by providing a telephone answering service 24 hours a day in most towns so that people talk to someone unknown to them about their problems.
Shelter	Concerned with the plight of the homeless. Concentrates on trying to alter government policies so that more decent housing is made available.
Oxfam	Tries to reduce poverty and malnutrition in the poorer countries of the world. Concentrates on providing assistance that will enable the poor to help themselves (e.g. irrigation schemes).
The Salvation Army	Concerned with the poor and underprivileged as part of their religious ideals. Still concerned with original aim of housing and feeding the poor, but now also operates houses and schools.

Voluntary organisations like the Salvation Army provide important welfare services.

5.4   HEALTH

In 1882 the average expectation of life in Britain was 40 for a man and 42 for a woman. The death rate (**mortality**) among young children was particularly high, with almost a quarter of all children dying before the age of five, mainly from whooping cough, measles and scarlet fever.

Today at birth, a man can be expected to live until he is about 73 and a woman until she is about 79. This expectation is known as **life expectancy** and can be measured at any age; obviously the longer you live the greater, on average, is your chance of surviving beyond this initial expectation. It has been estimated that the number of people over 85 in the UK will rise from 800,000 to 1,400,000 by the year 2025.

In general, women live longer than men, although in agricultural societies the gap between their life expectancies will be narrowed and in a few cases be reversed. This is because women are expected to have children and look after them while continuing to work in the home and fields; they have many children as few survive and medical attention may be unskilled. In Britain today only 10 per cent of women die before the age of 45; in 1850, 50 per cent were dead before reaching that age.

Infant mortality, that is death before the age of one year, has improved remarkably in Britain, dropping from 154 babies dying for

A poor district of Newcastle in 1889. The death rate among children was particularly high.

A refugee camp in the Sudan today. In many parts of the world, life expectation is lower than it was in Britain in the 19th century.

every one thousand that were born in 1891 to less than 11 per thousand in 1991. But infant mortality in Ecuador, for example, remains similar to our 1911 figure of 130. This is mainly because underfed children have low resistance to pneumonia and diarrhoea, while epidemic diseases (whooping cough, diphtheria, measles) still flourish where children have not been immunised.

Immunisation is one of the main medical advances that have contributed to rising life expectancy. If we contract a disease, our body produces antibodies to fight it and these remain for a time afterwards, giving us immunity from further attacks of the disease. In the case of measles, mumps and some others, immunity is usually for life. In 1798 Edward Jenner discovered that a person could be immunised against smallpox by being given a mild attack of cowpox, although the idea of inoculation was not new, having come to Britain from Turkey in 1714. Such immunity can now also be achieved for many other diseases including poliomyelitis, cholera, yellow fever, measles and typhoid.

However, although medical advances have been important in reducing mortality, improvement in diet and hygiene (particularly improved living conditions, pure water and efficient sewage systems) have been even more important.

While fewer people now die from epidemic diseases, there has been a considerable rise in deaths from cancer and heart disease. This may be partially due to the fact that more people are surviving to an age when they are likely to suffer from these diseases, but there is no doubt that the stress of modern urban life, pollution and some of the processed foods we now eat are major factors. Road accidents also increase the mortality rate to a greater extent today than in the past.

However, modern methods of treatment can now prolong life a good deal. In fact, we now have a situation in which the body can be kept living although the mind has permanently ceased to function. When should a life support system be switched off?

Euthanasia, or 'mercy killing', arouses a great deal of debate. In many nomadic peoples, such as the Eskimos and Native Americans, it was accepted that the death of the old should be hastened. Do you think that the old or the incurably ill should be killed in our society today, and if so, under what circumstances?

1. a. Consider Figure 5.3. Bear in mind some of the less obvious reasons for the development shown. For example, in the past people may have died of other diseases before cancer could develop. Cancer may also have been considered in some way shameful in the past and so the true cause of death may not have been recorded. What are the current statistics?
    b. In 1986 140,801 people died from cancer, but none died from typhoid. Even more died from heart disease. Find

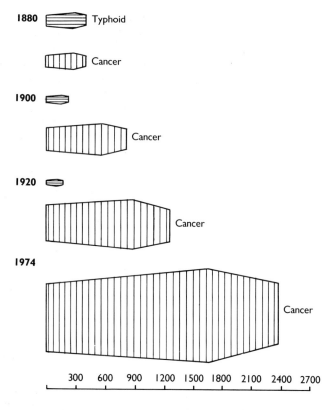

**Figure 5.3
Typhoid and cancer
deaths.**

Number of deaths per million people in England and Wales.

out how many. (Try the *Annual Abstract of Statistics*
which should be in the reference section of your local
library.)

2. Polluted water is the source of typhoid, cholera and dysen-
    tery. The purification of drinking water has eliminated
    these death-dealing diseases in Britain. Find out why
    deaths from tuberculosis, poliomyelitis and diphtheria are
    now also rarer in Britain.

3. Consider the following passage:

    Without cleanliness, within and without your house, ventilation
    is comparatively useless. In certain foul districts of London,
    poor people used to object to open their windows and doors
    because of the foul smells that came in. Rich people like to have
    their stables and dung-hill near their houses. But does it ever
    occur to them that with many arrangements of this kind it
    would be safer to keep the windows shut than open? You
    cannot have the air of the house pure with dung-heaps under
    the windows. These are common all over London. And yet
    people are surprised that their children, brought up in large
    'well-aired' nurseries and bed-rooms suffer from children's
    epidemics. If they studied Nature's laws in the matter of
    children's health, they would not be so surprised.

There are other ways of having filth inside a house besides having dirt in heaps. Old paper walls of years' standing, dirty carpets, uncleansed furniture, are just as ready sources of impurity to the air as if there were a dung-heap in the basement. People are so unaccustomed from education and habits to consider how to make a home healthy, that they either never think of it at all, and take every disease as a matter of course ... or if they ever entertain the idea of preserving the health of their household as a duty, they are very apt to commit all kinds of 'negligences and ignorances' in performing it.

Florence Nightingale, *Notes on Nursing*, 1858

Add items to the following list of the ways in which most people care for their health better today than in Victorian days. To the other list add ways in which we injure our health to a greater extent.

Improve health	*Injure health*
Eat a more balanced diet	Eat too much
Use flush WCs	Smoke more

4. a. Carry out your own survey using the same questions as in this Gallup survey. (Gallup interviewed 1,060 electors in more than 100 districts.)

From: *The Daily Telegraph,* 11 November 1991

High marks fail to stand the test of time

GALLUP asked respondents to leave aside what they had read in newspapers or seen on television and to think only of their own experience: "Do you think the service provided by the NHS has got better over the past few years, got worse or stayed about the same?"

Those who believe the service has got worse constitute nearly half the electorate. They out-number those who think the service has improved by more than three to one:

	All voters	Con voters	Lab voters	Lib Dem voters
Service has got better	14	26	5	11
Has got worse	45	22	60	53
Stayed about the same	35	46	31	27
Don't know	6	6	4	8

Ratings of the NHS given in the new survey compare very unfavourably with past ratings. In 1956, Gallup asked electors whether they thought they were getting "a good service" or "a poor service" from the system.

At that time nearly nine out of 10 people thought they were getting a good service. Today fewer than two-thirds think the same:

	June 1956	Now
Good service	89	57
Poor service	10	35
Don't know	1	8

In the run-up to the June 1983 General

THE SATISFACTION TEST

In general, how satisfied or dissatisfied are you with the health and medical services provided for people like you? (Marks out of 10)

Average mark: Now 5.9, May 1983 7.4

Marks	Now	May 1983
10	9%	24%
9	6%	11%
8	17%	22%
7	14%	12%
6	9%	8%
5	15%	11%
4	8%	4%
3	6%	2%
2	3%	2%
1	3%	1%
0	6%	3%
Don't know	5%	2%

Election, Gallup asked electors to rate the health services being provided for people like themselves, with a mark of 10 at the top of the scale and a mark of 0 at the bottom.

The question was repeated in the latest survey. As the thermometer chart shows, the public's average rating of the NHS has fallen from 7.4 in 1983 to 5.9 today.

The proportion giving it one of the top three marks in 1983 was 57 per cent. The corresponding figure today is 32 per cent. The proportion giving it one of the lowest three marks has doubled since 1983 to 12 per cent.

Convert your answers into percentages (e.g. if you interview 20 people multiply by 5), then compare your findings with those in the first three upright columns of the
survey.

b. Also ask your sample to rate the health service in the
way described and compare your findings with those on
the 'thermometer' chart.

c. How **valid** is the comparison of 1991 with 1983 in the
thermometer chart? (Note that the respondents are
being asked to make a **value** judgement, to state what
their opinion is.)

5.5   HOUSING

The area in which we live and the kind of accommodation
that we occupy is likely to have a great influence on our health, our
personality, the sort of schools we go to and the sort of jobs we end
up with.

Many of our cities still contain cramped rows of terraced houses,
and tall tenements built by careless speculators during the 19th century to accommodate at a minimum cost the millions of people who
swarmed into the towns during the Industrial Revolution. As better

*A high-rise block in Liverpool
and modern suburban houses
in south London. How might
different housing conditions
affect people's expectations
and way of life?*

housing has been made available over the years, many of those who could afford to do so have moved out of the worst of the older areas, leaving behind mainly those least able to help themselves: the old, those with big families and low wages, those with personal problems such as alcoholism, and the families of criminals. These areas suffer the additional hazards of neglect and vandalism and become 'slums'. The emotive word 'slum' is now often avoided and the term 'deprived area' used instead. Of course, not all old inner-city areas are slums; the houses may be well cared for and contain members of a close-knit community that would object strongly to being moved. Areas which still have some sound housing, but which are in danger of becoming slums, are referred to as 'twilight areas'.

Often immigrants find that the deprived areas are the only ones in which they can find accommodation, and so like the Jews and Irish before them, one often finds Asian and West Indian communities in the deprived city areas. When an area becomes mainly inhabited by one ethnic group or social class, whose association with the area reduces their acceptance elsewhere, it is sometimes called a **ghetto**, although the term is more commonly used today in the United States than in Britain.

The fact that poor housing encourages crime and disease was recognised by the Artisans' Dwelling Act of 1875, which resulted in the destruction of the London 'Rookeries' – a maze of dilapidated tenements. Since then local authorities have had continuous programmes of slum clearance. However, the backlog of the 19th century has still not been cleared, and at the same time new slums continually appear.

Private philanthropists built homes for the poor. In 1862 George Peabody started the Peabody Buildings; the Lewis Trust and Guinness Buildings are other examples. Homes like these continued to be erected after the start of council house building towards the end of the 19th century. These 'Trust' buildings are now outdated and are themselves slums in many large cities. The large houses of the Victorian middle class are too large for many people to afford to run these days and have often been sub-divided into flats and bed-sitting rooms; these too have become slums in some areas. Much more recent buildings, particularly some modern council flats, have deteriorated to the point at which they too are likely to take on the characteristics of slums. This is particularly true of some 'high-rise' blocks where:

1. Families are isolated from their neighbours, no feeling of community develops, and loneliness and depression are rife.
2. Older children cannot be seen and supervised by family and neighbours.
3. Hidden staircases, lifts and corridors encourage unobserved crime and vandalism.

4. No one feels responsible for the common areas which remain neglected and vandalised.

There has been a move away recently from the wholesale pulling down of areas of older housing; instead housing that is still structurally sound is being modernised. This is called **urban renewal**.

Councils also encourage people to modernise their own houses and grants are available to install an inside toilet, a bathroom, hot running water and other basic amenities. From 1979, because of the need to save energy, local authorities have also offered grants to insulate loft spaces to prevent heat loss.

It has long been established that the quality of housing is not just a matter for private individuals. Councils can compulsorily purchase housing to make way for modern homes or amenities (do you think they should be able to do so?); they supply basic services such as a sewage system; they can make loans for house purchase; and they have planning departments to control building and plan the environment for the future.

---

1. *Town*   *Country*

    Parks more accessible than   Open countryside
        much country   Clean air
    Shops near by   Less danger from traffic
    Always piped water and   Services sometimes lacking
        electricity   Police not so likely to be
    Schools near by   needed
    Police at hand

    Complete these lists and say where you would prefer to live and why.

2. Where do you think old people should live? In an old people's home? If so, what sort? With children or near children? In a retirement area away from where they have spent most of their lives?

5.6   PLANNING

Town planning is not new. It was practised in Ancient Greece and Rome, in some medieval towns in Britain and later in the 18th century, with towns like Bath being developed to a careful design. However, the industrial towns of the 19th century were quickly and cheaply built without much attention to the comfort and safety of their inhabitants.

Towards the end of the 19th century, a number of people realised that a poor environment both ruined people's physical and mental health and also made bad economic sense in that people were less efficient as a result. This realisation resulted in a movement to improve the environment in which the majority of the population lived. In 1879 the chocolate manufacturer, George Cadbury, built the Bournville Garden Suburb, including playing fields and libraries, for his workers, while Lord Leverhulme founded Port Sunlight in 1888 to include his soap factory and houses for the workers there. Ebenezer Howard founded the Garden City Association in 1899 and the first town designed on his principles, Letchworth in Hertfordshire, was begun in 1904. Welwyn soon followed.

Since then a great deal more attention has been paid to improving our towns and cities. There are more open spaces in which children can play; shopping precincts which are closed to cars enable us to shop in safety; subways help us to avoid traffic; entirely enclosed shopping centres protect us from the weather (often with fountains, flowerbeds and sculptures); multi-storey car parks take parked cars off the roads. Perhaps it is the car that is becoming the main threat to our enjoyment of our towns: its fumes poison us; it is a danger, particularly to the young and old; it causes congestion that wastes both time and fuel. Some towns have already started to remove wheeled traffic entirely from the town centres.

The success of garden cities led to a plan to remedy the increasing congestion of London and other large cities by building a ring of New Towns around London and in various other parts of England. In 1946 the New Towns Act was passed which enabled land to be acquired, and compulsorily purchased if necessary, to establish these new towns, which were to have sufficient local industries and services to discourage people from commuting to other towns and cities for work. At the same time, housing would be laid out with plenty of open spaces and usually private gardens for every home.

The desire to live near green fields with one's own garden, however, is not new. **Commuting**, which means travelling from where one lives to where one works, became common at the beginning of this century. It resulted from a desire to live in a more rural environment on the fringe of large towns and cities where families could be brought up in more spacious surroundings with low-density housing. This development has had the result of separating families, so that husbands may rarely see young children; it has greatly increased the traffic flow, and damaged the community life of both the inner-city areas and the new suburbs, which are often referred to as 'dormitories' as the wage earners only seem to return there to sleep.

Commuting has also had the undesirable effect of removing many middle-class people from their communities. In many cases these people would have been the most active in insisting on high standards of services from the authorities. Their absence has also assisted in the decline of the central areas. In the 1991 census the population of Inner London was estimated to be 2,349,900 – a decrease of 5.9 per cent compared with 1981, while the 1981 figure was itself a decrease of 17.8 per cent on 1971. (This compares with an overall increase in the population of England and Wales as a whole over this period.)

New Towns have many advantages, but they proved to have some disadvantages too:

1. People missed their family and friends and many returned to their former neighbourhoods after a while.
2. New estates take time to become established, both in appearance and in the development of a feeling of community. Many people found the New Towns raw and uninviting.
3. Some people missed the bustle and readily available entertainment of inner-city life.
4. New Towns particularly appealed to young families looking for a home of their own. The communities were unbalanced, with few middle-aged and elderly people (the old were often left behind alone in the inner city).
5. As industries moved out of the inner-city areas to the more congenial factories of the New Towns, the problems of the inner-city areas increased, particularly unemployment.

In 1976 the government decided to slow the growth of New Towns and put money instead into redeveloping the inner-city areas themselves.

One of the reasons for the separation of the 'commuter belt' from its feeder town was the establishment of **Green Belts** round our towns and cities. They were intended to prevent **ribbon development** along the roads out of the town and subsequent **urban spread** as more houses are built round this ribbon development – a characteristic of the early years of this century. These undeveloped areas of green belt allow the built-up areas to 'breathe', by providing both fresh air and recreational opportunities for the inhabitants. They are largely the result of the writings of Alfred Maxhall, who in 1899 suggested a 'national fresh air tax'. He said, 'We need to prevent one town from growing into another, or into a neighbouring village; we need to keep intermediate stretches of country in dairy farms, etc., as well as public pleasure grounds.'

Voluntary societies such as the National Trust, founded in 1895, have taken over large areas of countryside and coastline to preserve them for our enjoyment and that of future generations. In 1949 an Act of Parliament was passed to establish National Parks to which the public would have certain rights of entry and which would receive special protection from development. These now include: Dartmoor, Exmoor, the Pembroke Coast, the Brecon Beacons, Snowdonia, the Peak District, the Yorkshire Dales, the Lake District, the North Yorkshire Moors and Northumberland.

Even the best-intentioned developments can have unfortunate

Town planning from scratch – the New Town of Milton Keynes.

consequences. We have seen that the development of the commuter belt caused problems; so too has the building of high-rise flats – and so has the development of New Towns. Planners thought that high-rise flats would create space and recreational land in the centre of big towns; they now admit that this may have been true, but other factors were more important. It is certainly true that planners have made mistakes and will continue to make them, but probably the majority of people would not wish to swap our modern cities and towns for the old industrial slums.

New Towns in England and Wales

	Main reason for creation
Basildon, Bracknell, Crawley, Harlow, Hatfield, Hemel Hempstead, Milton Keynes, Northampton, Peterborough, Stevenage, Welwyn	To relieve problems in the Greater London area (i.e. to reduce overcrowding, demolish slums, improve the communication system).
Aycliffe, Corby, Cwmbran, Peterlee, Washington	To bring new industries to areas of unemployment and improve local environments.
Newtown	To help stem rural depopulation in mid-Wales.

Runcorn, Skelmersdale	Overspill from North Merseyside and Liverpool.
Telford, Redditch	To take excess population from Birmingham.
Warrington	Expanded to take overspill from Liverpool and Manchester.
Central Lancashire New Town	New regional city based on existing towns of Preston, Leyland and Chorley.

---

1. Place the following in the order of priority which you feel they should have when living areas are being planned:

swimming pools	shops near by
playgrounds	car parks
parks and open spaces	a local college
theatres	local employment
indoor sports centres	local schools
gardens attached to homes	

2. Conduct a local survey as a group project. Interview about 100 people in total; all your interviewees should be working.
   a. Determine the average distance each person travels to and from work.
   b. Calculate the average amount of time spent daily in this travelling.
   c. Calculate the average cost per day of this travelling.

5.7   ENVIRONMENT AND POLLUTION

We saw in section 5.6 how attempts have been made to improve our environment by providing better amenities. However, the sort of house we live in and the absence or otherwise of pedestrian precincts are relatively unimportant compared to the atmosphere we breathe. If we breathe in asbestos dust we will die earlier than otherwise from lung disease; lead, either inhaled from exhaust fumes or drunk in water running from lead pipes, can cause brain damage, particularly to young children; other kinds of pollution cause cancer, while many people died from bronchitis during the severe London 'smogs' of the 1950s.

In recent years people have become very conscious of the dangers of smoke, dust and chemical fumes. All industrial pollution is closely

Dead trees above a phurnacite plant in south Wales.

monitored by Environmental Health Officers, although this does not in itself stop pollution. (One district near Billingham-on-Tees receives an estimated 100 tons of grit and ash each month from the local chemical works.) Many councils have also introduced Clean Air Zones (under the Clean Air Acts of 1956 and 1968); in these the burning of anything but smokeless fuels is prohibited. People may mourn the loss of liberty in not being able to have cheerful coal fires, but the London smogs are now no more. Many countries have already prohibited the use of lead in petrol.

Domestic pollution of water is now rare except along some stretches of the coast where untreated sewage is still pumped into the sea. However, industrial effluents such as sulphuric acid, ammonia and detergents are still discharged into many rivers and canals. Here too there is hope – for example, young salmon were reintroduced into the Thames in London in 1979 for the first time in more than 100 years.

Noise is another form of pollution. In excess it can cause deafness, but even at a lower level it causes irritability and reduced performance (e.g. people may work less efficiently).

Pollution from industrial dereliction of the past, as factories, mines and mills have been abandoned, is a major feature of many environments. Efforts are being made to improve the situation, for example by grassing over the slag heaps of the coal fields, or by using former quarries and brick workings for water sports.

Dangerous chemical wastes are still being dumped instead of being **recycled**, that is, used again for the same or another purpose. Efforts are also being made to encourage other items to be recycled, but in some ways the situation is growing worse (e.g. the growth in non-returnable soft-drink bottles).

We cannot gauge accurately the imbalances in nature caused by human action: the destruction of forests affects our atmosphere by removing a source of oxygen; the use of aerosol sprays damages the ozone layer round the earth which protects us from the sun's harmful radiation; the destruction of hedges and the use of agricultural chemicals destroy much natural wildlife and can cause nerve paralysis in humans.

Most serious perhaps are the risks involved in the growing use of nuclear energy. It may be that we must accept these risks, as our only hope of replacing the fossil fuels such as oil and coal may lie in the development of nuclear power. Others would say that there are other forms of energy that we have not yet really started to harness – solar energy, hydro power from rivers and tides, wind energy and geothermal energy using the heat from the centre of the earth.

1. **Planned obsolescence** is a term given to things which are deliberately made so that they do not last too long and replacement must be purchased. Such things may cause pollution. Can you think of examples?

2. Make a list of all the major forms of pollution in the order in which you think they are important.

3. Our environment not only affects our health, but our actions as well. For example, the problems in Northern Ireland appear to be religious and historical but there are other underlying causes. There is the permanently high unemployment rate, which is partly the result of the decline in shipbuilding and linen manufacture. In addition, many of the people live in very poor environments that encourage violence, tension and depression. For example, a 1982 survey found that 19 per cent of Northern Irish homes were 'unfit', compared with 7 per cent in Great Britain.

    Can you think of environmental factors in other areas that have a direct influence on the behaviour of the people who live there?

5 DISCUSSION

1 'People should stand on their own two feet, not depend on the government to help them out.' To what extent do you agree with this view?

2 'People who are living in need are fully and properly provided for' (Margaret Thatcher, House of Commons, 1983). Do you agree?

3 To what extent has the welfare state taken the place of voluntary organisations in our society?

4 Noise pollution can be a major problem. Outline some of the main sources of noise pollution and suggest ways in which it might be reduced.

5 Many people who are entitled to receive state benefits do not do so. Why do you think this happens?

5 ADDITIONAL ASSIGNMENTS AND INVESTIGATIONS

1. In *Poor Britain* (1985) Joanna Mack and Stewart Lansley discovered by survey what the majority of people believe to be 26 minimum necessities of life (including, for example, a bed for everyone in the household, two pairs of all-weather shoes, three meals a day for the children, a washing machine and a one-week annual holiday). Things which less than half of people regard as necessities (such as a telephone or a night out once a fortnight) are excluded. The poor are then defined as those who do not have, because they cannot afford, at least three of the 26 necessities.

On this measure, the Britons in poverty add up to five million adults and two and a half million children; seven and a half million people, or about one in seven of us. They are typically unemployed, low paid, members of single-parent families, sick, disabled or old. And they are concentrated in the North. Over two-thirds of them live in Scotland, the north of England and the Midlands.

Mack and Lansley then asked their sample if they would pay more in income tax 'to enable everyone to afford the items you have said are necessities'. An extra penny in the pound (about £1.20 a week for the standard-rate taxpayer on average earnings) would raise about £1,000 million a year. Three-quarters (74 per cent) would be willing, and only one-fifth opposed it.

The survey went on to ask if people would pay 5p in the pound which would raise £5,000 million. Such an increase would give substantial relief: 23 per cent on all National Insurance benefits, 43 per cent on Child Benefit, 10 per cent on Supplementary Benefit, and the ending of the denial of long-term supplementary rates to the long-term (1.2 million) unemployed. In that package a man out of work for over a year with a wife and two children could be given £12 more a week. It would be an act of national charity sufficient to lift one-third to half of the present poor above the level which the majority of the nation define as minimally decent.

At this point the charitable feelings of the electorate outran their willingness to act on them: only 34 per cent would definitely give the extra 5p, with 13 per cent saying 'don't know'.

   a. Establish your own definition of poverty by asking as many people as possible (say 25) to name 26 items which they believe everyone in Britain is entitled to expect to have (use the items given in the *Poor Britain* survey as a guide). Select the 26 items which appear most frequently in the replies you receive.
   b. Select a number of people paying income tax (say ten) and show

them the list of 'essential' items which you have established in survey (a). Point out that you are defining as poor those people who cannot afford *at least three* of those 26 items (i.e. they have to do without them). Ask (i) whether they would be prepared to pay an extra 1p in the pound income tax to alleviate the position, and then (ii) whether they would be prepared to pay an extra 5p in the pound income tax. See to what extent your findings correspond to those in *Poor Britain*.

2 'The poverty trap' is a situation where increased earnings lead to little or no increase in spending power because of the loss of earnings-related benefits. Find out, from leaflets obtainable from your local post office and/or Citizens' Advice Bureau, the following for a married couple with two children aged four and six, with the wife not earning.

  a. At what point in earnings does income tax begin?
  b. At what point in earnings does Family Credit end?
  c. At what point in earnings does Housing Benefit end?
  d. At what point in earnings do National Insurance payments stop rising with income?

(For explanations of welfare benefits see the *National Welfare Benefits Handbook*, published annually by the Child Poverty Action Group.)

3 Find out from your local council what their rules are in allocating council housing.

  a. How long, on average, do a young married couple have to be on a waiting list before being allocated a council house or flat?
  b. What 'points system' does the council operate to determine priorities for housing?

How fair do you think your local 'points system' is?

5 OUTLINE OF AN APPROPRIATE GCSE INVESTIGATION/PROJECT

(For guidance, see 'Coursework for GCSE' on pages ix–xiv.)

Title   An investigation into differing measurements of poverty.

Hypothesis   There is no general agreement on how to measure poverty today.

Secondary sources   Sociology textbooks for definitions.

J. Mack and S. Lansley, *Poor Britain* (1985).

Leaflets and other information from organisations such as the Child Poverty Action Group or the Salvation Army. (State that you are carrying out an investigation into poverty for the GCSE. Remember that these organisations are charities and include a stamped addressed envelope.)

Primary sources   **Questionnaire** You could ask people to name a number of items. This might include ten items such as a refrigerator, a damp-free home, a night out once a fortnight, a car, etc. You might make four columns and ask your **respondent** (the person answering your questions) to tick the column that they most agree with. The columns could be headed:

1. Necessity (everyone should be able to afford)
2. Desirable (most people should be able to afford)
3. Luxury (nice to have if you can afford it)
4. Not necessary

You must decide where you are going to make your Poverty Line – say why – and then calculate the number of people who agree with you.

You might also ask 'How much income do you think is necessary for a family with two children?' and offer six alternatives ranging from 'under £5,000' to 'more than £40,000'.

You might decide to obtain a representative sample, or to target particular groups, perhaps a group of old people receiving Income Support and a group of the same age and size who you identify as wealthy.

You might identify homeless people or people at a Benefit Office, but be careful if you are approaching strangers – always do so with others.

Say why you have chosen your sample and state any way in which your choice may bias your results.

Additionally you may support this investigation with interviews and observation.

Pilot surveys   It is desirable to test out aspects of your investigation before you commence your main survey in order to ensure that what you intend to do is likely to achieve usable results – this 'mini' investigation is known as a **pilot survey**.

For example, if you intend to question 25 people in your main survey, you may decide to try out your questions on just 4 people first, both to see whether your method of selecting your sample is likely to lead to it being representative and also to see whether people understand your questions and can give appropriate responses to them.

Pilot surveys can save a lot of wasted time and effort.

5 GCSE QUESTION

Note: GCSE questions often require answers using information from interrelated themes. This one is mainly, but not exclusively, concerned with poverty and the welfare state.

Study Item A and Item B. Then answer the questions which follow.

Item A

> In 1983 'Breadline Britain', a survey carried out for London Weekend Television, looked at 'relative poverty' as 'the minimum standard of living laid down in society'. The survey found that:
>
> 6 million people could not afford some necessary item of clothing;
>
> 3.5 million people could not afford carpets and washing machines;
>
> 3 million people could not afford to heat the living areas of their homes.
>
> 'Breadline Britain' stated that 7.5 million people (or 13% of the population) were living in poverty.

Item B

Percentage of people who described each of the following items as
necessary

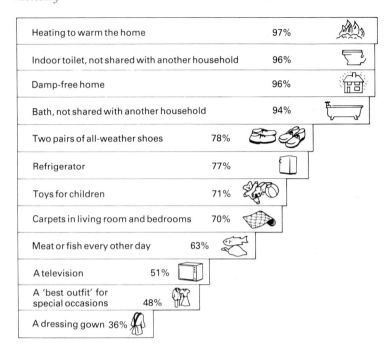

Heating to warm the home	97%	
Indoor toilet, not shared with another household	96%	
Damp-free home	96%	
Bath, not shared with another household	94%	
Two pairs of all-weather shoes	78%	
Refrigerator	77%	
Toys for children	71%	
Carpets in living room and bedrooms	70%	
Meat or fish every other day	63%	
A television	51%	
A 'best outfit' for special occasions	48%	
A dressing gown 36%		

Adapted from *Poor Britain*,
J. Mack and S. Lansley,
Allen & Unwin, 1985

(**a**)   Study Item A and state:
   (i) the number of people who could not afford carpets and
   washing machines;
   (ii) the percentage of the population who were living in poverty. (2)

(**b**)   Study Item B and state:
   (i) the percentage of people who considered a television as
   necessary;
   (ii) which of the following was considered most necessary – a
   television, a refrigerator, a dressing gown. (2)

(**c**)   Briefly state *three* reasons why women are more likely to be
   living in poverty than men. (3)

(**d**)   Identify and explain any *two* ways in which the welfare state or
   voluntary groups may help people in need. (4)

(**e**)   What may be seen as the main causes of poverty in the United
   Kingdom over the last ten years? (9)

SELF-TEST QUESTIONS

(Answers on pages 290–91)

1. What is 'relative poverty'?

2. What is the 'poverty trap'?

3. Membership of which social class is most likely to lead to earlier death?

4. What welfare measures were enacted in the following years?
    a. 1908
    b. 1909
    c. 1911

5. Which report in 1942 led ultimately to such developments as the National Health Service and Family Allowances?

6. Name three benefits which are available in our 'welfare society'.

7. What was/is the life expectancy for:
    a. a man at birth in Britain in 1882?
       40, 60, 75 or 80
    b. a woman in Britain today?
       52, 60, 79 or 86

8. What is the popular name for euthanasia?

9. What three disadvantages may a New Town have?

10. Give two examples of ways in which pollution can be reduced.

UNIT 6

CHANGING THE RULES

The threat of the use of force – an anti poll tax demonstration in central London in 1990.

6.1 POWER

Law and order rests on the threat, or actual use, of force. Most people behave themselves, but the few who will not may be compelled to do so by the police or the armed forces. The police and armed forces, therefore, have **power**, but the direction of this power usually rests with others, so they have power too, but we call their power **authority**.

Mrs Thatcher was elected as the first female Prime Minister of the UK in 1979. She was not elected because of her physical strength. Prime Ministers are not expected to fight terrorists or arrest criminals personally. However, their position of authority gives them the right to order others to take appropriate action. They **delegate** their authority which is given to them by Parliament.

157

Those who control the armed might of the nation are the Government, who in turn may be controlled by a Parliament, which may be controlled by a political party with a majority of representatives. The representatives may be elected by the ordinary people of the country, and they in turn may be influenced by the people who control the newspapers, speak on television or represent the churches. In their different ways all these people and organisations have power, although the actual amount each has will naturally vary a good deal.

The means by which people and organisations gain power and use it is usually referred to as **politics**. 'Politics' comes from the Greek word *polis*, meaning 'city', as some Greek cities decided their policy by a majority decision of the inhabitants.

People may want power for many reasons – they may regard it as a means of growing rich, for helping others, or merely because they enjoy being powerful. Desmond Morris in *The Human Zoo* claimed that all animals struggle among themselves to be the most important – they struggle for **status**.

Status is sometimes called **prestige** and it is suggested that people are expected to behave in certain ways to show that they occupy a particular position. This expectation is likely to influence their choice of friends, their clubs, how they dress and behave. Desmond Morris suggests that the same sort of behaviour can be observed in most animals and that all leaders follow 'ten golden rules' if they are to remain leaders:

1. They dress and move in a way that indicates superiority.
2. If challenged they must behave aggressively to those beneath them.
3. If physically attacked they must be able to win, or direct others who can win for them.
4. They must be able to outwit their inferiors.
5. They must stop arguments between subordinates.
6. Those immediately below them must be able to exercise power and have recognisable benefits.
7. They must be able to protect the weaker members of the group.
8. They must make decisions concerning the social activities of the group.
9. Weaker members must be reassured from time to time.
10. They must lead opposition to attacks from outside the group.

Think of someone you regard as a leader. How many of these rules does he or she follow?

Of course, power is not just exercised by governments or leaders of other organisations. A group of bank robbers may have power when they hold up a bank, but they have no authority to do so. Equally, many people are in a position of authority and may not only have a right, but a duty to control others. Who can you think of who has a duty to control you? Are you ever in a position of authority?

1. Read the following passage carefully:

> The male status-seeker ... is often driven to neglect his family.
> This forces his mate to take over the masculine parental role in
> the home. Even the older child, who comes to understand the
> super-tribal status race and boasts about his father's status
> achievements, will find them small compensation for the
> absence of an active paternal influence. Despite his mounting
> status in the outside world, the father can easily become a
> family joke.
>
> It is very bewildering for our struggling super-tribesman. He
> has obeyed all the rules, but something has gone wrong. The
> super-status demands of the human zoo are cruel indeed. Either
> he fails and becomes disillusioned, or he succeeds and loses
> control of his family. Worse still, he can work so hard that he
> loses control of his family and still fails ...
>
> In the status race it frequently occurs that a subordinate dare
> not express his anger openly towards a dominant. Too much is
> at stake. He has to re-direct it elsewhere. It may land on his
> unfortunate children, his wife, or his dog. In former times, the
> flanks of his horse also suffered; today, it is the gearbox of his
> car. He may have the luxury of staff subordinates of his own
> that he can lash with his tongue. If he has inhibitions in all
> these directions there is always one person left: himself. He can
> give himself ulcers.
>
> In extreme cases, when everything seems utterly hopeless, he
> can increase his self-inflicted aggression to the maximum: he
> can kill himself.
>
> Desmond Morris, The Human Zoo

   a. What do you think is meant by 'the super-tribe'?
   b. What problems can result during the pursuit of status?
   c. An old rhyme goes:

   > God bless the Lord and his relations
   > And keep us in our proper stations.

   Do you think it would be better to have a fixed position
   in society from which you could not rise, rather than be
   in a situation in which you are expected to improve your
   position?

2. Study the following extract:

> In some areas of the Great Basin a more reliable food supply
> permitted several Shoshone families to remain together and to
> cooperate. In these areas, both the larger population and the
> need to maintain peaceful relations with non-Shoshone
> neighbours created a role for leadership. The first White
> explorers to arrive in such parts of Nevada were delighted to
> find leaders with whom they could make treaties. The Whites,
> however, understood nothing about the band level of social
> organizations, and so they made the mistake of attributing to

this leadership more power than it actually possessed. The leaders of a Shoshone band possessed nothing like the political power of a chief. Agreements the Shoshone leader made with Whites in good faith were not kept by other Shoshone, because in band society no mechanism existed to enforce the leader's agreements.

Peter Farb, *Man's Rise to Civilization*

Did the Shoshone leaders have: (a) status, (b) authority and (c) power?

3.   You exercise power because you are strong, because you are clever, because someone has delegated their power to you, because you have inherited it, because you are rich – or because you are lucky! Here are some examples of power being exercised. Say which you consider reasonable and which unfair.

A big boy stops a small boy on his way to school and takes his dinner money.

A principal expels a student from college for not attending lectures.

A council evicts a family from their council house for not paying rent.

Your house is compulsorily purchased for a road-widening scheme.

A bank manager refuses to let you/your Dad/your Mum have a loan for a new car because you/he/she are not earning enough.

A hospital nurse prevents a patient from smoking because it is bad for him.

6.2   DICTATORSHIP

In section 6.1 it was said that a government may be controlled by a parliament. However, it may not be, or even if it is, the 'parliament' may not be an elected one, or perhaps only one section of the society may have been permitted to vote for it.

Clearly there are varying degrees of control by the people of a country and if only one person controls the state it is referred to as an **autocracy**, a **dictatorship** or a **totalitarian** state. One person could not rule without an inner ring of supporters so there is always an element of **oligarchy**, or rule by a group. Sometimes the small group runs things directly, as when a group of colonels seized power in Greece and between 1967 and 1975 ruled the country jointly.

In the Middle Ages, it was generally believed in Europe that kings were chosen by God. This 'Divine Right' to rule meant that anyone disobeying the king was disobeying God. This greatly enhanced the king's authority.

Sometimes people will voluntarily submit to a dictator because they think that only he has the power to improve their situation. The Germans voted Hitler into power; Franco might have had a majority of support in Spain; Castro probably does have the majority of Cubans behind him; Saddam Hussein appeared to be supported by most Iraqis before the Gulf War. However, whether they take power or are given it, dictators are usually unwilling to risk having their power confirmed in open elections, as such activities allow opposition to form, and this is potentially dangerous. Although dictators often do allow some form of parliament to be established, the members must usually only represent groups friendly to the dictator.

Dictators can usually find some excuse for avoiding open elections. A favourite one is that they are so popular that everyone would vote for their nominees in an open election, and that this would reduce public choice. However, by permitting only one political party they enable several candidates to be put forward for selection, thus increasing the choices open to the public at large. What do you think of this argument?

The sort of people who can attract the kind of support necessary for success often have a magnetic appeal which commands loyalty and obedience. This is called **charisma**.

Hitler was voted into power though not by a majority of the electorate.

Stalin ruled as the dictator of the USSR from 1924 until his death in 1953.

Saddam Hussein.

1. Sometimes people justify dictatorship by saying it is efficient – 'the trains run on time', was Mussolini's boast. What arguments can you think of for *not* having a dictator?

2. If Britain had a dictator, whom would you choose from the following list and why? (List your choice in order.)

   Prince Charles   Ken Livingstone
   Revd Ian Paisley   John Smith
   Margaret Thatcher   John Major
   The Queen

3. In order to ensure that an effective opposition does not arise, a dictatorship will seek to control the newspapers. In what other ways might it seek to impose its authority?

4. Originally elected in ancient Rome when the state was in danger, the dictator was given power over life and death for six months with no appeal against his decisions.

   Most modern dictators last a good deal longer than six months. Make a list of some of those ruling today, together with the countries they rule. Note also how long they have held power. (You may find *The Statesman's Yearbook* helpful.)

6.3   DEMOCRACY

The Greek city states which decided their laws by a joint decision of their citizens would not be regarded as democracies by us today, because slaves and women were not allowed to take part. Indeed women were not allowed to take part in British elections until 1918. Would you regard South Africa, where only white people have full voting rights, as a democracy?

The extent of democracy (literally 'rule by the people') in each country varies a great deal. It is now impracticable for every adult to vote personally on every major matter that affects the country. In countries that most people in the United Kingdom would recognise as democratic, the adult population exercise their democratic right by electing representatives whom they believe will put forward their views in Parliament.

In Communist countries in which free elections were not held (e.g. former East Germany), the countries claimed to be democratic because they claimed that collective ownership ensures the people will achieve what they wish.

As we shall see in later units, it is very difficult to establish a situation in which Parliament really does represent the wishes of the people. For example, there have been more people voting against the party that forms the government than in favour of it in every general election since 1945. In fact, the Conservatives formed the government in 1951 even though the Labour Party received more votes, while in February 1974 the opposite was the case. The voting system is, therefore, one way in which democracy may be limited, but there are also others. The press may be owned by people with the same kind of political views; the Civil Service may make it difficult for a minister to know all the facts; trade unions may make life particularly difficult for some governments.

However, there are some general features that we expect to see in a democracy and which are generally present in Britain:

1. We expect to be able to elect those who govern us.
2. We expect to be allowed to say what we like, with certain limitations to prevent injustice to others.
3. We expect to be able to join any non-criminal organisation we wish.
4. We expect not to be arrested without good cause, and if we are arrested we can expect a fair trial.

Can you think of any exceptions to these rules?

In Britain there are some people and groups which are more powerful than others – we call these **élites**. Britain can be said to be democratic because these élites cannot do as they like, but are subjected to the same laws as other people and can be criticised.

Democracy cannot, however, just rest on the will of the majority; minorities must also be protected. One of the problems in Northern Ireland is that there is a permanent majority of 60 per cent who favour unity with England, but an equally stable group of 40 per cent who want union with the rest of Ireland. For many years the minority group felt that the majority were depriving them of equal rights, particularly in housing and employment, and this was a major factor which led to some of their members resorting to terrorism to achieve their aims. Similar frustration has led to violence by minorities in other countries.

1. a. 'I am always in the minority. The only way I can be fairly treated is by using force.'
    b. 'I am in the majority, therefore I can do as I like. After all, that is what democracy is all about.'
    Is either of these attitudes right?

2.   *Money and power*

    It is almost impossible to assess how much influence advertising has on election results. Table 6.1 shows what happened in the general election of 1992.
    Table 6.2 gives the amount of money spent in the referendum campaign in the UK for entry into Europe.

Table 6.1 *Money spent and votes polled in the general election of 1992*

	Conservative	Labour	Liberal Democrat
Total expenditure[1]	£20,000,000	£10,000,000	£1,000,000
Total votes	14,231,884	11,619,306	6,083,661

[1] Approximately $\frac{1}{3}$ of total expenditure spent on advertising.

Table 6.2 *Money spent on the 1975 EEC referendum campaign*

Source of income	'Yes' Britain in Europe campaign	'No' National referendum campaign
Government grant	£125,000	£125,000
Contributions of £100 or more	£984,825	£2,796
Contributions of less than £100	£11,683	£5,815
Other receipts (mainly from the European Movement)	£360,075	£19
Total income	£1,481,583	£133,630
Votes polled	17,378,581	8,470,073

a. How important do you think money is in an election campaign?
b. How would you ensure fairness so far as finance is concerned?

6.4 POLITICAL PARTIES IN BRITAIN

In countries that we regard as democratic people have the right to vote – a right that has usually only been won after a hard struggle.

Because people have differing viewpoints, it is natural that they should join together with others who share their views in order to win power and put their views into practice. These groups establish organisations to win elections which become political parties.

In Britain, the earliest political parties were the Whigs and the Tories. The Whigs were established in 1679 and were named after a group of Scottish rebels; they wanted to increase the power of Parliament and lessen that of the king. In 1868 Gladstone became Prime Minister and the party became known as the 'Liberals'. The Tories were called after some Irish outlaws, and supported the king against the growing power of Parliament and were known as 'Conservatives' after the Reform Act of 1832, although the earlier name of the party is still often used today. The Labour Party as we know it was formed just before the 1906 election, after which the party had 29 Members of Parliament. This party replaced the Liberal Party as one of the two largest political parties in Britain in 1922 when it won 142 seats.

In March 1981 four former leaders of the Labour Party set up a new Social Democratic Party and were quickly joined by a number of sitting Labour MPs and one Conservative MP, which together with two victories in by-elections, made the SDP, with 25 MPs, the third-largest in the House of Commons by the end of 1981. However, the SDP lost most of these seats in the general election of 1983, although, in alliance with the Liberals, they obtained almost as many votes as the Labour Party (see page 171).

The general election of 1987 resulted in a very similar position to that of 1983, and in 1988 the Liberals and SDP merged to form the Social and Liberal Democratic Party (SLD). Part of the SDP retained its previous identity for a time but it officially ceased in 1991.

These three parties now represent most of the electors in England, although 'nationalist' parties of differing viewpoint have always been strong in Northern Ireland and developed in Scotland and Wales during the 1960s, polling strongly in the general election of 1974, but declining in those of 1979, 1983 and 1987 before recovering somewhat in 1992.

Each of the main political parties represents widely differing attitudes so that those on the 'left' of the Labour Party may have views near to the former Communists, while those on the 'right' may be difficult to distinguish from 'left'-wing Conservatives; a similar spread of opinion will be seen in the Conservative and Social and Liberal Democratic Parties.

However, there are so many possible answers to political questions that even these three major groupings cannot represent all viewpoints and so there are many smaller parties – Workers' Revolutionary, Socialist Workers, Green and British National Party are some of the more prominent ones. In Britain small parties of this kind attract little support, but in some European countries 'fringe' parties can be very influential as one party is unlikely to have a majority over all the others and so must look to the smaller political parties for support if it wishes to form a government. For example, in France, Italy and Germany, there are four or more parties which each have more than 10 per cent of the total number of MPs. In the UK, the two largest parties have about 95 per cent of the total number of MPs with all the rest sharing 5 per cent (although polling over 25 per cent of the votes).

We often think of political parties being in a straight line with the left on one side and the right on the other. However, the reality is more like a circle, as both extreme left and extreme right would not tolerate other political parties if they came to office, but would form some sort of dictatorship. Additionally, there are many different areas of government activity, and so it is unlikely that there is a single voter in Britain who would support all the policies of the party for which he or she votes.

Generally speaking, the Conservative Party wants to conserve, or keep things much as they are. For this reason, there is a tendency to think of the Conservative Party as the party of the wealthy who want to maintain their position. However, this is an oversimplification and many very rich people are members of the Labour Party, while the Conservative Party could not win elections if many working-class people did not vote for them. The Conservatives think that the state should intervene in people's lives as little as possible and that industry is most effective when fair competition exists. Equally it believes that people should be encouraged to pay for what they need themselves, that taxation should be kept to a minimum and that ideally the state should only help those who are unable to help themselves.

The Labour Party believes that wealth should be shared more evenly and that some kind of state direction of many essential industries and services is necessary for the economy to operate effectively. It believes that since people start life with uneven chances, there should be greater equality of opportunity. The Labour Party works closely with the trade union movement and might use public money to keep open factories faced with short-term losses in order to save jobs, although Conservatives would say that this encourages inefficiency and makes British industry less competitive abroad.

The SLD tend to be nearer the Conservative Party in believing in the necessity for competition in industry, but nearer to the Labour Party in supporting greater equality of opportunity. They believe that the future lies in giving everyone a stake in industry through shareholding rather than in state direction, and think that the other two main political parties concentrate too much on the differences between the two sides of industry rather than on their common interests.

All three major political parties have a headquarters with permanent staff in London, and some have full-time political agents in the country. The Conservatives have a full-time agent in most constituencies, the Labour Party a similar person in many and the SLD a few.

Each year the political parties hold annual conferences which decide what policies the party should follow, and to these each local constituency party sends a representative or delegate.

Other factors

Some research indicates that a number of factors can reflect the way people vote:

Age   Prior to 1992 it appeared that younger people were more likely to vote Labour; however, Gallup's survey after the 1992 election found that the Conservatives enjoyed a small majority over Labour among 18–24-year-olds.

Education   The longer one has spent in education the more
likely one is to vote Conservative. In 1992 those
with higher and further education voted 43 per cent
Conservative, 29 per cent Labour and 21 per cent
Liberal Democrat. University graduates voted 39
per cent Conservative, 30 per cent Liberal
Democrat and 27 per cent Labour.

Religion   Slight influence in England, Wales and most of
Scotland but is very important in Ulster.

Gender   Women in the past were regarded as more likely to
vote Conservative because more were engaged in
white-collar work in middle-class surroundings
away from trade union activity. They also appeared
to dislike change more than men. In the general
election of 1983 more women moved to the
'Alliance' than did men and by 1987 gender
appeared to have little effect on voting behaviour;
however, in 1992 the earlier pattern returned,
Gallup's post-election survey finding that 44 per
cent of women voted Conservative compared with
38 per cent of men.

The Liberals (now mostly part of the SLD) tended to draw their support more or less equally from all sections according to D. Butler in
'The Floating Voter' (*The Sunday Times*, 1973), a view confirmed in
respect of the Alliance in the general elections of 1983 and 1987 and of
the Liberal Democrats in 1992.

---

1. Draw up a simple questionnaire designed to indicate
   whether the factors above influence people in your
   neighbourhood when they vote (or if they were to vote).

2. Many children grow up to vote the same way as their
   parents. Suggest some reasons why this may be so.

3. Automation and mechanisation result in a drift from
   unskilled manual to white-collar jobs. Do you think that the
   Conservative Party is bound to become more and more
   powerful?

4. Look at Figure 6.1, which gives the results of an *Observer/*
   Harris public opinion poll taken just before the general election of 1992.
   a. Why would it be difficult for you to compare a poll taken
      by yourself with the results of this *Observer* poll?
   b. What political parties might be represented within the
      'other' category?
   c. Opinion polls always find a considerable number of
      'don't knows'. The results given in Figure 6.1 exclude

these people. What happens to the 'don't knows' in a general election?

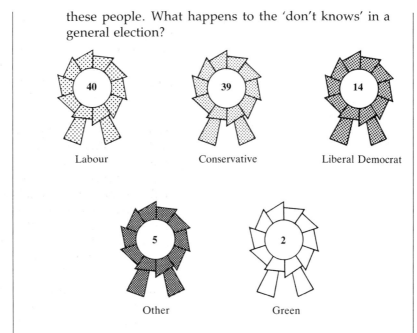

Labour Conservative Liberal Democrat

Other Green

Figure 6.1

From: *The Observer*,
8 March 1992

6.5   ELECTIONS

In Britain elections for Parliament must take place at least every five years, but the Prime Minister can choose any date within that period. This obviously gives an advantage to the ruling party. In local government, elections for county councillors are held every fourth year; elections for metropolitan district councillors are held for one-third of the council in each year which does not have county council elections; and non-metropolitan district councils can decide whether to have all their councillors elected together or one-third each year.

In all elections the political parties are very important. This is particularly so in general elections. At the local level they select the local candidate, 'canvass' by going round from door to door to persuade people to support their candidate and make a list of supporters so that they can ensure they get to the polls, distribute literature, put up posters, organise and speak at meetings, drive supporters to the polls on polling days and help to raise the funds necessary to fight the election.

At the national level the parties arrange advertising in the national press and big poster campaigns, prepare the party political broadcasts, issue manifestos stating what they will do if elected, and arrange for their most important speakers to visit the most important constituencies – usually the most marginal.

A marginal constituency is one that could be won or lost by a small

Party leaders campaigning in marginal constituencies in the 1992 general election.

margin. About half of British constituencies have not changed hands during the last 40 years. These are 'safe' seats – it has been the others that decide elections.

In the marginal constituencies the result will be decided by the 'floating voters'. Usually up to 8 per cent* of the electors will no longer be on the **electoral roll** (the list of those eligible to vote), perhaps because they have recently moved house or failed to register; between 12 and 15 per cent will abstain; and about 65 per cent will vote the way they always have without very much thought. This will leave the remaining 15 per cent to decide the outcome. Constituencies are more likely to change in **by-elections** which are held when an MP dies or resigns as the electorate feels they can protest without actually changing the government.

The 80 per cent who do vote in British general elections compares well with other countries – for example, only about 50 per cent of Americans bother to vote in Presidential elections. In Britain no one is compelled to vote, unlike Australia where it is compulsory.

The UK is divided into 651 constituencies, each electing one MP; each constituency usually has between 50,000 and 80,000 electors. However, in remote rural areas and the dying hearts of large cities the number may be much less. (Find out which was the largest and which was the smallest constituency in Great Britain during the last election. Try *Whitaker's Almanack*.)

In British general elections a 'first past the post' system operates, which means that a candidate could be elected by a majority of one. The system can result, as mentioned in section 6.3, in a party getting a majority of voters but fewer seats than another party which attracted fewer supporters. The system also results in smaller parties gaining fewer MPs than their voting strength seems to justify, with the

* In 1992 some electoral rolls had much larger numbers missing because people feared that they would be used to check on those not paying poll tax.

Table 6.3 *Votes cast in general elections (excluding Northern Ireland),*
1983 and 1992

Party	Votes cast		Numbers of MPs	
	1983	1992	1983	1992
Conservative	(13,010,000)	14,231,884	(397)	336
Labour	(8,460,000)	11,619,306	(209)	271
Alliance/Liberal Democrats	(7,780,000)	6,083,661	(23)	20
Scottish Nationalist	(330,000)	629,552	(2)	3
Plaid Cymru	(130,000)	154,857	(2)	4

result that some people are unlikely to vote for any other party than
one of the two largest. This strengthens the 'two-party system' even
further.

In the 1983 and 1987 elections the position was further complicated
by the emergence of the SDP in alliance with the Liberals, giving even
more bizarre results, as can be seen in Table 6.3, although this
imbalance reduced in 1992.

The two-party system is claimed to have the advantage that it
normally gives one party a clear majority and permits strong government. The party in power does not have to compromise or implement
policies favoured by small parties in order to gain their support.

The opponents to the two-party system say that it is undemocratic
and that dictatorships give even stronger government. They feel that
it is a good thing for governments to have to compromise as they will
then more clearly reflect the will of the people, and that the power of
back-bench MPs will increase.

Proportional representation

Most European countries, and many others, have a system
which more fairly reflects the support which political parties have in
the country, that is there is an attempt to ensure that the number of
representatives elected for each party is more or less proportionate to
the number of people who voted for that party. There are several
forms – here are two:

The single transferable vote	The alternative vote
Example: Ireland	*Example: Australia*
Method. Constituencies have several Members of Parliament. People vote for candidates in order of preference. A quota is calculated by dividing the number of votes by the	*Method.* Constituencies remain as at present in Britain, with one representative. Voters number candidates in their order of preference. The first preferences are counted and

Example: Ireland – cont.	*Example: Australia – cont.*
number of seats, and candidates who achieve this quota are elected. Later preferences are then counted according to a set formula. (Surplus votes not required by any winning candidate are transferred to the second choice.)	if one candidate gets more than 50 per cent of the poll they are elected; if not, the last candidate on the list is crossed off and their second preferences distributed. This continues until one candidate has 50 per cent of the poll.
Advantages. It very accurately reflects voting intentions in the number of MPs elected. It allows voters to prefer some individuals to others within the same party, and allows most constituents to have at least one MP who reflects their view.	*Advantages.* Same constituencies, simple to operate. It allows people to vote for the candidate they really want without fear of 'wasting' their vote.
Disadvantages. It is complicated and the link with one representative is lost. It is difficult for MPs to know their large constituency well, as if there are six MPs the constituency might be six times the size of the current single-member constituencies.	*Disadvantages.* It still does not give a completely accurate picture of the support that parties have.

There are variations to each of these models. For example, some countries like France use single-member constituencies with a second ballot. If no candidate has an overall majority (more than 50 per cent of the total vote) there is another election in the constituency, with parties doing 'deals' to decide who withdraws.

In countries like Italy, Belgium and Israel, there are multi-member constituencies, but people vote for a party rather than a person. The political party produces a list of candidates and the ones from the top of the list are elected according to the number of MPs the proportion of the vote won allows. This system has the disadvantage of reducing the personal link between elector and MP, but it has the advantage of increasing the representation of ethnic and other minority groups as parties will tend to put up a range of candidates to ensure the widest possible support.

It is sometimes suggested that other voting systems would lead to unstable governments (as in Denmark and Italy) but this does not appear to be inevitable. Canada, which has our own system, had five general elections in the eight years 1957–65, but Sweden and former West Germany (both with 'proportional representation') have had governments at least as stable as our own.

Which system of voting do you favour for this country?

---

1. What would have happened if we had had proportional representation (PR) in 1992?

    No one can answer that question because there are many varieties of PR. More importantly, the existence of PR would probably change the way that many people vote. Nevertheless, we can draw some conclusions by looking at the distribution of votes in particular areas.

    Devon is one of the most strongly Conservative areas of the United Kingdom, while South Yorkshire is a stronghold of the Labour Party. Tables 6.4 and 6.5 tell us what would have happened in these two areas if a 'party list' system of PR had existed or if each had been a 'multi-member constituency' and *if* voters had not changed their vote in consequence.

    Table 6.4 *Results in parliamentary constituencies in Devon (1992)*

Constituency	Con	Lab	Lib Dem	Others	Result
Devon West and Torridge	29,627	5,997	26,013	1,039	Con
Exeter	26,543	22,498	12,059	1,981	Con
Honiton	33,533	8,142	17,022	5,272	Con
Devon North	26,620	3,410	27,414	765	Lib Dem
Plymouth Devonport	17,541	24,953	6,315	2,407	Lab
Plymouth Drake	17,075	15,062	5,893	1,488	Con
Plymouth Sutton	27,070	15,120	12,291	256	Con
South Hams	35,951	8,091	22,240	1,073	Con
Teignbridge	31,272	8,128	22,416	671	Con
Tiverton	30,376	5,950	19,287	3,328	Con
Torbay	28,624	5,503	22,837	425	Con
	304,232	122,854	193,787	18,675	
Actually elected	9 MPs	1 MP	1 MP	0 MPs	

    Under PR, with total votes of 639,548 and 11 seats (giving 1 MP for every 58,141 votes), the results would have been:

Conservatives	5 MPs
Labour	2 MP
Lib Dem	4 MPs

Table 6.5 *Results in parliamentary constituencies in South Yorkshire (1992)*

Constituency	Con	Lab	Lib Dem	Others	Result
Barnsley Central	7,687	27,048	4,321	–	Lab
Barnsley East	5,569	30,346	3,399	–	Lab
Barnsley West & Penistone	13,461	27,965	5,610	970	Lab
Don Valley	18,474	32,008	6,920	803	Lab
Rotherham	10,372	27,933	5,375	–	Lab
Rother Valley	13,755	30,977	6,483	–	Lab
Sheffield Attercliffe	13,083	28,563	7,283	751	Lab
Sheffield Brightside	7,090	29,771	5,273	150	Lab
Sheffield Central	5,470	22,764	3,856	1,054	Lab
Sheffield Hallam	24,693	10,930	17,952	673	Con
Sheffield Heeley	13,051	28,005	9,247	–	Lab
Sheffield Hillsborough	11,640	27,568	20,500	–	Lab
Wentworth	10,490	32,939	4,629	–	Lab
	154,835	356,817	100,848	4,401	
Actually elected	1 MP	12 MPs	0 MPs	0 MPs	

Under PR, with total votes of 590,942 and 13 seats (giving 1 MP for every 47,454 votes), the results would have been:

Conservatives	3 MPs
Labour	8 MPs
Lib Dem	2 MPs

Now prepare a similar chart for your own area using the most recent general election figures (you will need a calculator). You will find the figures in an up-to-date *Whitaker's Almanack* or *Dodd's Parliamentary Companion* in the library. You will have to work your way through the results lists picking out the constituencies in your own area (in brackets after the constituency name; for example, if you live in Greater London you will see '(Gtr. London)' after Barking, Battersea, etc.) When you divide the number of votes achieved by a party by the 'qualifying' number of votes, the nearest 'whole number' will give you the number of MPs (e.g. 3.4=3 MPs; 3.8=4 MPs).

2.   *Becoming a Member of Parliament*
First, get involved with a political party at local level, helping with canvassing, etc. Perhaps become an officer of your local party or association or stand as a local government candidate.

In the case of the Conservative or Liberal Democrat parties, apply to the national headquarters asking to be put on the list of approved candidates (you do not have to be on the list, but it helps). If considered a possibility you will be invited to the HQ for an interview and if successful placed on the list.

In the case of the Labour Party you must be nominated by a trade union affiliated to the party or by a body, such as a local branch, attached to the constituency party.

When a vacancy occurs in a constituency (you do not have to live there) apply – or get nominated in the Labour Party. You may be shortlisted and interviewed by a selection committee in the Conservative and Liberal Democrat parties, who will recommend two or three candidates to go before a general meeting of the local association. Here you will make a short speech and a vote will be taken. If you are successful you become the PPC – the prospective parliamentary candidate. In the Labour Party the members of the local constituency party make the final selection of the PPC.

However, both the Standing Advisory Committee on Candidates in the Conservative Party, and the National Executive Committee of the Labour Party, can refuse to confirm the selection of a candidate, although this rarely happens.

Your first constituency is likely to be a 'hopeless' one and you will be expected to 'nurse' it and increase your party's vote. If successful, you may apply and be selected for a winnable seat.

In order to stand you must now get electors living in the constituency to nominate you and put up a **deposit**. You lose this deposit if you get less than a certain percentage of the total vote. This is supposed to discourage frivolous candidates but is very good value as once you have paid the deposit you are entitled to free postage of one communication to each elector (this is worth about £6,000 on average).

a. The selection of prospective candidates for Parliament is carried out by very few people and only party candidates have a real chance of winning. Some people see this as undemocratic. Can you think of a fairer system?

b. Find out how much has to be put up as a deposit if you wish to stand for election, and what percentage of the total vote you must attract in order not to lose it. Try looking in the index of *Whitaker's Almanack* under 'House of Commons'. (The information you are looking for is towards the start of the section.)

c. Recently there has been a growth of apparently non-serious candidates, including the Monster Raving Loony Party. Find out what other 'fringe' parties have been represented recently.

3.   Study Figure 6.2, which gives figures for the growth of the electorate.

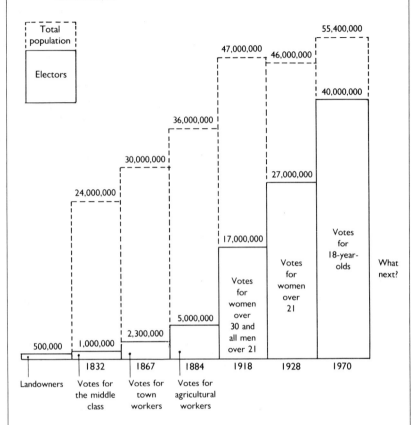

Figure 6.2
The electorate.

Before the Reform Act of 1832 the vote was effectively limited to male landowners over 21. Other males over 21 were given the vote by the Acts of 1867 and 1884, but up to 1918 voting was still conditional on the payment of rates – the 'poor's' rates.

a. Do you think the voting age should be lowered further?
b. Do you think any individuals or groups who currently have the right to vote should have their 'franchise' taken away?

4.   A **referendum** is when all the electors of a country are asked to vote for or against a particular change in the constitution or the law. The referendum is used often in some countries, but in Great Britain it has only been used twice – to decide whether or not to enter the (then) EEC (the 'Common Market'), and in Wales and Scotland to decide whether devolution of some power was wanted by the people of these countries. The main argument against the referendum is that it permits only a crude 'yes' or 'no' when the decision involved may have many alternatives.

On what kind of issues do you think a referendum would be appropriate?

5. In February 1974, Mr Heath's Conservative government was defeated in a general election. The Conservative Party gained more votes than the Labour Party, but won five fewer seats. The Liberal Party had gained 6 million votes, but won only 14 seats and Mr Heath approached the leader of the Liberal Party, Mr Thorpe, to try and form a **coalition** government. The Liberals were probably offered two places in the cabinet, with Mr Thorpe as Foreign Secretary. However, they refused and suggested a 'national government', that is a government made up of all the parties. This was unacceptable to the other parties and Mr Heath resigned.

    a. If you had been Mr Thorpe, do you think you would have accepted Mr Heath's offer? (Clearly you do not have all the facts; decide on the basis of what you know.)

    b. What do you think are the advantages and disadvantages of a national government such as we had during the Second World War?

6.6 PRESSURE GROUPS

Casting your vote at elections is one very important way of exercising your right in a democracy, but if going to a polling station once or twice every three or four years was all you were allowed to do in order to express your opinion, you would be justified in thinking that you had very little real power to influence those things and people who affect your life.

In fact one very important factor in a democracy, as we saw in section 6.3, is to be able to express our opinions and join any organisation that is not criminal. We can join a political party, even ones that wish to end democracy, or become a member of many other groups that seek to influence events.

There are hundreds of these groups in the UK – trade unions, employers' organisations, Oxfam, the churches, the National Council for Civil Liberties, the League Against Cruel Sports all try at some time or other to put pressure on the government, public authorities or other organisations in order to persuade or force them to follow the wishes of their members.

Sometimes organisations exist just for one purpose, to try and get something done or prevent something from happening.

In addition to national campaigns to bring pressure to bear on the government, there are hundreds of small campaigns throughout the country at any particular time: 'action groups' to try and get more jobs in an area; 'sit-ins' to try and stop a factory being closed; processions of parents across busy roads to force the local authority to have a crossing installed; squatters' groups to gain possession of empty homes. What groups are trying to get things done or prevent things happening in your area at the moment?

We can join many groups that seek to influence events – pressure groups allow people to express how they feel and ensure that their views are not ignored.

Sometimes **pressure groups** turn to violence or break the law in other ways in order to draw attention to their cause, but most do not. The main weapon of the pressure group is publicity.

Some pressure groups prefer to work quietly – they may **lobby** Members of Parliament. This means that they go to the lobby, or entrance hall, of the House of Commons and ask to see a Member of Parliament. (It is usual to check in advance that the MP will be available.) The MP will then come out to the lobby to hear the case for the group. Other groups, particularly big corporations and organisations such as the National Union of Teachers and the National Farmers' Union, will deal directly with ministers and departments of government.

It is this quiet form of pressure that worries some people as there is no opportunity to ensure that the opposite point of view is also heard. S. Finer called these groups the 'anonymous empire' because they were 'faceless, voiceless and unidentifiable'.

One big argument against pressure groups is that those that make the most noise – and perhaps spend the most money – may attract the most attention. They may also be selfish and put personal interests before national ones. Nevertheless, pressure groups are an essential part of life in a democracy. They allow people to express how they really feel and actively ensure that their personal needs or views are not ignored by officials.

1. *MPs and pressure groups*

One would expect MPs to have strong views and belong to interest groups themselves, and electors can take candidates' views into account when deciding whether to vote for them. However, many MPs are paid by various organisations as 'advisers', or they may be directors of commercial firms or sponsored by trade unions. In order to try and ensure that personal financial interests do not affect the work that Members do in Parliament a *Register of Members' Interests* was introduced in 1975. MPs are supposed to list any financial interests that they have in this annual record.

Try and find out if your MP is 'sponsored' or paid as an 'adviser' for any organisation. Make a list of all the organisations to which your MP belongs (these might include a church, a charity, a sports organisation, etc.).

2. Imagine that the local council has decided to pull down all the houses in the street where you live. Draw up an outline of how you would organise a pressure group to stop the scheme going ahead and what methods you would use.

3. Obtain a copy of a national newspaper and list all the pressure groups you can find mentioned on a particular day. You will be surprised how many you will find, particularly if you use one of the more serious papers like *The Guardian*, *The Independent* or *The Daily Telegraph*.

4. Here are the names of some 'permanent' pressure groups – you can find the addresses yourself. Some of these – and many others – are listed in *Whitaker's Almanack* in your school or college library. Look up 'charitable societies (various)' in the index at the front. Write to one of them and

report back to your group on how the organisation concerned tries to influence the Government or other official
bodies. (Many pressure groups are charities, so enclosing a
stamped addressed envelope would be helpful.)

> Age Concern
> Child Poverty Action Group
> Christian Aid
> Claimants' Union
> Community Service Volunteers
> Consumers' Association
> Help the Aged
> Joint Council for the Welfare of Immigrants
> National Children's Bureau
> National Council for Civil Liberties
> NSPCC
> Oxfam
> Shelter

6.7   SUPRANATIONAL AUTHORITY

The United Nations

After the First World War, the League of Nations was
established to prevent a repetition of global war. The United States
refused to join; the Soviet Union was largely ignored by other members; France and Britain were not particularly keen; Germany, Italy
and Japan simply ignored the pledges they had given. The League
was a failure.

During the Second World War, the main 'Allies' – the United
States, the Soviet Union, Britain and China – decided to try again
when the war was over. A 'Charter' laying down the rules was drawn
up and in 1945 50 countries signed. Its aim was to save succeeding
generations from the scourge of war, to reaffirm faith in fundamental
human rights, in the dignity and worth of the human person, and in
the equal rights of men and women and of nations large and small.

In theory the United Nations is open to any 'peace-loving' country.
In practice it is impossible to sort out which countries are peace-
loving and virtually any country can join, provided the others will
accept them. The United States vetoed the admission of China to the
United Nations for many years, as they regarded the 'government in
exile' in Taiwan as the legitimate one. However, in 1971 China was
admitted and Taiwan expelled.

All member countries are represented in the UN **General Assembly**
which gives every member nation an opportunity to express its point
of view. However, the real power is reserved for the **Security Council**
made up of the five most powerful countries in 1945 (the United

States, Russia, the UK, China and France), plus six others on a rota basis.

The responsibility for forcing nations to stay at peace lies with the Security Council, but important decisions can be vetoed by any one of the permanent members. This is why the United Nations has been unable to stop major wars like that in Vietnam.

Despite the lack of a permanent armed force that was once hoped for, the United Nations Forces in their light-blue helmets and berets were successful in restoring order in the Congo between 1960 and 1964, when the Belgians suddenly withdrew from their colony. They have also had some success in forming a buffer between conflicting forces in the Middle East in 1956 and 1973, between India and Pakistan in 1948–49 and 1965, and between Greeks and Turks in Cyprus.

The European Community

In 1973 Britain decided that its future was with Europe and joined the 'Common Market', the name by which the European Community (EC) is usually known. Decimal coinage had already replaced £.s.d. in 1971 and decimalisation of weights and measures has proceeded rapidly so that soon we will be using the same measurements as our partners in Europe for most things. By 1993 there was 'free trade' between the member states: frontier controls were mostly removed, some VAT and excise duties were standardised, professional qualifications were recognised throughout the Community, and other obstacles to free movement across the single market were removed.

The EC is run by a 17-member **European Commission**, to which France, Italy, Germany, Spain and the UK send two members and the smaller countries one each. This Commission is controlled by the **Council of Ministers**, one from each country, who must be unanimous for important decisions to be made.

In 1979 the first international general election took place when the voters of Europe returned 410 Euro-MPs to the Parliament in Strasbourg to represent the 260 million people of the then EEC. The European Parliament was at first composed of members nominated by the parliaments of their member states and is really only a forum for discussion with no real power. Many people consider that now that its members are elected it will increase its powers and ultimately be the sovereign body of a 'United States of Europe'.

The **European Court of Justice** sits in Luxembourg and rules on whether member states are acting in accordance with the Treaty of Rome, the treaty which first established the EEC in 1958.

Although theoretically it is possible for any member state to withdraw from the EC there would be problems in withdrawal as one of the objectives of the EC is to have free trade between its member states and over 40 per cent of Britain's trade is now with EC countries. One of the reasons why Britain joined the EC was because of the economic success it had achieved – the total value of production (the Gross National Product) of the original six members increased almost twice as fast as in Britain between 1958 and 1973.

It is now possible to work anywhere within the EC without restrictions, and most countries have joined in an attempt to harmonise their currencies. However, the UK left this Exchange Rate Mechanism (ERM) in 1992. There is continued debate on whether the European 'ecu' should become the common currency unit.

A substantial number of people opposed entry to Europe and some would still wish us to withdraw because:

1. We import more from Europe than we export.
2. The 'Common Agriculture Policy' supports inefficient farmers elsewhere in the EC and prevents Britain importing cheap food from elsewhere.
3. Britain alone in Europe has sufficient oil, gas and coal for its needs.
4. Britain will lose its independence and sovereignty.
5. We must obey policies which damage our own industry, for example limiting our fishing fleet.

However, a majority of people were in favour of European entry and they might say:

1. It would be foolhardy not to belong to the largest trading bloc in the world, particularly when it is next door.
2. Our old trading partners in the Commonwealth were already moving away from us to new markets before we joined the EC.
3. Europe is potentially the most powerful nation on earth and can provide a counterbalance to the United States.
4. In the modern world there is a loss of sovereignty by all successful nations; they cannot act alone.
5. If we wish for the benefits of membership we must tolerate the difficulties.

History of the EC

A united Europe was attempted several times by the Romans, Charlemagne, Napoleon and Hitler. It has also been advocated on the basis of agreement since the 17th century.

1944   The exiled governments of Belgium, the Netherlands and Luxembourg agreed to work together economically as 'Benelux'.

1949   The Council of Europe was formed. It consists of 25 members and its objective has been to achieve greater unity. Its major

In 1990 Germany became a united country once again.

achievement has been the European Convention of Human Rights.

1951 The European Coal and Steel Community (ECSC), Benelux plus France, West Germany and Italy, agreed to pool their coal and steel production. This meant that war between them became impossible. Britain was invited to join but refused.

1958 The Treaty of Rome. The European Economic Community was established by 'the six' members of the ECSC.

1959 The European Free Trade Association (EFTA) or 'outer seven' was established by Austria, the UK, Denmark, Norway, Portugal, Sweden and Switzerland.

1961
1964 Attempts by the UK to join the EEC failed.

1970 'The six' invited the UK, the Irish Republic, Denmark and Norway to negotiate on entry.

1972 Norway had a referendum on entry and withdrew its application.

1973 The Irish Republic, Denmark and the UK joined the EEC.

1975 A referendum was held in the UK on 5 June on whether to remain a member. The question asked was 'Do you think the United Kingdom should stay in the Community (the Common Market)?' (See Table 6.6.)

1981 Greece became the tenth member.

1986 Portugal and Spain joined.

Table 6.6 *Results of the 1975 referendum on EEC membership*

	Votes	% turnout	% 'yes'
England	21,722,222	64.6	68.7
Wales	1,345,545	66.7	66.5
Scotland	2,286,676	61.7	58.4
Northern Ireland	498,751	47.4	52.1
United Kingdom	29,453,194	64.5	64.5

---

1. Do any other countries want to join the EC?

2. Read the following passage carefully:

    > Thus has once more the unity of Germany been attained. That it may be permanent, and that so great a nation may for almost the first time in its long history have fair opportunities of developing its vast resources, cannot but be the prayer of everyone belonging to our own kindred folk of England; for it must never be forgotten that by race and speech Englishmen and Germans are brethren.

    > *The National Encyclopaedia*, 1882

    See if you can find any descriptions of Germany or Germans made by people in the UK between 1939 and 1945, and compare them with the one above.

6 DISCUSSION

1 where every man is enemy to every man ... In such condition, there is no place for industry; because the fruit thereof is uncertain; and consequently no culture of the earth, no navigation, nor use of the commodities that may be imported by sea, no commodious building; no instruments of moving, and removing such things as require much force; no knowledge of the face of the earth; no account of time. No Arts; no Letters; no society; and which is worst of all, continual fear, and the danger of violent death; and the life of man, solitary, poor, nasty, brutish and short.

Thomas Hobbes, *Leviathan*, 1651

This famous passage was written in 1651; Thomas Hobbes was describing a state of **anarchy**.

There are still anarchists – people who believe that it is possible for the 'State to wither away' (Engels, 1872) and for men to live together harmoniously without a legal system. Do you agree with Hobbes or the anarchists?

2 The British public is growing cynical and bitter, going through the motions of supporting a political system where, although traditional party politics may be the primary target of disillusionment, some of the disenchantment rubs off on Parliament. Close observers have questioned recently the degree of public attachment to Britain's representative institutions, and to the political system in general. The collapse of civil order in Ulster, the emergence of nationalism in Scotland and Wales, the strikes and demonstrations which have affected the stability of government, the emergence of direct action and the withdrawal to community politics have all been taken as testifying in different ways to a rejection of parliamentary authority.

S. Walkland, *The Commons Today*

To what extent do you think this passage is true today?

What faults do you think there are in our system of government? In what ways would you seek to improve the system?

3
  a. What advantages and disadvantages can you see in referenda?
  b. Consider some situations where you think a referendum would be appropriate, and some in which you think it would be unsuitable. Say why.
  c. Do you think Britain deserves the description 'a democracy'?

4 What disadvantages might there be to living in a totalitarian state? What possible advantages might there be in living within such a state?

5 Why do you think that some people do not vote in local and/or general elections? Do you think that voting should be compulsory as it is in some countries?

6 Consider the kind of power that may be held by people in Britain today – financial power, military power, trade union power, political power, knowing appropriate people, and so on. Which sort of power do you think is most important? Which kind of power do you think is justified?

 # ADDITIONAL ASSIGNMENTS AND INVESTIGATIONS

1 Look at Table 6.7.

Table 6.7 *Age of MPs elected, 1 January 1987*

Age on 1 Jan. 1987	Conservative	Labour	Liberal	SDP
20–9	4	–	1	1
30–9	70	44	4	–
40–9	146	94	7	2
50–9	111	63	4	2
60–9	43	27	1	–
70–9	4	1	–	–
Total	376	229	17	5
Median age				
1987	48	47	45	47
1983	47	51	43	45

Source: D. Butler and D. Kavanagh, *The British General Election of 1987*, Macmillan, 1988

    a. Which age band contains the most MPs?
    b. Which party has the youngest MPs as a percentage of their total number?

2 Look at Table 6.8.

    a. What kind of job is a Conservative MP most likely to have held before election?
    b. What kind of job is a Labour MP most likely to have held before election?
    c. How many MPs (so far as you can tell from the table) have held manual jobs before election?
    d. List the three most likely occupations to have been followed by MPs overall before election.

Table 6.8 *Occupation of Members of Parliament elected, 1987*

Occupation	Conservative	Labour	Liberal	SDP
Professions				
Barrister	43	9	4	1
Solicitor	21	9	1	–
Doctor/dentist	3	2	–	1
Architect/surveyor	7	–	–	–
Civil/chartered engineer	6	–	–	–
Chartered sec./accountant	17	2	–	–
Civil Servant/local govt.	13	8	–	1
Armed services	15	–	1	–
Teachers:				
University	6	11	2	–
Adult	2	15	–	–
School	17	29	2	–
Other consultants	3	2	–	–
Scientific research	3	6	–	–
Total	156	93	10	3
	(42%)	(40%)	(59%)	(60%)
Business				
Company director	39	2	–	–
Company executive	75	12	–	–
Commerce/insurance	18	9	–	–
Management/clerical	4	16	2	–
General business	3	2	–	–
Total	139	41	2	0
	(37%)	(10%)	(12%)	(0%)
Miscellaneous				
Miscellaneous white collar	8	18	1	1
Politician/pol. organiser	21	12	1	–
Publisher/journalist	26	14	2	1
Farmer	16	2	1	–
Housewife	7	–	–	–
Student	–	–	–	–
Local administration	–	4	–	–
Total	78	50	5	2
	(20%)	(21%)	(30%)	(40%)
Manual workers				
Miner	1	16	–	–
Skilled worker	2	44	–	–
Semi/unskilled worker	–	6	–	–
Total	3	66	0	0
	(1%)	(29%)	(0%)	(0%)
Grand Total	376	229	17	5

Source: ibid.

Table 6.9 *Education of candidates, 1987*

Type of education	Conservative	Labour	Liberal	SDP
Elementary only	–	4	–	–
Elementary +	–	11	–	–
Secondary only	25	32	3	1
Secondary +	26	50	2	–
Secondary & university	69	100	4	2
Public school only	41	1	–	–
Public school +	21	1	–	–
Public school & university	194	30	8	2
Total	376	229	17	5
Oxford	90	22	2	1
Cambridge	76	12	2	1
Other university	97	95	8	2
All universities	263 (70%)	129 (56%)	12 (71%)	4 (80%)
Eton	43	2	–	–
Harrow	8	–	–	–
Winchester	4	1	–	–
Other	201	29	8	2
All public schools	256 (68%)	32 (14%)	8 (47%)	2 (40%)

Source: ibid.

3 Look at Table 6.9.

    a. What percentage of MPs attended a university?

    b. What percentage of MPs attended a public school?

4 Do you think it is desirable or not for the background of MPs to reflect the backgrounds of those they represent?

5 Do you feel reasonably happy with the kind of Members of Parliament we have (so far as you can tell from the statistics)? Give reasons for your answer.

6 Borrow a copy of Hansard (the record of each day's proceedings in the House of Commons) from your local library. Find one with an interesting debate and use it as a script with members of your group, playing the parts of ministers and MPs. When you feel you have grasped the general idea of the debate, abandon your script and continue to a division (the name given to voting in the House of Commons, when each side goes through different doors) using your own words.

7 Find out how many people voted in the last election for councillors to the council responsible for education in your locality (e.g. Metropolitan District Council); work out what percentage these voters were of the total number entitled to vote. Bearing the figures you have discovered in mind, is it worth holding local government elections?

8 Find out as much as you can about the background, age, education, marital status, wealth and dwelling place of your MP. Assess whether or not you feel he or she is a suitable person to represent your constituency, ignoring any political loyalties you may have.

9 Visit a meeting of your local council (phone in advance if you will be one of a large party).
  a. Apart from your group, how many other members of the general public were present?
  b. How many councillors were present?
  c. Giving reasons based on your visit, state whether you would like to be a local councillor.

10 Obtain, draw or trace a large map of the world and colour this in appropriately using three colours to show:
  a. 'free' nations – those you regard as democratic;
  b. 'semi-free' nations – those you regard as partially free (i.e. there are elections with different political parties involved but some political parties are banned; some of the adult population cannot vote; or there are serious restrictions on what can be said or written);
  c. totalitarian regimes.

You may find some of the information you require in an up-to-date *Statesman's Yearbook*; a careful study of the press will provide even more up-to-the-minute information. (You may also try contacting Amnesty International for a list of countries currently holding political prisoners in gaol, often without trial.)

When you have completed your map, compare this with those completed by others in your group and try to resolve any differences of opinion that emerge.

6 OUTLINE OF AN APPROPRIATE GCSE INVESTIGATION/PROJECT

(For guidance, see 'Coursework for GCSE' on pages ix–xiv.)

Title   An investigation into the effectiveness of a pressure group.

Hypothesis   The decision to retain or close Littlewood Primary School will not be influenced by the 'Save LPS Group'.

(A similar study might relate to the closure of a local hospital, community centre, swimming pool, etc.)

This study relates to *power*; to the likely influence of a group of local people in an attempt to retain a local facility. There are a number of factors to be considered and only a few are listed here:

- How representative of the local community was/is the pressure group?
- Does the pressure group include powerful individuals (e.g. councillors from the majority party or their partners; wealthy business people or professionals such as lawyers; media people such as the local newspaper editor)?
- How and by whom will any decision to close the facility be made?
- What are the financial implications of a decision to close or to retain the facility? For example, if the decision is to keep it will other local services be lost instead?
- What financial resources does the group possess?
- What methods are/were used to exert influence (e.g. demonstrations, lobbying of councillors or MPs, petitions)?

Secondary sources   These are likely to be limited but may include articles from local newspapers; tapes of local radio programmes; minutes of council meetings (usually available from your main library or the Civic Centre/County or Town Hall).

(You may wish to compare the number of column inches devoted to comments in support of the pressure group as compared to those opposing it in your local newspaper. Simply mark the support or opposition in different colours in the newspaper for several editions and then measure the respective amount of coverage given to each.)

Primary sources   **Observation** of council meetings, demonstrations (if you are a member of a pressure group yourself this is likely to become *participant* *observation* because you are taking part in the demonstration – remember to avoid your views biasing the results).

Interviews with the main opponents and supporters of the pressure group. Make sure you ask each the same sort of questions so that you have **comparability** (i.e. you can compare statistically the responses given by both sides).

Questionnaires   You might limit these to individuals in the local community who are not actively involved in the dispute to see to what extent there is general support for the pressure group.

Statistical data   The actual facts relating to your survey in terms of the numbers involved and the financial facts.

Remember   The *point* of your survey. In this case you are studying *power*; you are *not* trying to decide whether the pressure group is justified or not.

6 GCSE QUESTION

Note: GCSE questions often require answers using information from interrelated themes. This one is mainly, but not exclusively, concerned with the sociology of politics.

People are often reluctant to disclose their true behaviour.

'If an election were held tomorrow, which party ...?'

Punch, 11 July 1984.
Reproduced by kind permission of *Punch*

(**a**) What is meant by a 'democracy'? Explain, using examples. (4)

(**b**) What aspects of government in Britain might be thought not to be democratic? (7)

(**c**) Social class is known to influence voting behaviour. Why do many working-class people not vote in the way they might be expected to? (9)

MEG, Sociology Paper 2, 1991

6 SELF-TEST QUESTIONS

(Answers on pages 291–92)

1. What are three alternative names for a state that is controlled by one person?

2. What does the word 'democracy' mean?

3. List three general features of life in a democracy.

4. What is an 'élite'?

5. What is the name of the new Party formed in 1988 by the amalgamation of the Liberal Party and part of the SDP?

6. How many MPs are there?

7. Describe briefly two methods of proportional representation.

8. When did women in the UK over the age of 21 get the vote?

9. List the names of ten pressure groups.

10. Which countries were full members of the EC (European Community) in 1992?

UNIT 7 THE MEDIA AND POWER

7.1   COMMUNICATING

All animals communicate with others. To stare at an aggress-ive dog is dangerous because the dog will recognise your stare as a challenge. When they wish to mate animals communicate particularly vigorously – their mating calls may travel many miles, they may pro-duce a powerful scent to attract the opposite sex, they may perform mating displays or even change colour.

Human animals may do all of these things as well, although the scent and the colour may be obtained from a shop. The difference between human beings and other animals is that humans can convey abstract ideas in the form of speech. This ability assists human society to develop instead of remaining virtually static, as with animal groups.

All normal human beings use speech in order to communicate, but they also express their thoughts and feelings in many other ways. We may kiss in order to convey affection, spit in order to indicate dis-taste, shake hands to indicate friendship. The armed forces recognise that it is possible to be insubordinate without saying or doing any-thing – you can be charged with 'dumb insolence'.

As we saw in Unit 1, human society has grown from small, isolated groups and these groups developed different ways of communicat-ing, both in speech and in other ways. Putting your thumb up indic-ates success in the UK; it may earn a punch on the jaw elsewhere!

Natural boundaries prevented people from mixing and allowed the development of different cultures, including language. These natural boundaries include:

> rivers
> mountains
> seas
> distance

The River Rhine separates the French from the Germans. Think of other cultures that have developed as a result of each of the natural barriers listed.

The ability of individuals to communicate has probably always had a great influence on the position that a person has occupied in society. Original thought is of little use unless it can be passed on to others. Powerfully expressed bad ideas may gain acceptance rather than poorly presented good ones. Think of some examples of bad ideas gaining acceptance because those who held them had the ability to communicate effectively.

The importance of our ability to convey our thoughts clearly and powerfully has grown enormously in recent years. The development of radio and television mean that ideas can now reach audiences of millions throughout the world.

Human beings, as we have seen in earlier units, like to be part of a group. We have to have strong personalities to stand apart and express views counter to conventional wisdom. You may feel privately that a police officer, a referee, a teacher or a politician is doing a good job in a difficult situation, but not be prepared to support him or her when everyone about you is in opposition. Crowds are dangerous as people become less critical, are more easily led and lack a feeling of responsibility when they become part of a crowd. Often we are not actually part of a crowd, but are still unwilling to be unpopular and express our real views. Fortunately, some people are prepared to stand by their opinions despite opposition. Others have given in to pressure, but been proved right in the end.

Below are listed a number of people who have had new ideas or opposed the conventional wisdom of those around them. Use the reference books in your library to find out what they believed and what happened to them as a result:

Alexander Solzhenitsyn
Nicolas Copernicus
George Fox
Thomas More
Socrates
Martin Luther King
Galileo

1. Esperanto is an international language invented by Dr Zamenhof of Warsaw, who published the first book on it in 1887. It is intended to bring the peoples of the world closer together, but has never attracted the mass enthusiasm necessary for it to achieve its aim. Suggest some reasons why Esperanto has not so far succeeded.

2. The following people need to be able to communicate effectively. Add at least six more groups to the list:

politicians
salespeople
police officers
parents

7.2   THE MEDIA

Quite early on in the history of humankind, it must have been found desirable to communicate with people at a distance. In the past minstrels could spread stories and news and town criers could make announcements, but communication was slow and reached only comparatively few people. Transport was slow, by foot and later by boat or horseback, but drums could send messages that could be received almost immediately, so could signals using smoke or fire. Later more sophisticated messages could be sent using semaphore or the heliograph, which used mirrors to reflect the sun's rays.

Books started to be widely available from the 16th century and newspapers and magazines in the 17th century. This was the start of what has come to be called the **media** or, as they now reach nearly everyone, the **mass media**. The mass media now include television, radio, newspapers and magazines, while advertising hoardings, films, videos, records and tape recordings are often also used for the same purpose.

Person-to-person communications have also greatly improved and telephone, fax and telex can put us in touch with people on the other side of the world within minutes. These are not, however, classified as part of the mass media as we usually communicate with only one person or a few people at a time.

The mass media can be an instrument for good or evil – they put an enormously powerful weapon into the hands that control them. Perhaps it is ironic that the television programme that was seen simultaneously by most people throughout the world in the 1970s was the *Miss World Contest*; could such a programme influence attitudes and opinions?

The media may have had a major influence on the American withdrawal from Vietnam in 1973 by showing the American public the misery and destruction it caused. The media certainly had a powerful influence in respect of the recent changes in Eastern Europe. The media can improve standards of all kinds of things by raising expectations and spreading knowledge; they can alert us to dangers that affect us all; they can bring people together by demonstrating similarities and common interests.

The media can also be used to encourage us to accept stereotyped views, or may numb our senses by constant contact with horror. News items can be selected in order to influence our views. The need to dramatise in order to attract audiences or sell papers may mean that our view of events is unreal. As we look at individual aspects of the media bear in mind this tendency to stereotype, dramatise and select.

1. Read the following passage carefully.

I am concerned here with the way in which the situation was initially interpreted and presented by the mass media, because it is in this form that most people receive their pictures of both deviance and disasters.

5   On the Monday morning following the initial incidents at Clacton, every national newspaper, with the exception of *The Times* (fifth lead on main news page), carried a leading report on the subject. The headlines are self-descriptive: 'Day of Terror by Scooter Groups' (*Daily Telegraph*), 'Youngsters Beat Up Town –

10   97 Leather Jacket Arrests' (*Daily Express*), 'Wild Ones Invade Seaside – 97 Arrests' (*Daily Mirror*). The next lot of incidents received similar coverage on the Tuesday and editorials began to appear, together with reports that the Home Secretary was 'being urged' (it was not usually specified exactly by *whom*) to

15   hold an inquiry or to take firm action . . .

It is difficult to assess conclusively the accuracy of these early reports. Even if each incident could have been observed, a physical impossibility, one could never check the veracity of, say, an interview. In many cases, one 'knows' that the interview

20   must be, partly at least, journalistic fabrication because it is too stereotypical to be true, but this is far from objective proof. Nevertheless, on the basis of those incidents that were observed, interviews with people who were present at others (local reporters, photographers, deckchair attendants, etc.) and

25   a careful check on internal consistency, some estimate of the main distortions can be made. Checks with the local press are particularly revealing. Not only are the reports more detailed and specific, but they avoid statements like 'all the dance halls near the seafront were smashed' when every local resident

30   knows that there is only one dance hall near the front . . .

The major type of distortion in the inventory lay in exaggerating grossly the seriousness of the events, in terms of criteria such as the number taking part, the number involved in

35   violence and the amount and effects of any damage or violence. Such distortion took place primarily in terms of the mode and style of presentation characteristic of most crime reporting: the sensational headlines, the melodramatic vocabulary and the deliberate heightening of those elements in the story considered

40   as news. The regular use of phrases such as 'riot', 'orgy of destruction', 'battle', 'attack', 'siege', 'beat up the town' and 'screaming mob' left an image of a besieged town from which innocent holidaymakers were fleeing to escape a marauding mob.

45   During Whitsun 1964 even the local papers in Brighton referred to 'deserted beaches' and 'elderly holidaymakers' trying to escape the 'screaming teenagers'. One had to scan the rest of the paper or be present on the spot to know that on the day referred to (Monday, 18 May) the beaches were deserted

50   because the weather was particularly bad. The 'holidaymakers' that *were* present were there to watch the Mods and Rockers.

The full flavour of such reports is captured in the following
lines from the *Daily Express* (19 May 1964): 'There was Dad
asleep in a deckchair and Mum making sandcastles with the
55 children, when the 1964 boys took over the beaches at Margate
and Brighton yesterday and smeared the traditional postcard
scene with blood and violence.'

This type of 'over-reporting' is, of course, not peculiar to the
Mods and Rockers. It is characteristic not just of crime reporting
60 as a whole but mass media inventories of such events as
political protests, racial disturbances and so on . . .

The repetition of obviously fake stories, despite known
confirmation of this, is a familiar finding in studies of the role of
the press in spreading mass hysteria. An important example in
65 the Mods and Rockers inventory was the frequently used '£75
cheque story'. It was widely reported that a boy had told the
Margate magistrates that he would pay the £75 fine imposed on
him with a cheque. This story was true enough; what few
papers bothered to publish and what they all knew was that the
70 boy's offer was a pathetic gesture of bravado. He admitted three
days later that not only did he not have the £75 but did not even
have a bank account and had never signed a cheque in his life.
As long as four years after this, though, the story was still being
repeated and was quoted to me at a magistrates' conference in
75 1968 to illustrate the image of the Mods and Rockers as affluent
hordes whom 'fines couldn't touch'.

S. Cohen, *Folk Devils and Moral Panics.*
The same incidents are referred to in S. Cohen and J. Young,
The Manufacture of News.

a. What examples does the writer give that prove the
reporting of the incident to be exaggerated?
b. In what ways, as illustrated in this extract, may the mass
media misrepresent incidents?
c. What is meant by:
   (i) 'journalistic fabrication' (line 21)?
   (ii) 'too stereotypical to be true' (lines 21–2)?
d. How do you think the kind of reporting described might
influence future events?
e. Think of a recent incident of sensational reporting and
say how 'over-reporting' may have influenced subsequent events.

7.3   THE PRESS

The mass media are unlikely to have existed at all if printing
had not been invented. Strangely we are not really sure who invented
it, but movable type was first used successfully by a German called
Gutenberg about 1450 and Caxton brought the idea to England 25
years later. Movable type allowed quick, cheap printing and made

books available to thousands who would otherwise never have been able to afford them. In 1272 the pay of a labourer was just under 1p per day; the price of a bible was £33 (his pay for ten years).

Books were the first kind of media to reach masses of people and have had a tremendous influence on the world in which we live today. The writings of Dickens helped with social reform, those of Karl Marx spread Communism throughout the world and Hitler's *Mein Kampf* helped his evil cause.

Books take quite a long time to print, need time to read, are comparatively expensive and reach comparatively few people. The development of newspapers, commencing with the *Weekly News* in 1622 and the first daily paper in 1703, has meant that printed information has reached the masses quickly and cheaply. (Stamp duties, however, in the 18th and early 19th centuries restricted circulation by making newspapers expensive.)

The average person in Britain buys more newspapers than the average person anywhere else in the world, and although we can overestimate the impact of the media in general we can also assume that newspapers would not be able to sell advertising space if readers were not influenced by what they read. In fact, advertising accounts for about 75 per cent of the 'quality' papers' income and about 40 per cent of that of the 'popular' press.

A few men control all the national newspapers in Britain. They and the editors whom they appoint are in a very influential position, both because they can select which items of news they wish to print and because they can decide how to 'slant', or put across, the selected news.

British newspapers buy news items from the three main press agencies:

> Reuters
> Exchange Telegraph
> Press Association

They also buy news from freelance reporters and employ their own correspondents and journalists. The newspapers can only use a fraction of the items submitted to them and so the news we see is what the editor and sub-editor of the newspaper think we should see.

In putting the news across to us, the newspaper may create bias by sensational headlines, by adding favourable or adverse comments, by exaggerating certain aspects of news, selecting photographs or by publishing cartoons supporting the general view of the paper. The power of the 'press barons' is, however, limited in a number of ways:

1. If a newspaper offends its readership by blatant bias contrary to the general opinions of the readers, it will lose sales.
2. If a newspaper offends its advertisers, it will lose revenue.

Photos an infringement of privacy, says friend ● People can make up own minds, says palace

Court refuses to block pictures of duchess

FERGIE'S STOLEN KISSES

Storm breaks over topless photos of the Duchess

FERGIE IS OUT IN THE COLD

FERGIE TOE-JOB SCANDAL

Lawyers fail to stop Duchess photos

Newspapers have very different approaches to reporting the news. Which of these headlines gives the most accurate picture?

3. If important news items are not covered in the paper, but appear on television, the readership may suspect bias.

4. Since 1953 the **Press Council** has investigated complaints about the conduct of newspapers.

5. There is legislation to prevent newspaper owners from taking control of independent television or local radio stations in:
   a. the Television Act 1963
   b. the Sound Broadcasting Act 1972

6. Further concentration of power is limited by the Monopolies and Mergers Act 1965.

7. The Department of Trade and Industry has to agree to any proposal for the transfer of ownership of a newspaper in order to prevent the further concentration of ownership of the press.

If the political opinion of newspapers was a crucial factor in influencing public opinion, it is likely that the Conservative Party would always be in power, but clearly this has not been the case. However, it is sensible to be aware of the bias that our newspapers have and to take this into account when interpreting the news we read.

One assessment of the political inclination of the national press is given in Table 7.1. Ask the members of your group to obtain different newspapers on a day when a major political news story 'breaks' and see if you agree with the assessments made.

Table 7.1 *Political allegiances of British national newspapers*

Newspaper	Political allegiance
The Sun	Formerly continued Labour tradition of *Daily Herald*, now mainstream Conservative.
Daily Mirror	Generally supports Labour; did give some Liberal support when party was popular.
Daily Express	Conservative, but can be critical.
Star	Generally supports Conservative.
Today	Supported the SDP/Liberal Alliance when first founded; now appears to favour the Conservatives.
Daily Mail	Has supported several parties in past; now right-wing Conservative.
The Daily Telegraph	Generally supports official Conservative Party line.
The Times	Fairly independent, some Conservative bias.
The Guardian	Generally supports Labour, has supported the Liberals in the past and has been favourable to the Liberal Democrats.
The Financial Times	Conservative, but supported Labour in the 1992 election.
The Independent	Independent line as name suggests.
News of the World	Mainstream Conservative.
Sunday Mirror	Generally supports Labour.
Sunday People	Generally supports Labour.
Sunday Express	Conservative, but can be critical.
The Sunday Times	Fairly independent, some Conservative bias.
The Observer	Generally supports Labour; Liberal and progressive Conservative sympathies; now also favours the Liberal Democrats.
The Sunday Telegraph	Supports official Conservative Party line.

1. In 1978 Polly Toynbee made the following comments on the girls' magazines then available:

Pink, Mates, Blue Jeans, Oh Boy! and *My Guy*. They make a lot of money and get a wide circulation...
   This new genre aimed at the 11 to 16-year-olds is devoted almost entirely to boys, how to get them, how to entice them, what to do to them when you've got them. Reading through a stock of them, this monomania is quite overwhelming and verging on the pornographic...
   Nowhere is there a single suggestion that girls of this age might be even a little interested in anything else at all...
   Their own ambitions have disappeared and they have settled for getting a boy who does exciting things instead...
   The joke is that after all these years of battering on for a new

deal for women ... striving to release young girls from the stultifying role stereotypes of the past, magazines like these are actually travelling fast in the opposite direction.

The Guardian, 1978

Consider the girls' magazines available today and say whether Polly Toynbee's comments are still valid.

2. Read the following extract.

In *Society Today 5* on Crime I was especially interested in the pictures produced at the bottom of pages 4 and 5 showing various aspects of a policeman's life. My criticism on objectivity is derived from what the photograph on the bottom right of page 5 depicts. To the normal reader the photograph would seem to show the conflict between the police and the coloured population during the recent Notting Hill carnival. However, whilst reading an article in the *Police Review* (4th February 1977 'A suspicious charge') I came across the identical picture which was enlarged and showed more of the background. By looking at this picture one gains *better knowledge of what the photograph is really depicting*. The youth in question is not aiming his abuse at the policeman but he is, in fact, aiming it at another member of the coloured population who is standing behind the police officer's left shoulder. Therefore I believe that much has been made by the media, i.e. *Society Today* and other publications who have printed this photograph. In other words, a situation has been portrayed which didn't occur in reality.

Letter in *Society Today*, 11 March 1977

a. What does the author mean by
    i. objectivity?
    ii. what 'the photograph is really depicting'?
    iii. the media?
b. This letter was published by a very reputable magazine and concerns a photograph which the writer claims was misleading. Consider other ways in which the media can exercise bias, either inadvertently or deliberately.
c. See if you can find examples of misleading or biased reporting or examples of important news which is not reported.

7.4 SOUND AND VISION

In the 1920s the invention of radio meant that people could hear the news and the comment on it almost as soon as it occurred. They did not have to make the effort of buying a newspaper – they did not even need to know how to read.

At the same time films were becoming increasingly popular. They had the advantage that, within the limitation of what was selected, people could judge for themselves, but they had the same disadvantage as books in that they took quite a long time to produce and people had to make a special effort to see them.

Television has developed rapidly since the 1950s, until today virtually everyone in Britain has a television in their home (about 98 per cent of households). It can be viewed by nearly everyone from babies to the very old. It brings news and views to us quickly, dramatically and with no effort on our part; the outside world comes right into our homes. It has been suggested that television, combined with fast travel, has turned the world into a 'global village'.

The National Viewers' and Listeners' Association is a pressure group that registers a complaint if there is what they consider to be too much sex or violence on television. Many people think that television lowers moral values, increases crime and blunts our feelings by showing real and imaginary scenes of horror. The opposite view is that television is educationally and socially a tool for good, encouraging our individual development by opening up new ideas and experiences to us.

It is impossible to be certain which point of view is correct; probably both are partially right. Adults will already have developed opinions and attitudes and will tend to select those items which reinforce their views while subconsciously rejecting contrary opinions. It has been shown, for example, that party political broadcasts have little effect on the majority of viewers.

Children, however, are still developing and are most likely to be influenced by what they see on television. In the 1950s many people were worried that TV, which more and more people were watching, would have a bad influence on children. In *Television and the Child* (1958) Dr Hilde Himmelweit drew a number of conclusions from the studies she had made on the influence of television on children, and these were reported to the committee set up by the government to investigate the issue. (This committee produced the Pilkington Report in 1962.) Himmelweit's conclusions were:

1. The less critical the child, the more influence television has; most affected were the less intelligent 13–14-year-olds.
2. The more able the child, the less television he or she viewed; brighter children tended to turn to other interests.
3. Television drama tended to devalue working-class life-styles, making the average child dissatisfied.
4. Tastes could be developed because the child would watch informative programmes in between the less constructive.
5. Children did not become more aggressive as a result of watching television.

Other investigations, however, have suggested:

1. Aggressive children could become more aggressive by television violence.

2. Television has a 'drip effect', so that repeated doses can have an increasing influence, perhaps to suggest that violence is normal.

3. Television provides ideas and technical knowledge to potential criminals.

4. Television creates greater tolerance of 'deviant' behaviour.

---

1. The influence of television on home life is often discussed. Do you think that it:
   a. causes people to stay at home more, thus increasing family control?
   b. prevents friction in the home by lessening boredom?
   c. stimulates conversation in the home by introducing new ideas?
   d. opens up new interests for the family?
   e. reduces conversation and discussion on family affairs?
   f. deadens the development of children by reducing creative play?

2. The following tables give some statistics for television viewing. (The figures are averages which may vary from year to year.) Consider them carefully.

   5–15-year-olds
   In February I watched TV for 24 hours a week.
   In August I watched TV for 19 hours a week.

   16–19-year-olds
   In February I watched TV for 18 hours a week.
   In August I watched TV for 15 hours a week.

   20–29-year-olds
   In February I watched TV for 18 hours a week.
   In August I watched TV for 14 hours a week.

   30–49-year-olds
   In February I watched TV for 19 hours a week.
   In August I watched TV for 14 hours a week.

   50–64-year-olds
   In February I watched TV for 20 hours a week.
   In August I watched TV for 15 hours a week.

   65+
   In February I watched TV for 22 hours a week.
   In August I watched TV for 15 hours a week.

   Social Trends 22, HMSO, 1992

	I belong to*	I watched	
		In February	In August
5% Doctors, lawyers, clergymen, architects, senior civil servants, etc.	Social class A	14 hours	13 hours
25% Bank clerks, teachers, senior clerical, etc.	Social class B	17 hours	14 hours
The remaining 70%	Social class C	20 hours	16 hours

* BBC definitions

Source: Broadcasters' Audience Research Board Audits of Great Britain, 1984

a. Which age group watches most television?
b. List some of the things each age group might be doing when not watching television which would help explain the differences in the amount of television viewed.
c. Why are the August figures always less than those for February?
d. Can you give any reasons which might account for the differences in television viewing between the social classes?
e. Ask the family, school or college students and teachers/lecturers how much time they spend watching television and compare your findings with the survey results shown. (You will have to question fairly closely to ensure the information you are given is correct.)

3. Make a survey of the television programmes watched by the members of your group, listing the total time spent during one week in watching the various categories of programmes:

comedies	pop music and variety
plays with a serious theme	educational
films	panel games
sport	children's
documentaries	ballet and opera
news and political	soap operas
programmes for ethnic	
minorities	

a. Do you think any of these categories of interest receive
  i. too much coverage,
  ii. too little?
b. Do you think the BBC and IBA have a duty to ensure that minority interests are catered for?

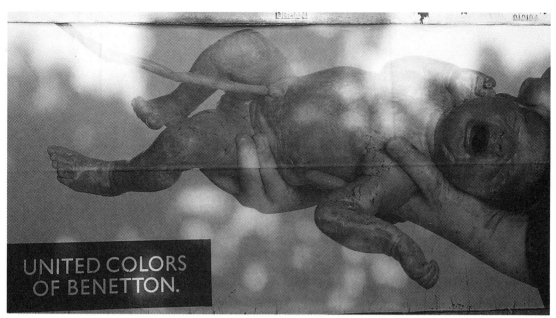

UNITED COLORS
OF BENETTON.

*Would you be offended by this
advertisement?*

7.5   ADVERTISING

You will find some kind of advertising almost everywhere in the world today, but particularly in the western 'free enterprise' countries where different firms compete with each other to sell their products.

In its most simple form, advertising merely tells us that something is available: 'Room to Rent', 'For Sale', 'Tobacconist'. Increasingly, it seeks to persuade us to buy one product rather than another. Advertising is also used to give information: 'Smoking damages your health', 'You are entitled to these welfare benefits', 'Exemption from NHS prescription charges'. Few people disagree with this 'informative' advertising. It is 'persuasive' advertising that tends to attract criticism.

Persuasive advertising is biased because it is trying to sell us something. Few people are foolish enough to take it at its face value. An advertisement for Optrex eye drops which stated 'A boyfriend or your money back' was permitted because it was clearly not intended to be taken seriously. However, there are many ways in which advertising can be used unfairly. One of our main defences against advertising is our awareness that it *is* advertising. For this reason **subliminal** advertising is banned in Britain. (This form of advertising involves flashing a message on a screen for a split second or reducing its intensity so that we do not consciously perceive it. The idea is that the advertisement will act on our subconscious without our reasoning defences coming into play.)

The British advertising industry produces a voluntary 'British Code of Advertising Practice' which is accepted by almost all the mass media. This code lays down rules which control the use or abuse of:

1. appeals to fear
2. 'knocking copy' (discrediting rivals)
3. guarantees
4. testimonials (they must be real!)
5. 'free' offers
6. appeals to children's credulity
7. 'scientific' claims.

The poster advertising industry also has a viewing committee which can ban certain types of posters, for example those:

1. showing obscenity
2. depicting acts of violence
3. inciting social disorder
4. advertising treatment for serious diseases
5. offending religious feelings.

The *IBA Yearbook* lays down strict rules for advertisers; for example, mirrors and glass cannot be used to create an illusion when advertising polish.

In addition to the voluntary rules, there are many Acts of Parliament which affect advertising, though there is no law relating specifically to it. Here are a few; see what others you can discover:

1. Adoption Act 1958
2. Cancer Act 1939
3. Children and Young Persons (Harmful Publications) Act 1955
4. Defamation Act 1950
5. Indecent Advertisements Act 1889
6. Misrepresentation Act 1967.

Some of the advantages of advertising are given below.

1. It brings new products to our attention.
2. It boosts demand, and therefore increases production and creates employment.
3. By increasing sales, it allows mass production and therefore reduces the cost per item.
4. It provides useful information.
5. It permits newspapers and magazines to be sold at prices all can afford.
6. It increases competition.
7. It raises living standards.
8. It raises money for charities.
9. It makes our world more colourful.

Some of the dangers of advertising are as follows.

1. It increases vanity, fear, envy and snobbery by appealing to these traits.
2. It devalues sex by using it to sell products.
3. It increases expectations which cannot be realised and makes people discontented.
4. The price of advertising is passed on to the consumer and increases costs.
5. It makes people buy things they cannot afford and may not need.
6. It often misleads (if you read *Which? Magazine* you will see that the most advertised product is often not the 'best buy').
7. It is a nuisance (interrupting television programmes, etc.).
8. It encourages us to damage our health (sweets, tobacco, alcohol).

Do you think that the advantages of advertising outweigh the disadvantages?

---

1. Make a collection of advertisements that:
   a. use the following to sell the product:
      i. envy
      ii. vanity
      iii. fear of failing our children
      iv. fear of being different
      v. our wish to be sexually attractive
      vi. sexual desire.
   b. give information
   c. warn

2. Decide on a product or service you wish to sell. Keeping within the law, devise an advertising campaign to sell it including:
   a. a 30-second TV commercial
   b. an advertising hoarding
   c. a newspaper advertisement
   d. one publicity 'stunt' – you may hire a famous personality if you wish

---

7.6 POWER AND CENSORSHIP

What should we be allowed to see, hear and read? Who should decide?

Cigarettes, the services of marriage bureaux and political opinion are some of the things that cannot be advertised on British television. The amount of violence and the degree of explicitly sexual material that can appear in magazines, in newspapers, books and on the screen is considerably more now than in 1963, when the publishers of *Fanny Hill* (first published in 1749) were charged with obscenity. However, there are still limits to what can be written or shown, and some people think we have already gone too far and more restrictions, or **censorship**, should be introduced. Do you agree?

There has been no press censorship in Britain since 1695. During both world wars it was an offence to publish anything likely to be useful to the enemy, but although censors were appointed to whom material could be submitted for approval, this was not compulsory. This does not mean that today newspapers can publish what they like. For example, there are laws prohibiting:

1. libel – writing anything untrue which will damage another person
2. blasphemy – insulting God in such a way as to offend Christians
3. incitement to racial hatred – under the Race Relations Act 1965
4. obscenity – anything likely to 'deprave or corrupt'
5. publication of matters threatening national security.

Again, there is no government censorship of films, although films can only be shown for commercial purposes in a building licensed by a local council who can forbid the showing of films. Usually these councils accept the grading of films by the Board of Film Censors, an organisation operated by the cinema industry itself, but occasionally films passed by the Board are banned by local councils.

In 1968 the Theatres Act abolished stage censorship. However, it is an offence for plays to be performed that offend against the rules already listed for the press.

We tread a delicate path between liberty and licence, between having the right to decide for ourselves what we do and living in a society where anything goes – where people can be cheated, slandered, brutalised or corrupted with impunity. Who should decide the position of the path? In the case of films and plays, perhaps it is fair to leave the decision to the courts, for if a show is likely to offend us we can avoid it. In the case of the press we can choose to some degree, but children may be influenced by what they see lying about or on display in newsagents.

Television comes right into our homes and so needs special care. The BBC and IBA do control what is being shown and material likely to cause offence is usually shown late at night.

Censorship is more severe in many other countries than in Britain. You could write a letter extolling the virtues of socialism to the editor of the *Daily Mail* but it is unlikely to be printed. In some countries you would not have dared to write the letter.

Only the enormously wealthy could afford to start a newspaper.

Gerry Adams, Sinn Fein MP from 1983 to 1992. The British government now censors discussion of the use of violence for political purposes.

However, television and radio in this country do try and present a range of opinion. Local radio in particular does encourage local people to express their views.

Dictators insist that everyone must think as they do; they fear views different to their own. Democracy is essentially concerned with a right to communicate freely. The problem remains how to ensure that everyone has the right and the opportunity to express their views if they wish, and yet respect the right of others not to be insulted, humiliated, embarrassed or threatened.

1. a. What programmes or scenes from programmes would you ban from current television programmes if you were an official censor?
    b. Do you think political views should be censored?

7 DISCUSSION

1 The following advertisement appeared in a magazine in America. Do you think such an advertisement would, and should, be permitted in Britain?

Is it true the amazing secret of TELECULT POWER

AUTOMATICALLY BRINGS YOU ANYTHING YOU DESIRE . . .

And in 10 seconds starts to draw Riches, Love, Fine Possessions, Friends, Power, Secret Knowledge, and much more into your life? See for yourself!

Yes a staggering miracle has happened. A brilliant psychic researcher has discovered a secret—so powerful that it is said to bring your desires to you, from the invisible world, like a blazing streak of lightning!

Yes, how would you like to be able to sit in your living room, give the command for love, and instantly have your loved one appear at your side? Or give the command for money, and suddenly find a big, thick roll of dollars in your hand?

Now, a daring new book called TELECULT POWER lays bare this magic secret, and shows how it can bring fortune, love, and happiness. And Rees P. Dubin — the man who discovered it — makes this shocking claim.

From: *True Life Secrets*

2 Do you feel that a greater degree of censorship is needed in Britain? (In 1988, for example, the government introduced a ban on television appearances by members of a political wing of the IRA, Sinn Fein. Was this justified?)

3 The Blasphemy law in Britain is restricted to insults which offend the Christian religion. Should this law be extended to prevent the publication or broadcasting of insults which offend other religions? Should the Blasphemy law be abolished altogether?

4 Attitudes and values can also be learned from television, and incorrect notions and stereotypes about life and other people and groups can be picked up. Children are particularly susceptible to stereotyped presentations of groups, situations, occupations, etc. when they have little or no related knowledge or experience. Children (and, for that matter, adults) find it difficult to tolerate uncertainty and ambiguity, they look for meaning and they welcome definitions. Television can give meanings and definitions which the individual who finds himself faced with unfamiliar situations may find helpful and comforting. Short-term personal 'adjustment' is often gained at the cost of long-term social disorganisation. The role of television and the other media in the development of racial and ethnic stereotypes is a case in point, and one which requires urgent investigation. If the only time the media present immigrants is in crisis situations, ought we to be surprised if there is a wide-spread use of racial stereotypes?

It is in the areas of the unfamiliar, the uncertain and the unknown, then, that television may have its maximum effect on attitudes and values. Children are likely to be particularly vulnerable to outside influences, including the influence of television, if they have few guidelines, lack relevant experiences, or if the family and other 'primary' agencies in the socialisation process have not made their point of view clear or provided the necessary standards. If these conventional sources in the learning process are not available or are not felt to be adequate, then other sources including television are more likely to be used.

J. Halloran, 'The Social Effects of Television', in *The Effects of Television*, ed. J. Halloran.

a. Which group does the author consider will be most susceptible to the influence of television?
b. Bearing in mind the points made in the source material, would you make any changes to the present programmes on television?
c. What benefits can or could arise from television?

ADDITIONAL ASSIGNMENTS AND INVESTIGATIONS

1 Advertising has to make an impact to be successful. Some people suggest that the most effective advertisements are those that appeal to our vanity, our envy of others, our sexual appetite or fear (e.g. that we are failing our children in some ways).

Make a collection of ten advertisements that you consider effective and write on each one the emotion(s) that you consider the advertisement appeals to.

2 a. Obtain at least one newspaper from each of these three groups on the same day, and fill in the chart below.
   A *Sun, Daily Mirror, Daily Star*
   B *Daily Express, Daily Mail*
   C *The Daily Telegraph, The Guardian, The Times.*

	Group A	Group B	Group C
Number of pages altogether			
Number of pages of advertising			
Number of pages of sport			
Number of photographs			
Number of pages of general articles including editorial			
Approximate percentage of paper occupied by photographs			
Approximate percentage of paper occupied by foreign news			
Approximate percentage of paper occupied by British news			
Approximate percentage of paper occupied by general articles including editorial			
Approximate percentage of paper occupied by main headlines			

If you wish to do this more scientifically use a ruler to calculate the number of centimetres (or inches) of each column in the newspapers devoted to the above.

   b. Which paper do you regard as the best value for money?
   c. Check with *Social Trends* which newspaper is read by the greatest number of people.

3

Table 7.2 *Reading of national newspapers: by sex and age, 1971 and 1990*

Great Britain	Percentage of adults reading each paper in 1990			Percentage of each age group reading each paper in 1990				Readership (millions)		Readers per copy (number)
	Males	Females	All adults	15–24	25–44	45–64	65 and over	1971	1990	1990
Daily newspapers										
The Sun	25	20	23	29	24	21	16	8.5	10.2	2.6
Daily Mirror	22	17	19	20	18	21	18	13.8	8.7	2.8
Daily Mail	10	9	9	7	8	11	11	4.8	4.2	2.5
Daily Express	10	8	9	7	7	10	11	9.7	3.9	2.5
Daily Star	8	5	6	8	8	5	3		2.8	3.0
The Daily Telegraph	6	4	5	3	4	7	7	3.6	2.3	2.2
Today	5	3	4	5	5	3	1		1.7	3.0
The Guardian	4	2	3	3	4	3	1	1.1	1.3	3.1
The Times	3	2	3	2	3	3	2	1.1	1.2	2.7
The Independent	3	2	2	3	3	2	1		1.1	2.7
The Financial Times	2	1	2	1	2	2	–	0.7	0.7	3.6

Source: Social Trends 22, HMSO, 1992

a. According to Table 7.2:
   i. What percentage of men read the *Daily Mail*?
   ii. What percentage of women read the *Sun*?
   iii. Between 1971 and 1990 the relative popularity of the *Sun* and the *Daily Mirror* changed. Give *one* possible reason for this change.

b. According to Table 7.2:
   i. Which is the most widely read 'quality' daily newspaper?
   ii. How many people read each copy of *The Guardian* actually bought?

c. Give *two* differences in content that you would expect to find between a 'quality' daily newspaper and a 'popular' newspaper.

d. The prices paid for newspapers rarely cover the cost of their production. What other sources of finance may a newspaper have?

e. What factors should be taken into account in deciding whether the information you read in a newspaper is reliable?

4   In Table 7.3 the first column gives the classification often used by researchers who are seeking to establish what kind of people are likely to use particular products or behave in a particular kind of way. (It is no use advertising in a particular paper if the people you are trying to 'get at' read another.) In the second column you see some suggestions as to which newspaper each of these social classifications is most likely to read.

Produce a questionnaire asking what occupation your respondents have and which newspaper they read. This is a simple survey and so you should be able to ask a number of people. Try and ensure you have representatives from each class listed. Compare your results with the suggestions listed.

Table 7.3

Social class	Newspapers most likely to be read
Class A. The head of the household is a successful business person or leading professional; senior civil servant; or has considerable private means. Class A covers about 3 per cent of the population.	*The Daily Telegraph, The Times, Daily Express, The Independent*
Class B. Most professional people. Teachers, clergy, lecturers, solicitors, accountants and librarians. Class B covers about 12 per cent of the population.	*The Daily Telegraph, The Guardian, Daily Express, Daily Mail*
Class C1. Small tradespeople and non-manual workers who carry out less important administrative, supervisory and clerical jobs. Class C1 covers about 22 per cent of the population.	*Daily Mirror, Daily Express, The Sun*
Class C2. Skilled manual workers, covering about 32 per cent of the population.	*Daily Mirror, Daily Express, The Sun*
Class D. Manual workers, generally semi-skilled and unskilled, about 23 per cent of the population.	*Daily Mirror, Daily Express, The Sun*
Class E. Old age pensioners, widows, casual workers, and those on social security with household income little above basic flat-rate social security benefit. Class E covers about 9 per cent of the population.	*Daily Mirror, Daily Express, The Sun*

OUTLINE OF AN APPROPRIATE GCSE INVESTIGATION/PROJECT

(For guidance, see 'Coursework for GCSE' on pages ix–xiv.)

Title A study of those magazines which claim to be directed at the 'more liberated' women to determine whether they counter stereotyping.

Hypothesis 'Liberal' women's magazines reinforce the traditional gender roles and strengthen the lower status position of women in our society.

(NB This hypothesis has two interconnecting features and it would be necessary to outline what the traditional gender roles are and justify the statement that women have a lower status position.)

Secondary sources These could include a number of books, for example *The Sociology of the Mass Media*, D. Glover (1984); *Learning the Mass Media*, M. Alverado, R. Smith and T. Wollen (1987); *Media Studies*, B. Dutton (1986), all of which deal with women's magazines.

Primary sources These could include a number of magazines depending on which you decide are directed at the 'more liberated' women; for example, *Company*, *Cosmopolitan*, *Woman's Journal*, *Spare Rib*.

You may also use one of the more traditional women's magazines as a comparison, for example *Woman's Own*.

- You might decide that certain topics reinforce traditional gender roles, for example fashion, beauty, food, childcare, and that others indicate a wider role, for example careers, sex and emotions, politics. (Note that you are making value judgements, i.e. your own opinions and prejudices are influencing your decisions; this indicates the difficulty a social scientist has in taking a truly unbiased, scientific approach. It is relevant to state this in your investigation report.)
- In order to compare the magazines you can use the contents list of each magazine to see what is featured and calculate the number of articles in each of the categories which you have decided are relevant in each of the magazines.

  You may then wish to assess the length, prominence and contents of these articles (e.g. if the article is about careers, is it to do with traditional female jobs such as secretarial work, or non-traditional ones such as engineering?).

- You might also assess the advertising in each magazine, e.g. clothes, DIY, perfume, cars; deciding again between traditional and non-traditional purchasing by or for women. But you may also wish to distinguish between types of a particular topic (e.g. if cars are advertised do these tend to be small cars rather than executive, high-performance vehicles?).
- You might also wish to carry out similar assessments of photographs, covers, etc.

Interviews　You may limit your further investigation to interviews. If so say why, for example the problem of assessing depth of feeling, emotional responses from questionnaires. Remember to be non-judgemental when asking questions even though you are still trying to prove or disprove a particular hypothesis.

Your interviews may seek to find out which magazines women read and why (e.g. are they more comfortable with a stereotypical role?); as well as seeking their opinion on particular magazines.

7 GCSE QUESTION

Note: GCSE questions often require answers using information from interrelated themes. This one is mainly, but not exclusively, concerned with the media and power.

**A new generation
of skin care**

AGE-LINE CONTROLLER

Our exclusive formula helps skin stay
younger looking longer – replenishes vital ingredients
found in the skin's structure – softens and reduces existing
facial lines. (Up to 37% on average in just 14 days.)
– Protects against new lines where you need it most: around
your eyes and mouth, on your forehead and throat. Use it day
and night and smile at a younger looking you.

Those in favour of advertising claim that it gives shoppers useful information and so helps us choose wisely. But those against say exactly the opposite – advertisements don't tell us very much – they only persuade.

There is no doubt that many advertisements do give us *some* information, but we need to be very careful over this, for information can be given in such a way that it can be at the same time both informative and persuasive. It is also true that, sometimes, what appears to be information is not of much real help.

(**a**)   What does the passage warn shoppers to be careful about when looking at advertisements?   (2)

(**b**)   How does the advertisement try to persuade people to buy the product?   (4)

(**c**)   Is the information of 'much real help'? What else would you want to know in order to be able to judge whether the product is worth buying?   (6)

(**d**)   'The advantages of advertising are more important than its disadvantages.' Do you agree? Give reasons for your answer.   (8)

WJEC, Sociology GCSE Paper 1, 1988

7 SELF-TEST QUESTIONS

(Answers on page 292)

1. What ability in communication do human beings have that is not possessed by other animals?

2. What four natural boundaries assisted the development of different cultures?

3. What is Esperanto?

4. List the three main forms of mass media.

5. Give three advantages and three disadvantages of the mass media.

6. Which body investigates complaints against newspapers?

7. What percentage of households in Britain have television: 56, 79 or 98 per cent?

8. According to Himmelweit, what sort of child will be most influenced by television?

9. List five advantages and five disadvantages in advertising.

10. What have Libel, Blasphemy, Incitement to Racial Hatred and Obscenity in common?

UNIT 8 EARNING OUR LIVING

8.1 THE ECONOMY

We saw in Unit 6 that the way political power operates in a country will influence our own lives. Even more important is the **economy** – the way that production is organised, distribution arranged and wealth exchanged. These aspects in turn will influence and be influenced by the sort of political structure we have.

Early in the history of humankind, demand was based on basic needs: people were contented to produce enough to satisfy their hunger and their need for shelter. This was a **subsistence economy**, and there are still places in the world today with just such a situation.

In Unit 1 we saw how people managed to achieve a surplus of food and so could afford to keep people who were not meeting basic needs – people who built cities, taught or invented new things – and expectations grew. Today we want all sorts of things that we do not really need in order to survive: television sets, records, fashionable clothes. In fact, in Britain, there are more people employed in producing and distributing such luxuries than in producing essential things.

In the modern situation two economic systems have developed: **capitalism** and **socialism**. In a capitalist system the means of production, distribution and exchange are in private ownership, and people try and produce a surplus in order to create a profit. In a socialist system production, distribution and exchange are run by the state and theoretically for the public good. Much of modern politics is concerned with which of these systems operates most effectively, and in fact most countries have a **mixed economy**, that is a mixture of private enterprise and state ownership.

In the UK, railways, coal mines and the postal service are owned by the state, that is they are **nationalised**; food production, banking and retailing are run by private enterprise. Some private enterprises, such as shipbuilding, have some of the shares owned by the state.

In the 1980s the government started to **privatise** some nationalised undertakings. This meant that the state sold all or most of its ownership to private shareholders; for example, the telephone system which was previously operated by the Post Office became 'British Telecom'. What other nationalised enterprises have been sold?

Long ago when people produced more than they could use them-

222

selves they could barter, or exchange this surplus for a surplus that someone else had created. However, this was a very awkward way of operating and money was invented to exchange for surplus goods. Perhaps the money would be specially shaped stones or shells; today it is little bits of paper or metal. The important thing is that people recognise the value of the money. If they begin to think of the tokens as of less value they will want more of them; when this happens we have **inflation**.

If prices rise more than earnings, the standard of living we have will decline; but if earnings rise more than prices, the living standards of those actually receiving the wages or salaries will go up. People are

German inflation, 1923 – a single dollar was worth 4,200,000,000 Reichsmark.

always trying to improve their relative positions, so there is always a tendency for earnings to increase; this **wage drift** may not result in an increase in what we actually have to spend (called **real wages**) if prices also increase accordingly.

If inflation becomes severe and people are being paid more but producing the same amount, wage increases raise the price of the goods when sold abroad. This can reduce sales and lead to lower production and unemployment. If people are unemployed they cannot afford to buy so much and this lowers **demand** still further and leads to more unemployment!

Controlling the economy so that people are encouraged to buy enough at home, but the **balance of payments** is maintained – that is, exporters manage to sell enough abroad to balance the goods being imported – is a very tricky operation, and one of the jobs the Chancellor of the Exchequer has to do each year when producing the Budget.

---

1. Get a copy of a newspaper that quotes share prices (e.g. *The Financial Times, The Daily Telegraph, The Guardian,* etc.). Imagine you have £1,000 to spend. Selecting not more than five companies, use the 'Bid' (or buying) price column, work out how many shares you can afford in the companies you have chosen and write them down. In one month's time look up your shares in the 'Offer' (or selling) price column and see how much you would have gained or lost if you really had invested £1,000.

2. *Unit trusts*
    People who only have a small amount to invest may not wish to risk it all in one company. Unit trust companies buy shares in many companies and then sell 'units' made up of part of the total shareholding to the public.

    By buying unit trusts you reduce your risk of losing your money, but you also reduce your chances of making a big profit! You can buy units on a monthly subscription scheme if you wish.

    Look up the unit trust section on the share prices page of newspapers, as in Question 1. Select a unit trust and imagine you have £2,000 to invest in it. Two weeks later check the same unit trust and see how much you have made – or lost.

3. *Bullock Report 1977: Worker directors*
    All large firms in the former West Germany have ordinary workers on their board of directors and elected works councils, even in small firms. It is suggested that this partnership of management and workers contributes to German industrial success.

In 1977 the Bullock Committee recommended that such 'industrial democracy' should be introduced in Britain. The report recommended that these 'employee directors' should be appointed by the trade unions; a minority felt that these directors should be elected directly by the work-force. However, most companies have still not appointed employee directors.

What advantage and/or disadvantage might there be in having employee directors?

8.2   CHANGES IN INDUSTRY AND COMMERCE

Worldwide inflation has led to a **slump**, or decrease, in world trade, and this is one reason why unemployment rose in most countries, including the UK, during the early 1980s and the 1990s.

However, in the UK and many other Western countries there were additional reasons for the growth in unemployment:

1. automation and mechanisation
2. the increase in married women working
3. an increase in the number of young people coming onto the labour market.

Mechanisation is the process by which work is taken over by machines. Machines of various kinds have existed for thousands of years, but machinery began to become really important in the middle of the 18th century. At first the introduction of machinery threw people out of work, and in 1811 groups called the Luddites started destroying the textile machinery that was replacing them. Although many Luddites were hanged or transported, the real reason they died out was that the growing industrialisation caused by the introduction of new machinery eventually created more jobs than were lost. Is the same process occurring now?

Automation is the process by which thinking processes get taken over by machines. Computers can instruct machines so that they not only make goods, but can control the flow of raw material, link different processes together, detect flaws and perform other jobs that only people could do in the past. Today computers, often linked to the more sophisticated machinery mentioned above, are replacing large numbers of people, particularly those previously engaged on routine manual and clerical work. It may be that in the future automation will increase the number of jobs in the service industries, but if this is to happen the additional wealth created by computers will have to be used to support these 'unproductive' workers.

However, even if automation had not become important during the 1960s and 1970s, we would still have needed an additional 4 million

Automation in the car industry.

jobs in order to keep unemployment to the same level as in the 1950s. The reason for this is that many more women work now because:

1. families are smaller and women can return to work earlier
2. increasing educational opportunities have increased the expectations of fulfilling careers for many women
3. pressures to consume more and a wish for higher living standards make a joint family income desirable
4. a greater number of women need to look after themselves because of rising divorce rates. (This is a fairly minor factor.)

Now more than 50 per cent of all married women work and this percentage can be expected to increase. In 1984 58 per cent of all women between the ages of 16 and 60 were working (33 per cent full-time), by 1989 the figures had risen to 66 per cent (37 per cent full-time). Find out the current statistics. In addition, up until 1981 there were more young people coming onto the job market because of the 'baby bulge' in the early 1960s, but the numbers of young adults then started to decline. (By 1989 the number of people aged 16 was only slightly higher than in 1971; after 1993 the numbers start to rise again, to peak about the year 2010.)

A further and less important factor is the increasing number of people who have two or more jobs; this is called 'moonlighting'.

Despite unemployment, there are unfilled vacancies. This is because of the following factors:

1. The jobs are in the wrong place. Most vacancies in the past have been in the South-East whereas most jobs until 1991 were being lost in the old industrial areas of the North,

North-West and North-East. The government tried to encourage jobs to move to people, for example by giving grants for new factory building in the declining areas and by moving government departments out of London to places like Glasgow and Newcastle. In addition, the government tries to encourage people to move to new areas by offering 'resettlement grants', but people have been reluctant to do so because they have to leave relations and friends and because the cost of living, particularly the price of housing, is greater in the more prosperous areas.

2.   The working hours are unattractive. People are increasingly reluctant to work shifts or at weekends; they are becoming more family centred and want to be free at the same time as their partners and children.

3.   The jobs are poorly paid. Benefits such as Family Credit mean that there can be very little financial difference between working and not working as benefits are lost as income increases.

4.   Although there may be suitable employment elsewhere it is often very difficult to move, because of housing problems. If an area is hit by redundancies house prices often fall and owners cannot move to more prosperous areas with much higher house prices; equally, council tenants will find transfer difficult.

5.   The people who are unemployed may not have the skills required for the vacant posts. There is a decreasing need for unskilled labour as many routine tasks have been automated, and many skills previously needed in heavy engineering, steel manufacturing, etc., are now outdated.

8.3   THE WORLD OF WORK

Some people like to look back at a golden age when happy peasants danced round maypoles and craftsmen glowed with pride. Of course, in reality, the vast majority of people laboured in miserable conditions, and although it is true that there were people doing satisfying, interesting work, it is possible that a greater percentage of people today do enjoy their jobs.

However, there are many people who get very little job satisfaction; automation and mechanisation have removed many boring routine jobs, but they have also replaced some satisfying skilled processes with machines requiring little more than button pressing. This development is not new – **production-line** (or 'conveyor-belt') methods developed from 1910 in the United States and became established during the First World War when it was necessary to speed up output. In this system each job is broken down into simple operations and each worker performs just one task before passing it on to the next person. People could be trained quickly and became

Child labour in the 1840s contrasted with modern office conditions.

very fast at repeating their operation, although they might not even know what they were making. In this sort of situation the operator may feel part of the machine and be dehumanised. There is no way the operator can show ability or have pride in such monotonous and repetitive work, a state of affairs which sometimes leads to accidents and mistakes.

Production-line methods and automation have increased the **division of labour** which had become general during the Industrial Revolution. People ceased to work in small units where many had been experts in a number of different skills – growing crops, rearing animals, building their own houses, making their own clothes or brewing their own beer – and specialised in one area of work, often in large factories.

1. About 100 years ago, Karl Marx said that men were becoming slaves of the machine and that the factory system made people feel that their work was meaningless and that they had no power. He called this feeling of separation **alienation**.

   It is suggested that alienation is increasing today. Do you agree, or do you feel that in some ways work is becoming more satisfying?

2. Why do we work?

   - personal satisfaction
   - more money
   - gain other people's approval
   - status
   - sinful not to
   - nothing else to do
   - keep fit
   - meet friends
   - get out of the house

   Put these reasons in the order of your priority.

   Carry out a small-scale survey among your friends and compare the results with your own views.

3. You could say we work for 'CISSES':

Contribution	Most people want to feel useful and to contribute something.
Integration	The way that most young people become part of the adult community, that is integrate with it, is through work.
Status	When people are asked what they do they will almost automatically state their job. Being a bus driver or a bank manager gives status.
Satisfaction	For many people their major satisfaction in life is their job.
Economics	Yes, we do work for money – but remember, some people work even though they could be as well off without.
Socialising	Meeting friends, or a future husband or wife.

> Consider the following occupations and give each one a mark from 5 (a lot) to 1 (very little) for each of the six criteria listed above. Total your marks and see which one receives the highest score; then compare your results with that of others in your group; if there is a big difference between your results discuss why this is so.
>
> nurse   dentist
> publican   typist
> police officer   stockbroker
> night-club hostess

8.4   WOMEN AND EMPLOYMENT

A greater proportion of women in Britain are now in paid employment than at any previous period of history. This is the result of many factors:

- Increasing educational opportunities arouse greater expectations of a satisfying career.
- It has become socially acceptable for married women to work. In the past women nurses, teachers and, until fairly recently, police officers had to give up their jobs if they married.

Women are increasingly doing jobs that were once considered a male preserve.

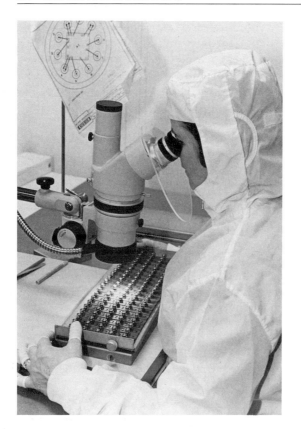

- Increased expectations of higher living standards require two incomes if those expectations are to be realised (e.g. the increased pressure towards home ownership means that both the male and female partner need to work in order to pay the mortgage).
- Legislation has made it easier for women to continue and progress in their career, e.g. maternity leave, Equal Pay Act 1970, Sex Discrimination Act.
- Smaller families are both the cause and the effect of women wishing or having to work.

It has also been suggested that women wish to work because of lack of status, isolation and boredom. Motherhood no longer seems to confer much status and the young mother may feel that she loses her own identity and becomes just an extension of her husband and her child. Because the nuclear family is now the norm the young mother may be isolated with her child for much of the day and she may wish to return to work in order to participate in society rather than for economic reasons.

1.

Women 'expected to make tea while men do real work'

By Clare Hargreaves

MANY working women are still expected to make tea and type while their less qualified male colleagues get on with the "real" work, according to a report for the Brook Street employment bureau and Elle magazine published today.

More than half the women and nearly three quarters of clerical staff who took part in a survey found they were expected to do things at work that men were not.

"Sexual discrimination is still rife in many areas of women's working lives, despite years of campaigning against entrenched and discriminatory attitudes,"

says the report, Is Work a Four-Letter Word?, which questioned more than 1,000 women mostly in their early to mid twenties.

"It is clear that, in many employment areas, women are still expected to type and make tea while male colleagues get on with the real work, despite having less experience and fewer qualifications."

From: *The Daily Telegraph*, 13 October 1988

Women 'will take the lead in business'

Chris Mihill
Medical Correspondent

WOMEN are the natural business leaders of the future because they have personality traits which motivate and encourage staff, an occupational psychologist said yesterday.

However, their managerial gifts are being wasted by male bosses and male assessment techniques, which are attuned to male ways of working.

Although the women appeared to be just as capable, they were perceived by their male assessors as less efficient because their methods were different. Instead of relying on rewards or punishments, women succeeded by motivating staff.

. . . even organisations dominated by women, such as the National Health Service, were unconsciously sexist.

Of 170 general managers, 27 per cent of the men had been placed on the top performance-related pay scale but only 13 per cent of the women. "This is an indictment of the NHS."

From: *The Guardian*, 8 January 1992

Dr Cathy Cassell and Dr Susan Walsh, from Sheffield Polytechnic and University respectively, argued that women were often "too nice" to indulge in the "back-stabbing" sometimes needed to succeed. Those that did make it, they said, also felt guilty about the long hours required to get on at work and that they were neglecting domestic duties by adopting a "male way" of behaviour.

"The rhetoric of equal opportunities may worsen the situation for women," said Dr Newell. A survey of 66 Birmingham women found most of those who worked did most of the housework and were responsible for the children.

"They continue to strive to fulfil their traditional role in the family while at the same time there's pressure on them to return to work to demonstrate that we live in an equal opportunities society."

From: *The Daily Telegraph*, 8 January 1992

a. What proportion of women in the survey for the Brook Street Employment Bureau found that they were expected to do things at work which men were not?
b. What is meant by 'sexual discrimination'?
c. Outline *two* ways in which an attempt has been made to stop sexual discrimination in recent years.
d. What factors reduce the effectiveness of legislation in combating sexual discrimination?
e. Are women likely to achieve full equality with men in the foreseeable future?

2. The Equal Pay Act 1970 became fully operational in 1975

and lays down that women doing the same job as men shall receive the same pay. Do you think this is right?

3. In 1976 1,985 cases were taken to industrial tribunals under either the Equal Pay or Sex Discrimination Act. Of these cases 42 per cent proceeded to hearings, and of those, 29 per cent were upheld.

In 1987 the figures were as follows:

Cases dealt with under the Equal Pay Act	517
Percentage proceeding to hearings	31
Percentage upheld (found proved)	27
Cases dealt with under the Sex Discrimination Act	612
Percentage proceeding to hearings	33
Percentage upheld	24

a. What was the reduction overall in the number of cases dealt with under Acts in 1987 compared with 1976?
b. How many cases (not percentages) were found proved in 1987 under:
   i. the Equal Pay Act?
   ii. the Sex Discrimination Act?

8.5   WAGES AND SALARIES

Traditionally, manual workers are paid a weekly **wage**; non-manual workers are often paid a monthly **salary**. This is because in the past 'blue-collar' workers were paid less than 'white-collar' workers and it was assumed that the manual worker would not be able to survive for four weeks without payment. Is this still true today?

In the past the length of time for which you were paid also established the length of notice that was given if your employment was to be terminated. This is no longer true today as the Protection of Employment Acts 1975 and 1978 make the length of notice for most people dependent on how long you have worked in the job.

The fact that some workers are paid weekly and others monthly, and that some had greater security of employment than others, helped to establish different **life-styles**. Salary earners had to budget their earnings to last over a longer period and paid many of their bills monthly; they often had bank accounts in order to keep their money safe and this encouraged them to save so that they could take on longer-term commitments such as buying a house. Wage earners tended to spend their money in the week in which they received it, paid rent for their homes and did not plan for the future. Is this still the situation today or are things changing?

In manual work there are two normal ways of payment – an hourly rate and piece-work rate. There are advantages and disadvantages in both:

1. *Hourly (or time) rate:*
    - Unfair to workers who work harder or better than others.
    - Simple to operate.
    - Workers know how much they will earn and can plan accordingly.
    - Needs more supervision to make sure everyone does a fair day's work.
    - Workers can relax and take more pride in the job.
2. *Piece-work rates:*
    - Workers can increase their earnings if they work harder.
    - More is produced, goods can be cheaper, profits higher (on average, one-third more is produced).
    - Because of the faster pace there are more accidents and poorly produced goods.
    - Machinery breakdowns or strikes elsewhere can reduce earnings.
    - More complicated to work out earnings.

Which system do you think is best?

How much a job is worth has always been a matter of opinion and probably always will be. There are a few people who think everyone should be paid exactly the same; the old socialist slogan is 'To each according to his need, from each according to ability'. Would this work well in practice?

The difference in pay between one job and another is called a **differential**. Skilled workers object when the differential between themselves and unskilled workers is reduced. People in positions of responsibility also often feel annoyed if the gap narrows between the pay they receive and that which is obtained by their juniors.

1. Study the information in Figure 8.1 and Table 8.1.

    Table 8.1 *Wage comparisons with earlier years*

	1984	% of 1938 purchasing power[1]
Doctor	£21,290	97%
Solicitor	£17,000	114%
Accountant	£14,500	157%
Sales assistant	£3,731	121%
Civil service executive officer	£7,215	74%

    [1] Doctors, for example, were able to buy almost exactly the same goods and services with their pay in 1984 as they could in 1938.

Figure 8.1
Gross annual earnings, 1991

Data from Department of Employment, New Earnings Survey, 1991

Adapted from an illustration in the *Independent on Sunday*, 8 March 1992

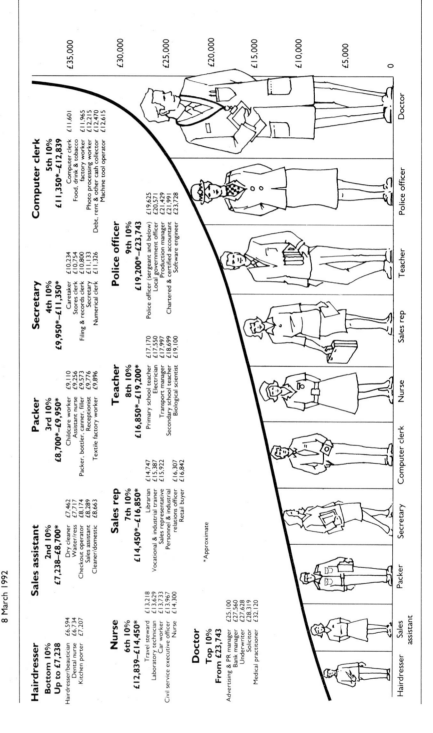

Hairdresser
Bottom 10%
Up to £7,238

Hairdresser/beautician	£6,594
Dental nurse	£6,734
Kitchen porter	£7,207

Sales assistant
2nd 10%
£7,238–£8,700*

Dry cleaner	£7,462
Waiter/ress	£7,717
Checkout operator	£8,174
Sales assistant	£8,289
Cleaner/domestic	£8,663

Packer
3rd 10%
£8,700*–£9,950*

Childcare worker	£9,110
Assistant nurse	£9,256
Packer, bottler, canner, filler	£9,573
Receptionist	£9,776
Textile factory worker	£9,896

Secretary
4th 10%
£9,950*–£11,350*

Caretaker	£10,234
Stores clerk	£10,754
Filing & records clerk	£10,800
Secretary	£11,133
Numerical clerk	£11,326

Computer clerk
5th 10%
£11,350*–£12,839

Computer clerk	£11,601
Food, drink & tobacco factory worker	£11,965
Photo processing worker	£12,215
Debt, rent & other cash collector	£12,470
Machine tool operator	£12,615

Nurse
6th 10%
£12,839–£14,450*

Travel steward	£13,218
Laboratory technician	£13,629
Car worker	£13,733
Civil service executive officer	£13,967
Nurse	£14,300

Sales rep
7th 10%
£14,450*–£16,850*

Librarian	£14,747
Vocational & industrial trainer	£15,387
Sales representative	£15,922
Personnel & industrial relations officer	£16,307
Retail buyer	£16,842

Teacher
8th 10%
£16,850*–£19,200*

Primary school teacher	£17,170
Electrician	£17,550
Transport manager	£17,997
Secondary school teacher	£18,699
Biological scientist	£19,100

Police officer
9th 10%
£19,200*–£23,743

Police officer (sergeant and below)	£19,625
Local government officer	£20,571
Production manager	£21,429
Chartered & certified accountant	£21,991
Software engineer	£23,728

Doctor
Top 10%
From £23,743

Advertising & PR manager	£25,100
Bank manager	£27,560
Underwriter	£27,628
Solicitor	£28,319
Medical practitioner	£32,120

*Approximate

Axis values: £35,000, £30,000, £25,000, £20,000, £15,000, £10,000, £5,000, 0

Categories (axis): Hairdresser, Sales assistant, Packer, Secretary, Computer clerk, Nurse, Sales rep, Teacher, Police officer, Doctor

a. i. Which job shown has improved its relative position most since 1938?
    ii. Which job shown has improved its relative position least since 1938?
    iii. Why do you think the job you have named in (i) above has done comparatively well?

b. Select one occupation listed which you regard as over-paid and one which you regard as underpaid. Give reasons for your selections.

2. Many people receive other rewards for their work apart from their wage or salary. These are called **fringe benefits**. Fringe benefits are sometimes more welcome than pay increases because they are more difficult to tax. Here are a few:

   subsidised meals
   company car
   low-interest loans for house purchase
   fees for private schools
   membership of private health schemes
   removal expenses

   Do you think such 'perks' should be allowed?

8.6   TRADE UNIONS

The conflict of interest between management and workers has resulted in various groups of workers organising together to improve their position. Such groups have come and gone for more than 2,000 years; however, scattered populations without common interests made it difficult for such groups to form or survive – agricultural workers are still one of the least unionised groups.

It was not until the Industrial Revolution of the 18th century, when people were packed together in towns and factories that trade unions could organise effectively. Perhaps the first modern industrial strike was that of the London hatters in 1696 who stopped work to protest at a reduction in wages.

At first trade unions were illegal and 'Combination Acts' were passed by Parliament, which in those days just represented the employers. These Acts made it illegal to 'combine' together to improve working conditions or earnings.

In 1824 unions became legal, but they were in the form of hundreds of isolated groups who had no legal protection and were not effective. An attempt was made to form just one 'Grand National Consolidated Trade Union' for the whole country in 1833 by an enlightened employer, Robert Owen, but different occupational groups had differing interests, and it failed, despite the fact that half a million people joined in the first few weeks.

The **Tolpuddle Martyrs**, members of the Grand National Consolidated Trade Union, were six farm labourers from Tolpuddle in Dorset, accused of taking an illegal secret oath when forming their union branch in 1834. Transported to Australia, they were released after only four years because of public concern at the severity of their sentence.

In the 1850s the first effective trade unions were formed by the skilled workers, who could afford high subscriptions to cover such things as sickness, unemployment, pension and funeral benefits and the wages of full-time officials. The accounts of some of the biggest unions in 1886 show that most of the subscriptions were handed out in benefits. This welfare aspect of trade unionism is often overlooked today.

In the last part of the 19th century, the unskilled workers' unions began to develop and they are now among the most powerful. One of the earliest successful strikes by unskilled workers was that of the London match girls, who in 1888 demanded the same wages as men doing the same work.

The most recent development has been the growth of the 'white-collar' unions. This is for a number of reasons:

1. There are more white-collar jobs because of the growth in the service sector, and fewer manual jobs in heavy industry.
2. Clerical pay has declined relative to that of manual workers. This is partly the result of de-skilling, as some clerical tasks are now performed by computers instead of people. This leads to a reduced status for clerical workers who then feel they need union representation.
3. Large office organisations are growing and, like factories, these encourage unionism.
4. There are fewer opportunities for promotion because more educational opportunities allow recruitment directly to higher grades, rather than by working up through the organisation. Therefore, those on the lower scales no longer identify with management.

Trade unions have been substantially responsible for changes in social conditions during the last 100 years. In 1910 there were 2.5 million trade unionists; by 1979 there were 13 million, but by 1990 membership had dropped to less than 10 million. This was partly the result of increased unemployment, and although the increase in the number of women working means that there are more people actually in employment today than there were in 1979, many of these are part-time or in service industries which are traditionally less likely to be unionised. More important is the decline in the numbers of those employed in heavy industry, such as steel manufacturing, or mining, which were historically committed to trade unionism. The new hi-tech industries, which have to some extent replaced traditional industries, tend to be small scale and more highly paid and are not so easily unionised as the large, less personal factories of the past. Decline in trade unionism also results from the growth in self-employment; legislation which has restricted the 'closed shop' (i.e. the rule that to be employed in a particular organisation or in a particular job you had to belong to a trade union); and the reduction in the number of public service employees, for example in the civil service. About 38 per cent of all employees are now members of trade unions.

In order to increase their effectiveness and to cope with the decline in membership, the number of individual unions has been reduced by almost a half to less than 400 during the last 25 years, with more than half the members being in the largest nine unions. The Trades Union Congress (TUC) is the central controlling body of the trade union movement and is effectively controlled by these nine huge unions. (Find out which they are.)

Trade unions are often blamed for encouraging strikes; actually more working days are usually lost each year through unofficial or 'wildcat' strikes not supported by the trade unions than by 'official' strikes. Most disputes are settled by discussion between the union representative and management. In 1984 a Trade Union Act was introduced which means that a ballot has to be taken and a majority for strike action must result before an official strike can take place.

The Employment Act 1980 limited 'secondary' picketing and 'secondary' blacking in industrial disputes (that is, the picketing of firms or the blacking of workers in firms not directly involved in the dispute). It also tightened up the procedures for introducing closed shops, and provided state aid for unions to hold elections for their full-time officials.

The Act also ended a number of legislative protections for workers employed by small firms, such as length of time required on notice of dismissal and on maternity leave, on the grounds that these steps would encourage employers to hire more workers.

Many people would say that the conflict between management and workers is now old-fashioned and would encourage worker representation on company boards of directors, as in Germany, so that the employees have a say directly in how their firm is run. See also the question on the Bullock Report on pages 224–25.

Glossary of trade union terms

Blacking
The instruction to union members not to work for a particular firm or with a particular individual.

Black leg (or 'scab')
An insulting term used to describe someone who refuses to go on strike.

Do you think individuals have a right to refuse to support a strike?

Closed shop

This refers to a place or employment where only members of a union are allowed to work. It may be set up if a majority of workers vote for it.

Advantages of the closed shop include:

1. Prevents those benefiting who have not worked (or gone on strike) for better conditions.
2. Makes negotiations more straightforward.

Disadvantages of the closed shop include:

1. Limits the freedom of individuals to join a union or not.
2. Puts too much power in union hands.

Under the 1980 Employment Act an employee can only be dismissed for refusing to join a closed shop if the agreement came into being *after* the employee started work or, in the case of agreements after 15 August 1980, if it had the support of 80 per cent of employees voting in a secret ballot.

Demarcation dispute ('who does what')

These are disputes between unions when they feel that their members' jobs are threatened. They occur particularly when new processes are introduced – a number of unions may feel that their members are the only ones qualified to perform the operation.

Lock-out

The opposite of a strike. The employer refuses to allow the employees into the factory or office until they agree to his or her conditions. It is rare today.

Pickets

These are groups of strikers who assemble outside premises where a strike is in progress. They do not have the right to block entrances, merely to persuade *peacefully* others not to work. Assault while on picket duty is treated the same as assault anywhere else.

Political levy

This is a sum included in subscriptions for political activities, usually donated in one way or another to the Labour Party. A member may 'contract out' by signing a document saying they do not wish to pay.

Many people who support other political parties do not in fact contract out. Why do you think this is so?

The 1984 Trade Union Act makes it necessary for unions to ballot their members before making a political levy.

Shop steward

The shop steward is the immediate representative of groups of workers on the 'shopfloor'. Under the Employment Protection Act 1975 the shop steward has a right to time off with pay to engage in

The miners' strike, 1985.
Picketing and policing should
be conducted peacefully.

collective bargaining, meeting with full-time officials, talks with new
employees on union matters, training, etc.

Work-to-rule; go-slow

These types of industrial action are very similar in their effects. In a
work-to-rule every minor rule is rigidly adhered to; in a go-slow the
workers will deliberately slow their normal rate of work.

---

1. Consider the following headlines:

PAY STRIKES RULED OUT BY NURSES

Ambulance crews plan fresh walk-out

Should any group of people be banned from taking strike action? What about:

- the police
- firemen
- soldiers
- shop assistants

2. Consider the following headlines and articles:

Troops answer

SOS calls after

strikers' revolt

STRIKING ambulance men brought chaos yesterday following a revolt against their union leaders who called off the ban on SOS calls.

Troops moved in to maintain emergency services in London and Cardiff after shop stewards admitted: 'Our members are out of control!'

In other areas Red Cross and St John Ambulance Brigade volunteers handled 999 calls.

And in hospitals patients had to make do with cold meals, staff went hungry, and out-patients clinics were shut.

Last night Social Services Secretary David Ennals urged ambulance men to step back from the brink after threats of more strikes.

Furious

A leader of the 2,300 London men, furious at troops being called in, threatened an indefinite 'life or death' strike.

From: *The Sun*,
9 February 1979

THE SUN SAYS

Send in troops

THE GOVERNMENT should send in troops
to shift the mountains of rubbish in our cities.

From: *The Sun*,
23 January 1979

Already in London rats are pouring out of the sewers and colonising the rubbish heaps in the streets.

What are Ministers waiting for?

Bubonic plague?

The cry will go up that the use of troops will provoke the unions.

Let it!

Under what circumstances would you wish troops to be used in a strike situation?

8.7   LEISURE

The idea of a distinct time devoted to leisure is quite new. During the Industrial Revolution the only people to have a problem deciding what to do were the very rich, most of whom devoted most of their time to leisure so that it was merely a normal way of life. The other people worked while it was daylight and, if they were lucky, went to bed when it was dark.

Leisure is the time in which we can choose for ourselves what we wish to do. People who are not paid for working, such as students and housewives, may find it difficult to distinguish clearly between work and leisure. In some ways they are in the same position as people in pre-industrial Britain when most people worked on the land. It is difficult to estimate working hours then, as ordinary people made most of their own clothes, prepared their own food and generally spent more of their time doing essential things. However, although the time spent on informal 'work' was probably no more than we spend today, the Industrial Revolution changed this way of life and working hours increased dramatically during the 18th century, peaking at approximately 102 hours per week per person by about 1800.

After 1800 the working week gradually became shorter, mainly due to legislation such as the 'Ten Hours Act' of 1847 and trade union legislation. By 1900 the average working week had almost halved to 56 hours. There was a reduction of a further eight hours in average working hours by 1950 and now the average nominal working week is about 40 hours for male full-time manual employees, although overtime working increases this to about 44.

For those fortunate to have a job and not be subject to 'enforced leisure' as a result of unemployment, it is likely that automation and

mechanisation will encourage working hours to drop to around 35 a
week during the next ten years, with an average of six weeks'
holiday. (By 1990, all full-time manual employees were entitled to
four weeks or more – nine out of ten were entitled to more than four
weeks, with three out of ten receiving at least five weeks. In 1961,
97 per cent of full-time manual employees had a basic entitlement of
only two weeks.)

At the same time as working hours reduce, convenience foods,
modern equipment and smaller families increase the spare time that
people, particularly women, have, although a great many more
women work today (see Unit 2).

Until recently it seemed that work rationing would result in a later
start to the working life and earlier retirement; both trends have
already begun. But some views suggest that the drop in the birth rate
and the reduction in the number of people available for work may
halve or reverse the trend towards earlier retirement.

It has been suggested that already we are leaving the era in which
leisure was a time to refresh ourselves for work and approaching a
time when work is a time to earn money to spend in our leisure.
Many people find they need more money during leisure time and this
is recognised by some firms in Europe who pay double time for
holiday periods.

Those too young to work, those who have retired and those unemployed are likely to be the people with least money to spend and it
will be necessary to ensure that satisfying leisure activities are available. We already have increased vandalism and crime from the young
and boredom is often blamed. Are we likely to see rampaging groups
of old age pensioners?

There have been many changes since Dennis, Henriques and
Slaughter wrote *Coal Is Our Life* in 1956 but some of the attitudes to
leisure they described do still exist to some degree in working-class
areas. In the Yorkshire coal-mining community they described men
who spent all their working time in exclusively male company, and
this resulted in their leisure also being spent with their mates. This
tendency still exists, but there is now a greater likelihood of married
couples spending their leisure time together, even in such traditional
communities.

The way we spend our leisure can be influenced by the job we do.
Those in professional jobs have a more active leisure life than those in
clerical and skilled manual jobs; those in unskilled manual jobs tend
to spend their leisure most passively. Is this because those in the most
physically tiring jobs just want to rest when not working, or because
they are just less interested in other activities?

Not only our work but also our sex, age and income will influence
our leisure activities. Girls do not do much motorcycle racing, rugby
or chess playing – why? Boys do not do much knitting, netball or
cookery – are there any reasons for this? We might expect older
people to play less sport and spend more time reading, but they also

greatly increase the amount of time they spend gardening and reduce the amount of time they spend listening to music. Do you find this surprising?

Increased leisure can be an opportunity for people to express themselves, or it can mean an aimless drifting with a loss of the pride and the status which a job can provide and an opportunity merely for violence and destructiveness.

---

1. We work for about one-third of our time, sleep for one-third and spend one-third at 'leisure'. We also spend one-third of our money on our leisure, if we include holiday clothes and food like sweets.

   Some examples of leisure expenditure (1986 figures):

Alcohol	about 7% of income
Tobacco	about 3.2% of income
Recreation, entertainment and education	about 9.4% of income

   a. Which item included above might not be regarded as leisure?
   b. Which other forms of consumer expenditure should be included?
   c. Check in *Social Trends* and see whether percentage consumer expenditure on the following are increasing or decreasing:
      i. alcohol
      ii. tobacco.

2. **Source A**

   The Shoshone had nothing but time on their hands, which is what made them appear unusually lazy to White settlers. Their leisure is explained not by laziness but by an absence of technology to store and preserve food. They might cache some seeds or nuts for the winter, but a bonanza in rabbits did them no good because they did not know of any ways to preserve the meat. Once a Shoshone caught a fish he had to consume it immediately before it spoiled, because he had never learned to dry and smoke it. He had no way to cope with a surplus. There were times of the year when the Shoshone were surrounded by an incredible abundance of game animals, but they derived no benefits from it. Even though pronghorn antelopes might suddenly become abundant, the Shoshone ceased further hunting until they consumed what they had already killed. The inability to cope with a surplus is true of hunting societies everywhere, with the sole exception of the Eskimo. They inhabit a natural deepfreeze that preserves the surplus, and so they manage to survive the harsh Arctic winter.

   Even when their food supply was nearly exhausted the

Shoshone still did not work very hard. Since they consumed a wide variety of foods, they had the choice of going after whatever was most readily available at the time. If fish were migrating upstream, the Shoshone merely went out and harvested that resource. If not, they probably knew some place where a supply of seeds was ripening. They might have to trudge many miles from their supply, but there was nothing haphazard about the undertaking: they knew exactly what was available and in which direction it lay. Despite the theories traditionally taught in high-school social studies, the truth is: the more primitive the society, the more leisured its way of life.

Peter Farb, *Man's Rise to Civilization*

Source B

I'm not talking about a world in which people work less and consume more – that's still impossible. I'm talking about a world in which, above a certain level, people are not driven like lemmings to work more because they are persuaded they must consume more. And more. And more. That world is possible. The goal in this world is not consumption, but the use and enjoyment of life.

In a rational life-style, some people could find contentment working moderately and then sitting by the street – and talking, thinking, drawing, painting, scribbling or making love in a suitably discreet way. None of these requires an expanding economy.

J. K. Galbraith

a. Why did the White settlers regard the Shoshone as lazy?
b. Try and find out more about the Shoshone Indians. For example, how did they acquire status? How did they spend their leisure?
c. In Source B the writer seems to be suggesting that in the future we should work less. Why?
d. At the moment we acquire status largely by the amount we own and spend. How could status be acquired in the future?

8.8 PROVIDING FOR LEISURE

Perhaps television arrived just in time to keep many people fairly harmlessly amused during the 'age of leisure'. In 1951 only 9 per cent of homes had television: by 1964 there was a television in 91 per cent of all homes. Now virtually everyone sees some television every week, and it is consistently listed as a major leisure activity of most people, male and female.

One great advantage of television over other forms of leisure activity is that it requires no additional space or facilities. Holidays away from home do, and these have vastly increased in recent years. Twice the number of people took holidays away from home in 1975 compared with 1950, while the number taking overseas holidays increased by over half between 1981 and 1990. A car in 1911 had one mile of road to itself; now it has thirty yards. Fortunately, all cars are not in use together, but car ownership has dramatically changed the way that the majority of people spend their leisure – they are able to come and go when they want and choose their own destinations. In some popular holiday areas such as Cornwall, saturation point must be approaching.

Package tours abroad have maintained their popularity, but the use of hotels has declined in proportion with more people preferring to camp or caravan, presumably mainly on the grounds of cost. Can you think of any other reason?

Leisure is now big business. Sports centres, discotheques, stately homes and gambling clubs have all boomed. The only serious decline in leisure activities are in cinema attendance and cycling. In the cinema, the weekly audience was 26 million in 1951 – find out what it is now.

The decline in cinema attendance would seem to be caused by the availability of television, which shows almost free of charge similar entertainments to the routine films of the past, and by the recent growth of the video industry. The cinema has turned to films of sex and violence regarded as unsuitable for television in this country to attract audiences, although exceptional films not in these categories still attract large crowds.

Membership of the two major cycling organisations in Britain has also declined sharply, from 121,000 in 1950 to an all-time low of 30,000 in 1970. Numbers had, however, increased in the 1980s.

The increasing number of sexually explicit and violent films, the considerable increase in gambling, particularly since the introduction of betting shops in 1960, the growth of alcohol sales and the availability of drugs arouse pessimism for the future in many people. Others point to the growing interest in the theatre, art, music, reading and creative hobbies and suggest that there is a tendency towards a more creative use of leisure when facilities are made available.

---

1. *What's My Line?*, *Coronation Street*, horror comics and glossies, bingo and the pools, are infinitely to be preferred to the mindless, drink-sodden, blood-splashed pastimes of our eighteenth-century forefathers.

   Part of J. H. Plumb's review of *Life in Georgian England* by E. Neville Williams, quoted in J. Brown, *Techniques of Persuasion*.

   Find out which pastimes were popular in 18th-century Britain. From what you know do you think our leisure activities are better than those in the past?

2.   Study Figure 8.2.

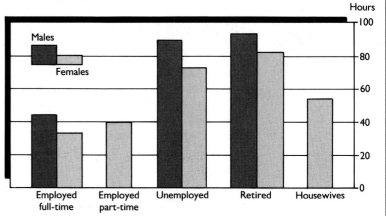

**Figure 8.2
Leisure time in a typical
week, 1990–91**

From: *Social Trends 22*,
HMSO, 1992

a.   i. Which group in the chart had the most leisure time?
     ii. Which group had the least leisure time?
b. Why do you think the group in (ii) had the least leisure
     time?
c. How would you define 'leisure time'?
d. What problems in coping with leisure time might there
     be for the four largest groups (i.e. the male and female of
     two of the categories shown) in the chart?

8 DISCUSSION

1. Consider the following notice issued in an office in Lichfield in 1852 (name of firm not known).

   a. Compare this notice with the situation in a modern office. Why do you think working conditions have changed?

   b. Do you think different work rules are appropriate to different kinds, or grades, of staff?

Rules for the Office

1. Godliness, cleanliness and Punctuality are the necessities of a good business.

2. This firm has reduced the hours of work, and the Clerical Staff will now only have to be present between the hours of 7 a.m. and 6 p.m. on weekdays.

3. Daily prayers will be held each morning in the main office. The Clerical Staff will be present.

4. Clothing must be of a sober nature. The Clerical Staff will not disport themselves in raiment of bright colours, nor will they wear hose unless in good repair.

5. Overcoats and topcoats may not be worn in the office, but neck scarves and headwear may be worn in inclement weather.

6. A stove is provided for the benefit of the Clerical Staff. Coal and Wood must be kept in the locker. It is recommended that each member of the Clerical Staff bring four pounds of coal each day during cold weather.

7. No member of the Clerical Staff may leave the room without permission from Mr. Rogers. The calls of Nature are permitted and Clerical Staff may use the garden below the second gate. This area must be kept in good order.

8. No talking is allowed during business hours.

9. The craving of tobacco, wines or spirits is a human weakness and, as such, is forbidden to all members of the Clerical Staff.

10. Now that the hours of business have been drastically reduced, the partaking of food is allowed between 11.30 a.m. and noon, but work will not, on any account, cease.

12. Members of the Clerical Staff will provide their own pens. A new sharpener is available, on application to Mr. Rogers.

12. Mr. Rogers will nominate a Senior Clerk to be responsible for the cleanliness of the Main Office, and the Private Office, and Boys and Juniors will report to him 40 minutes before Prayers, and will remain after closing hours for similar work. Brushes, Brooms, Scrubbers and Soaps are provided by the owners.

13. The New Increased Weekly Wages are as here under detailed.

Junior Boys (to 11 years)	1s. 4d.
Boys (to 14 years)	2s. 1d.
Juniors	4s. 8d.
Junior Clerks	8s. 7d.
Clerks	10s. 9d.
Senior Clerks (after 15 years with owners)	21s. 0d.

The owners recognise the generosity of the new Labour Laws but will expect a great rise in output of work to compensate for these near Utopian conditions.

2
We find that instances occur in which children are taken into these mines to work as early as four years of age ... while from eight to nine is the ordinary age at which employment in these mines commences.

In 1842 Report of the Children's Employment Commission (Mines)

a. At what age do you think people should be allowed to start work?
b. At what age do you think people should retire? Should this be compulsory?
c. What do you think is a reasonable length for a working week in hours and days?
d. Should overtime be banned?

3
The Sex Discrimination Act came into force at the end of 1975. This prohibits jobs being advertised as solely pertaining to one sex, or people being refused employment because of their sex. Do you think that this ruling is reasonable?

4
Peasants urged to make cash
After years of opposition to private enterprise, in 1979 the Chinese government urged the peasants to make as much money as they could from private market gardens and spare-time livestock raising. 'Facts have proven that it amounts to sheer illusion to suppose socialism can be built by deliberately preventing people from getting rich', says a commentary by the New China News Agency.

Do you think the 'profit motive', that is personal monetary reward, is essential if people are to work hard?

8 ADDITIONAL ASSIGNMENTS AND INVESTIGATIONS

| **1** | Consider the following sources: |

Unemployment rates: international comparison

	Annual averages (%)		
	1970	1980	1990
United Kingdom	3.0	6.4	6.9
Belgium	2.1	8.8	7.9
France	2.4	6.3	9.0
Italy	5.3	7.5	9.9
Netherlands	1.0	6.0	7.5
Spain	2.4	11.2	15.9
Australia	1.6	6.0	6.9
Canada	5.6	7.4	8.1
Japan	1.1	2.0	2.1
Sweden	1.5	2.0	1.5
United States	4.8	7.0	5.4

The 1970 figure is from an earlier edition. Germany has been excluded as reunification makes comparison unrealistic.
Source: Adapted from *Social Trends 22*, HMSO, 1992.

> On the dole? – lovely life if you happen to be a turnip. But I'm not a turnip, mate. I'm a thoughtful, sensitive, widely-read man, with cultivated tastes in music. Am I filled with bitterness? Yes – indeed. Why? The short answer is, of course, because I am a bloody pointless waste of a good citizen.
>
> Adapted from: 'On the dole' by J. Keenan, from R. Fraser (ed.), *Work*

a. Which country had the largest number of unemployed in 1989?
b. Which country had the smallest percentage of unemployed in 1989?
c. Describe the trends in the rate of unemployment in the United Kingdom between 1970 and 1989 quoting detailed figures.
d. Find the comparative figures for Germany (Federal Republic).
e. Why might the figures obtained for different countries in the chart above be 'not strictly comparable'?
f. Why could unemployment be described as a social evil: (i) from the point of view of a person out of work, and (ii) from the point of view of society?

2 Here are some general conclusions on leisure activities in the UK during the 1980s; try and establish whether these conclusions are now true in your own locality and then try and give reasons for your findings.

 a. About half the population over the age of four listened to the radio on an average day.

 b. Radio 1 was the most popular channel (15 per cent listened to it). Independent Local Radio had the second biggest audience (12 per cent).

 c. About 24 per cent of the adult population do not read a daily newspaper. More men read newspapers than do women.

 d. Women are twice as likely as men to play bingo; men are twice as likely as women to do the pools.

 e. Participation in sporting activities declines with age – the most active are in the 16–19 age group. (However, more men in the 20–34 age group played squash.)

 f. Many more men watch sporting activities than do women. Football is by far the most popular sport watched by men, followed by rugby.

 g. Spain is the most popular overseas destination for holidaymakers.

 h. About 40 per cent of people did not go away for an annual holiday.

 i. About 25 per cent of people had more than one holiday away each year.

OUTLINE OF AN APPROPRIATE GCSE INVESTIGATION/PROJECT

(For guidance, see 'Coursework for GCSE' on pages ix–xiv.)

Title   A study of the effect of work on the leisure activities of the individuals concerned.

Hypothesis   That Parker's division of work into patterns of Extension, Neutrality and Opposition is no longer true in terms of its effect on leisure.

Background   This enquiry seeks to test the theory put forward by S. Parker in *The Sociology of Industry* (1967) that there are three patterns of work and that the leisure activities of individuals will be determined largely by the work they do.

Secondary sources   The starting point would be Parker's book (above) and his division of work into three categories:

1. *Extension.* A person with an interesting job may be absorbed in it and not distinguish easily between 'work' and 'non-work' (e.g. a businessman discussing business on the golf course; a teacher preparing a lesson at home; a doctor attending a patient out of hours; an off-duty policeman arresting a suspect).
2. *Neutrality.* Applies to those with jobs that need not involve the whole personality, that have regular hours and a generally pleasant environment. There is little relationship between work, family and leisure other than income (e.g. bank employees; Civil Service clerical officers).
3. *Opposition.* Those with a dirty, dangerous, physically tiring or psychologically exacting job may seek complete escape from it in their non-work activities (e.g. coal miners; deep-sea fishermen; refuse collectors).

Other secondary sources might be the books of the same period to see if they supported Parker's theory at the time he developed it, for example:
Dennis, Henriques and Slaughter, *Coal Is Our Life* (1956)
Hollowell, *The Lorry Driver* (1968)
Tunstall, *The Fishermen* (1962)
Goldthorpe and Lockwood, *The Affluent Worker* (1969)
Hill, *The Dockers* (1976)

Primary sources **Questionnaire** directed at people drawn from each of the three categories used by Parker. Perhaps 12 in each category, divided 50/50 between those aged 20–30 and those aged 50–60 and between male and female. (It is for you to decide precisely what you propose to do and to explain your reasons in your final report.)

Your questionnaire might consist of closed questions (i.e. Yes; No; Don't know) to questions asking about the nature of the job and similarly to questions asking about the *kind* of leisure activities pursued.

Interviews directed at a smaller sample in each category trying to determine in greater *depth* the degree of opposition, etc., they had to their work; and the *degree* of involvement in leisure activities (e.g. someone may say 'gardening' in their questionnaire; does this mean cutting the hedge once a month or growing all their own vegetables?).

Observation carried out at a local leisure centre, with informal conversation seeking to obtain a picture of the employment followed by those attending. The manager or the instructors may also be prepared to give you information.

Limitation Remember to outline in your report your own understanding of the limitations of your enquiry, for example:

- How *representative* were your samples?
- Was your leisure centre in a middle-class or working-class area?
- Were some people more likely to have refused an interview to you than others?

8 GCSE QUESTION

Note: GCSE questions often require answers using information from interrelated themes. This one is mainly, but not exclusively, concerned with work and leisure.

Study the information given below and then answer the questions printed after it.

FORECAST CHANGES IN EMPLOYMENT
1986–1995

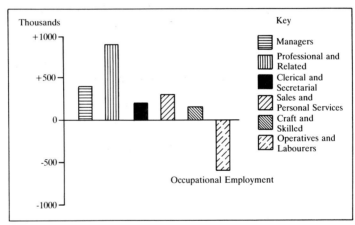

From: *IER – Review of the Economy and Employment 1987*

(a) Which two important ways of spending our leisure were not possible for most people a hundred years ago? (1)

(b) Between 1986 and 1995 which sort of occupation will
(*a*) decrease most,
(*b*) increase most? (2)

(c) State and explain *two* reasons for working which are not directly related to earning money. (4)

(d) How might the work we do affect the way we spend our leisure? (6)

(e) Explain the expected changes in the trends of employment outlined in the source material. (7)

8 SELF-TEST QUESTIONS

(Answers on pages 292–93)

1. Briefly define 'automation'.

2. State three reasons why more women work today than formerly.

3. Name two reasons why unfilled vacancies may co-exist with unemployment.

4. In addition to reduced working hours, name three factors that have increased leisure today compared with the past, particularly for many women.

5. Suggest three ways in which available work may be 'rationed' in the future.

6. Which leisure pastime has developed most rapidly since 1950?

7. Name three other forms of leisure activity that have increased considerably since 1950.

8. Name a leisure activity that has declined sharply since 1950.

9. State two reasons for the increase in the proportion of people in white-collar trade unions.

10. Give three reasons for the decline in the number of people in trade unions during the last 20 years.

9 KEEPING THE RULES

9.1 WHY HAVE RULES?

A gang of boys may find a tin can in the road and enjoy themselves for a few minutes kicking it about. However, aimless kicking becomes boring and they start passing to each other. Within a short time they are likely to have divided into sides: perhaps they make goals – they have started to have rules. But arguments about the rules are likely and one member of the gang may become the referee to sort problems out. In most games it is rules that make it possible to play.

If we all did whatever we felt like doing, the human society might last a few months but it would be unlikely to last much longer. At first, the strong and least controlled might enjoy themselves – they could take what they liked, beat up whom they wished and destroy anything they did not like! After a while, people would not work just to be robbed, or build just to see their construction destroyed. Most people do not like having to obey rules for which they see no reason, but in general most of us are prepared to put up with such restrictions on our freedom because we see that if individuals break rules they do not like, an ordered community would disappear.

So far as we know, all human societies have had rules, even the most tyrannical ones, and although some people (called 'anarchists') think that we could survive without rules and that people would get on better without authority, most people think that rules are necessary to ensure some degree of fairness and protection.

Most people do not have to be rewarded or punished to keep the rules, for in nearly all societies most people will believe that the officially **sanctioned** (or approved) behaviour is right and good for the community, and that conduct which breaks the rules is wrong because it is bad for the community ('anti-social'). The belief that some behaviour is good is the basis of morality.

Morality varies from group to group, and from situation to situation. For example, the Jains of Southern India wear masks over their mouths as they regard the killing of even an insect as evil, while other groups do not think it is immoral at all. We would probably condemn a man who poisoned his wife, but give the same man a medal during a war if he led a bombing raid that wiped out 2,000 enemy troops. Some people, however, would argue that there is a natural law that

Morality varies from group to group and from age to age – naturists on a Yugoslav beach in the 1980s contrasted with bathing costumes from a hundred years earlier.

never changes, and that something cannot be right in one society or context and wrong in another. What do you think?

Moral views can also change with time. Before 1967 in the UK, a doctor could have been imprisoned for performing an abortion. Now many thousands of abortions are performed each year by reputable doctors quite legally.

Perhaps the reasons why some people's attitude to abortion has changed is that it is no longer so likely to endanger the mother's life, population increase is seen as a threat to living standards, a woman's role is no longer regarded as being just in the home, and sexual relations outside marriage are no longer condemned so much as once they were. But other people would still claim that killing a foetus is murder. These two groups have different moral standards although they live in the same society. Do you think that abortions should be legal? If so, under what circumstances?

The state will decide that a particular form of action is right up to a certain point. This will usually be the majority view and represent the national morality. But groups within the society controlled by the state may have more stringent views; this stricter morality will often have a religious background.

Up to 1961 suicide was a crime in Britain. This did not matter much if you were successful in your attempt; however, if you failed you could be charged with attempted suicide. Now suicide is no longer a crime, but many people would still regard it as immoral. Catholics, for example, regard it as leading to almost certain damnation.

The majority of people in Britain would probably support killing people in a defensive war; Quakers would not. Muslims regard the drinking of alcohol as immoral, and Christian Scientists regard the giving and receiving of blood in blood transfusions as wrong. Many other religious groups have differing moral views on other issues.

Some rules are much more important than others and some are trivial. Nevertheless, people tend to obey them because they wish to feel fully part of their group. One example is fashion: in the 1990s a girl would not be arrested for wearing an 1890s-style swimming costume on the beach, but she might feel rather foolish. In the 1890s she would have been arrested for wearing a bikini!

---

1.   a. What laws do you think are out of date?
     b. Are there any additional rules which you would introduce
         if you had the opportunity?

9.2   RELIGION

Religious beliefs are likely to have a strong influence on morality. Religion, however, is not just concerned with making and enforcing rules of conduct – it usually involves a belief in powers superior to human beings and gives people a reason and objective for their lives.

Nevertheless, most law in a society does stem from the religious heritage of that society, and in the past it has often been religion that has been the major force ensuring that the rules were kept. This is still true in some societies today. For example, in rural Ireland the parish priest is still often treated with great respect and has considerable influence.

*Sikhs, Muslims and Anglicans
after worship.*

Generally, religions are opposed to changes in accepted standards of personal behaviour (for example, in permitting divorce). However, they may be willing to accept, or occasionally encourage, drastic changes in society such as industrialisation, which may ultimately have a profound effect upon the way in which people behave.

Sometimes religions will actually try and change society, perhaps peacefully as with Jesus Christ, perhaps violently as with Hsui-ch'uan, who claimed to be the brother of Jesus Christ and led a rebellion in 19th-century China, hoping to overthrow the Emperor and establish a heavenly 'kingdom on earth' where everyone would be equal.

Often, however, religious leaders will connect changes in standards of behaviour with other changes in society, and lead political movements to encourage or force a return to earlier beliefs. The Muslim Brotherhood was founded in 1928 to force a return to Islamic principles in Egypt, and a similar movement was successful in Iran in 1979.

Sometimes religions are accused of supporting the status quo for the benefit of those in power, thus attracting their support. Indeed, religious leaders have often also been secular leaders too – Popes ruled large areas of Europe up until 1870, while the Dalai Lama ruled Tibet until 1959.

Despite increasing secularism religion is still a very potent force in politics; for example, the Christian Democrats are a major political party in several European countries.

Secularism is a disregard for religion and spiritual matters; **secularisation** is used to describe a general decline in religious practice; for example, in the UK the government has taken over the functions of religion such as education, care of the poor or the operation of hospitals. Non-religious bodies are taking over other 'social' functions of religion in the field of entertainment and 'group togetherness'; law and government are leaving their religious origins behind; people do not need to believe in a better life after death as life on earth improves. But many other people would disagree – do you?

---

1. In Britain most people still seem to accept that religion is good for children because it teaches them morality. Those preaching a religion may or may not be more moral than those who do not, but there is evidence that those practising a religion are less likely than other people to become criminals. This may be less a sign of deep religious beliefs than an unwillingness to be rejected by a social group which may judge unlawful behaviour more harshly than others in the community.

    Do your religious beliefs influence the way you think? Do they influence the way you act?

2. **Secularisation** is a term used to describe a general decline in

the practice of religion and the significance of religious thinking. It also describes the process by which religious groups
and institutions are seen as focal points for social activities
within the community rather than important as centres of
worship.

a. Is it necessary to attend a place of worship in order to be a
    'religious' person?
b. Do you think practising a religion makes people 'better'
    people?
c. Would you like to be married and/or buried from a place of
    worship and/or have your children christened or
    otherwise accepted into a religion with some ceremony? If
    so, why?

3. *Religious strife*

a. Christians and Muslims   e.g. The Crusades
    Catholics and Protestants   e.g. The Inquisition
    Muslims and Hindus   e.g. 1947 Partition in India
    Christians and Jews   e.g. Persecution of Jews in
                                     Europe, culminating in
                                     the Holocaust
    Hindus and Sikhs   e.g. 1984 in India
    What signs of religious strife are there today?
b. The 'ecumenical movement' is currently trying to encour-
    age the various Christian churches to draw together. How
    successful do you think ecumenism will be?
c. Overall, do you think religion does more good than harm,
    or vice versa?
d. Your library should have an up-to-date copy of *Social
    Trends* (HMSO). Look in the index under 'Churches' and
    answer the following questions:
    i. Which Christian church in the UK has most members?
    ii. Which religion in the UK has grown the most during
        the period shown in the *Social Trends* chart you are
        using?

9.3   WHY KEEP THE RULES?

Most of us probably understand that some rules are necessary; but why should we as individuals bother to obey rules? Perhaps
in some cases there is no reason why we should. If we are not a
Muslim or a Jew there is no reason for us to obey religious laws which
ban the eating of pork. This law itself probably developed because
both these religions arose in an area where pork is liable to deteriorate
rapidly and cause food poisoning. With modern refrigeration it may
no longer be necessary for Muslims and Jews to obey the rule for

health reasons. However, they may choose to obey the religious ban and this may be, at least partially, because it helps to assist their 'group identity' – the feeling of belonging to a special group, *us*.

Most of the rules in a society reflect the **values** which most of the people in that society hold. These values are the standards by which most people in a group think conduct can be judged. The rules in a society are based on these values and so the rules reflect the expected pattern of behaviour of most people. It is assumed that most people will obey the rules for they reflect the normal behaviour of the majority of the people – the **norms** of the society.

Most people do choose to obey the rules: in fact they may never seriously question many of them. Certainly, it would be impossible to enforce any rule that the majority of people were determined to disobey. This is one reason why most forms of gambling were legalised in Britain in 1968 and public opposition led to the abolition of the 'Poll Tax' in 1991. The 'prohibition' on the drinking of alcohol in America during the 1920s and 1930s had to be repealed; an attempt to enforce a generally unpopular law may bring all of the law into disrepute, as the growth of the gangster gangs in America during the prohibition years illustrates.

The majority of people in society do, then, tend to accept the rules for they have been brought up, or 'socialised', to obey them. One of the difficulties of halting violence in Northern Ireland is because large numbers of people involved on both sides have been socialised to believe that what they are doing is right.

Laws do become out of date and no one bothers to repeal them because they are ignored. For example, lorry drivers are entitled to urinate against the offside wheel of their lorry in a busy street, providing they are not within 100 yards of a public lavatory – this is so that they can keep control of their horse! In 1819 a court was horrified when a man accused of murder claimed the right to challenge the victim's relatives to trial by combat with battle-axes; it was found that the old Norman Act of Parliament was still in force! The challenge was declined and the law abolished.

However, some old laws that many people would say are outdated still affect us. Until recently the opening hours of pubs were strictly regulated by licensing laws that were introduced to reduce widespread drunkenness and these rules have now been relaxed. Find out what the current rules are and say whether you think they should be altered (i.e. relaxed further or tightened up).

---

1.   Put these rules in what you consider to be their order of importance. Put a tick against those that you would not disobey even if punishment did not result.

     You must:

     • pay your television licence
     • marry only one partner at a time

- pay your income tax
- send your child to school from age 5 to 16
- report a birth or death to the registrar

You must not:

- kill people (unless licensed to do so, e.g. a soldier)
- beat up your wife, or husband
- build a house without planning permission
- import a dog without quarantine
- drink more than the legal limit of alcohol and then drive

2. **Is 'aggro' a harmless ritual?**

By trying to eradicate aggro we end up with something far more sinister. Instead of social violence*, we get non-social violence that manifests itself in random, gratuitous injury ... By learning to live with aggro ... we begin to see that illusions of violence are much preferable to the very real violence which maims and kills ...

On the football terraces, fans have discovered just one way of being tribal. They don't live in tribes. In fact the housing estates on which many live are about as far removed from the image of a community as you can get. [Football fans are like those who support different kinds of music –] by dressing up and talking and dancing in a particular way, you can become a member of a highly distinctive tribe.

The displays of hostility, the issuing of threats and the conventions of challenge and counter-challenge make up a distinctive and important part of a man's social means of coping with the problems of survival in a competitive world.

Peter Marsh, *Aggro: The Illusion of Violence*

a. In what ways do football fans resemble 'tribes'?
b. To what extent do you think football 'hooliganism' is just an 'illusion'?
c. Do you think violent behaviour associated with football should be prevented? If so, how?

9.4 INFORMAL CONTROL

Even if we do not agree with rules we may obey them because we do not want people to think badly of us. Most people, whatever they may say in public, do care what others think about them and it is this need for 'social approval' that is the most potent force in ensuring that the rules of our society are obeyed. The force of social pressures particularly applies to the unwritten rules; for

---

* By 'social violence' the author means violence that is contained within a particular social group and consists, normally, of minor acts of violence and posturing.

example, we are expected to wash and if we do not many people will avoid us – and our smell! But in Tibet we would smear yak's butter on our body instead of washing and this would be socially acceptable.

As we saw, most of the behaviour that is defined as wrong by society, or by the groups within our society that are most influential, is also regarded as wrong by the majority of people as well, so that informal pressure is an important factor in maintaining the law in a general way as well as ensuring that our 'social behaviour' is acceptable. A woman may be restrained from shop-lifting much more by the fear of the humiliation to herself and her family if she is caught than by the threat of a £10 fine.

If a woman is ill-treating a child or a man assaults a girl, most groups within our society will be very critical of them and this will reduce their **status**. This status is the degree of esteem in which a person is held by others within a given social situation. This prestige position is very important to most people and much of their behaviour may be geared to improving their status – keeping up with, or passing, the Joneses. However, if we belong to a group which gives status to those who break the rules, our desire for approval will have the opposite effect to that which would be the case in the outside society. In the case of young offenders in particular, most offences seem to be committed for excitement, competition and action rather than gain – to be 'one of the boys'.

1. Imagine you have invited a friend and he/she has behaved in the ways mentioned below. Now list those aspects of behaviour which would make it unlikely that you would invite him/her again. Imagine your friend
    - spat on the floor
    - gave your brother a black eye
    - swore at your mother
    - did not flush the toilet after using it
    - put feet up on the dining table
    - kicked your cat
    - took any food he/she could find without asking
    - was then sick in an armchair

2. Study the photographs on page 267.
    a. What similarities do the men in the two pictures share?
    b. What background do you think the men in the top picture come from?
    c. Who do you think might respect the men in this picture, dressed as they are?
    d. Why do these men dress like this?
    e. What background do you think the people in the bottom picture come from?
    f. Who do you think might respect the people in this picture, dressed as they are?

Masons in full regalia.

Punks in full regalia.

g. What do you think most people would think of them?

h. Why do they dress like this?

3. In 1876 an Italian, Lombroso, studied the skull of a notorious bandit and came to believe that there was a criminal physical type which was a 'throwback' to an earlier stage of human development. No expert now believes this, although some still think there is an inherited element in criminality – do you?

Study the photographs above and say who you think are or
were criminals. (The identities are given on page 273.)

4. Study the following passage:

> ... troublesome boys go in for crime, whereas troublesome girls
> merely go with boys. At one time, when the school-leaving age
> was fourteen, the peak incidence of conviction for both sexes
> was at the age of thirteen. Some authorities confidently predict
> that the peak will occur at age fifteen when the school-leaving
> age is raised again.

M. Schofield, The Sexual Behaviour of Young People

(*Note:* the peak age when this was written was 14 and the
school-leaving age was 15.)

  a. i. What is the school-leaving age now?
      ii. What is the peak age for conviction now? (Try *Social
          Trends* – information of conviction by age is
          sometimes included.)
  b. About six boys are convicted for indictable offences for
      every girl who is convicted. What reasons can you give
      to account for this?
  c. There now seems to be less social disapproval of girls
      who 'go with boys' than once there was. Do you think
      this may affect the number of girls who become
      delinquent in other ways?

9.5   FORMAL CONTROL

Although informal social pressures have a considerable
influence in helping to ensure that the law is obeyed, they are
assisted by the formal recognition of behaviour which is regarded as
being particularly worthy of merit, for example by the award of an
MBE, OBE or knighthood.

Equally, social disapproval is assisted by punishments ranging
from life imprisonment to a small fine. These punishments are particularly necessary in ensuring that the rules are kept among those
who do not accept them and where informal control cannot operate.

Social pressures will also be insufficient to ensure that members of
society will obey the rules when temptation is particularly great or
where there is no strong pressure of public opinion to ensure enforcement. Can you think of some examples?

Where there are a number of people who do not accept the normal
rules and who have a number of counter values in common they are
said to form a **sub-culture**. In such a sub-culture criminal behaviour
may be regarded as normal: stealing may be the family 'business' and
prison may be regarded as an occupational hazard, to be compared
with an industrial disease among the law-abiding.

Where people diverge, or deviate, from the expected pattern of
conduct they are called **deviants** and their behaviour is described as
deviant. People who are deviants or who belong to a sub-culture are

not necessarily criminal. For example, there is now no law against being a practising homosexual in private if you are over the age of 21; the Hari Krishna sect parade around London in saffron robes and shaved heads quite legally; people in the 1960s and 1970s rejected the 'materialistic society', left the cities and lived in communes in the countryside. These activities are and were all legal, although the groups may be regarded as 'deviant' by many people. There may be informal pressures which deter many people from engaging in particular activities, but the activities are not regarded as being a sufficient threat to our society's values to make it necessary for punishment to be inflicted.

Punishment usually has four motives:

1. *Retribution* – so that society revenges itself on people who break its rules.
2. *Prevention* – to stop the crime being repeated.
3. *Deterrence* – to persuade others not to engage in similar conduct.
4. *Reformation* – to cure the offender, thus preventing a repetition of the offence.

It would appear that the structure of a society will have a considerable influence on the form that punishment will take in that society. In ancient Ireland there is no reference to a death penalty, and most crimes were dealt with by the payment of compensation. It is probable that there was very little ordinary crime; since most land and property were held communally by the whole clan, theft and murder in the furtherance of theft were unlikely. Attempts to gain more property were directed against other clans. In China, on the other hand, under the Manchu dynasty, capital punishment was very prevalent – strangulation, decapitation and worse being the normal modes of death for robbery with violence, smuggling salt and many other crimes. This may have been necessary in a country dominated by a few rich people who were surrounded by a great many poor and yet possessing no efficient police system. It was thought necessary to be very severe on the few criminals caught, in order that others would be scared off from following their lead.

As most criminals think they will not be caught, the thought of their possible punishment is relatively unimportant. And when the criminal's personal belief is borne out by the fact that the conviction rate for robbery in London gives the criminal at least an 8:1 chance of not being caught, the deterrent effect of punishment diminishes further. Thus the crime detection rate is an important key to the prevention of crime.

Prison, or the threat of prison, is the normal way of dealing with criminals in our society, but until the late 18th century, criminals were usually sentenced to death, mutilation or transportation, prisons being reserved for those awaiting trial, confined for political reasons or detained for debt. John Howard helped to establish the prisons as places of confinement combined with work and this reform was included in an Act of Parliament in 1778, although Pentonville, the first prison designed for this purpose, was not built until 1842. This aim of reformation was repeated in the Criminal Justice Act of 1948 which laid a duty on prisons to prepare prisoners for their release.

However, the reformation of prisoners is hindered by overcrowding, lack of suitable work and the difficulty that released prisoners have in finding employment. This means that some people who experience prison find themselves constantly returning, often for petty offences. They are then known as **recidivists**.

---

1. Experiments with rats have ... shown that even when given ample food they will start fighting when their numbers increase above a certain level. In a ten-year study from 1950 to 1960 in London F. H. McClintock found that violent crime was most prevalent in areas of high population density. This sort of research suggests that there are limits to the crowding human beings can tolerate without strain, and that the amount of violent crime may be directly related to the degree of crowding.

    It is clear that there are many reasons for crime and the ways to seek to punish criminals must, if they are to be effective, be various and flexible. If crowding encourages violence it may not be appropriate to crowd three prisoners into a cell intended for one.

    G. O'Donnell, *The Human Web*

    What examples can you think of that may also suggest that overcrowding leads to violence?

2. The act of injecting heroin into a vein is not inherently deviant. If a nurse gives a patient drugs under a doctor's orders, it is perfectly proper. It is when it is done in a way that is not publicly defined as proper that it becomes deviant. The act's deviant character lies in the way that it is defined in the public mind.

    H. Becker, *Sociological Work*

    a. Can you give some other examples of behaviour which many people will regard as 'wrong' or 'deviant' in one context but not in another?
    b. To what extent do you think that the threat of hell or the promise of heaven still influence people's behaviour?
    c. Find out who was awarded an honour in your area in the last 'honours list' and what for. (You could do this by looking at back numbers of your local newspaper for the first week of the year or the second week in June.)

9.6   LABELS

Although most young people act in a responsible manner and find acceptable outlets for their energy and desire for adventure, others engage in activities which hurt or offend other people. The rise in vandalism, assault and other crimes committed by the young has led some people to demand the return of National Service or the 'birch'. Do you feel that the return of compulsory military service or flogging would solve the modern problems of danger to the community and damage to property caused by some young people?

There is a tendency to **label** people as belonging to a certain category. If people see a group of young people hurling bricks through windows they may go away with the impression that all young people are vandals. When we put everyone with a certain characteristic, whether it be age, colour or religion, into a particular category, we create a **stereotype**. We accept particular individuals as typical of an entire group.

Once a stereotype has been created, it is **reinforced** (emphasised and made clearer in people's minds) by the media, which, by constantly reporting only those aspects of the subject's behaviour that fit into the stereotyped image of the group concerned, confirm the view that people have. Two boys and a couple of girls walking quietly through a park chatting are not very newsworthy. The public wants to have drama on television and in their newspapers so that if in a Bank Holiday crowd of 600 young people ten are fighting with metal-studded belts, it is on these that the press will focus. The dress, hair styles and manner of the fighting ten will be noted and soon perhaps all young people similarly dressed will be expected to be violent.

If an individual is labelled in this way, they are likely to start acting out the role expected of them.

---

1. Look at Figure 9.1.

    a. i. From the evidence given, between which ages are people most likely to commit an offence?
       ii. Can you suggest any reasons for this?
    b. i. Are males or females more likely to commit an offence?
       ii. Can you suggest any reasons for this?
    c. What sort of punishment might someone who was given a non-custodial sentence receive?
    d. Make contact with the probation service and establish whether your answers for (c) are correct. Add any others which you now discover.
    e. In what way might someone who receives a custodial sentence be 'labelled'?

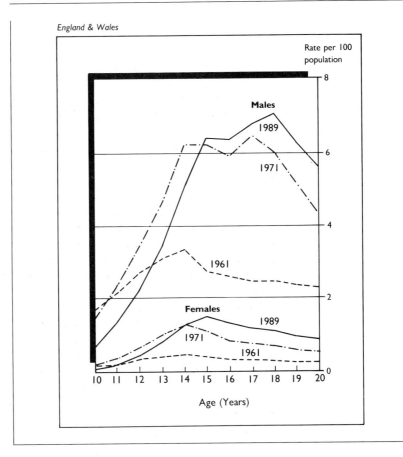

England & Wales

Rate per 100 population

**Figure 9.1
Offenders sentenced for
indictable offences by sex
and age**

From: *Social Trends 22*,
HMSO, 1992

Subjects of the photographs on page 268:
a. Thomas John Barnardo (1845–1905), English philanthropist and founder of homes for destitute children
b. The author of *Sociology Today*
c. The Kray twins, notorious gangland leaders imprisoned in 1969
d. Hawley Harvey Crippen (1861–1910), American murderer executed in 1910
e. Benjamin Disraeli, 1st Earl of Beaconsfield (1804–1881), British Tory statesman and Prime Minister

9 DISCUSSION

1

The waltz

I have watched closely and thought deeply on the subject, and now I have no hesitation in saying that the Waltz is immoral. I am happy to say that there still remain numbers of careful fathers who will not allow their daughters to dance it, although a vast proportion of the fashionable and a majority of the middle and lower classes do not seem as yet awakened to its iniquity. Dancers of today come in altogether too close contact. In the old time a gentleman merely touched a lady's waist, at the same time holding her right hand in his left. Now he throws his arms clean round her form, pulls her close to him as though fearful of losing her, brings his face into actual close contact with her soft cheek, and, in a word, hugs her. The Waltz is calculated to do more injury to the young than many of the vices that are preached against in private life ... I have no hesitation in saying that I attribute much of the vice and immorality now prevailing to the insidious influence of the Waltz.   Prof. J. Welch,
                                                'Promiscuous Dancing', 1897

a. In what ways is the argument used above similar to that used against some activities today? Give some examples.
b. Is the waltz immoral? Give reasons for your answer.
c. Here is a list of 'leisure activities' which some young people today may engage in. For each one state whether you regard that activity as immoral and give brief reasons for your answer:
   i. Glue sniffing
   ii. Topless sunbathing
   iii. Watching striptease shows
   iv. Drinking excessive alcohol
d. Is refusing to make a donation to help relieve famine in Africa immoral?

2

'It doesn't make any difference to me how many we have. I like large families ... If you aren't supposed to have them, you won't, if you are, you will. Having children has never been too bad for my wife. She isn't sick very much and she never seems to mind it.

'She says I'm crazy and I should do something to keep from getting her pregnant. She says we have enough now and should not have any more children. I just laugh at her and tell her if she isn't supposed to have them she won't get that way.'

(Mr Arthur Nelson. Aged 26, married five years with five children. Unskilled and unemployed.)

                                      Lee Rainwater, *And The Poor Get Children*

a. The book from which this passage has been taken was published in the USA in 1960. Do you think there are people similar to Mr Nelson in Britain today? What would be your attitude towards Mr Nelson?

b. In what way has the situation in the field of birth control changed since 1960?

c. What size of family would you think is ideal? Why?

3 Read the following information and then consider the questions which follow.

Drug taking has increased considerably in recent years. Nearly all of us take caffeine – it is the substance in coffee and cocoa that gives us a bit of 'lift'. Alcohol and nicotine are also widely used and are legal if used by those over 18 and 16 respectively.

Although both men and women are now more likely to drink alcohol than ten years ago there has been a reduction in the proportion of heavier drinkers. Consumption by semi-skilled manual males increased by 30 per cent between 1987 and 1989 while consumption by all other socio-economic groups fell. With only one exception male consumption was more than double the equivalent female consumption: among professionals female consumption increased by 25 per cent to more than half that of male professionals.

The number of people smoking cigarettes is decreasing. But both men and women smokers are smoking more. The death rate from cancer continues to rise (see page 138) despite the banning of cigarette advertising on television in 1965 and the health warning on packets since 1971. About 10 per cent of secondary school pupils smoked regularly in 1990, compared with 11 per cent in 1982, but smoking is now more common among schoolgirls than among schoolboys. Although the proportion of smokers is much higher among male manual workers than among non-manual, in 1982, for the first time, smokers were in a minority among unskilled workers.

In addition to these socially acceptable drugs, there has been a considerable increase in the legal prescribing of amphetamines (stimulants) and of barbiturates (sleeping tablets) to people who find they cannot cope with anxiety, depression, loneliness or stress.

a. Why are some drugs socially acceptable while others are not?

b. Consider the arguments for and against a total ban on alcohol for social purposes.

c. Should further action be taken to restrict cigarette smoking?

4 **Source A**

Violence no worse than in past, says London police chief

TODAY'S VIOLENCE at football matches and among Britons abroad is no worse than previous generations, Mr Richard Wells, Metropolitan Police deputy assistant commissioner, said yesterday. People were wrong to say it was much worse now.

'Every generation believes it is suffering more than in previous years,' he told the annual conference of the Association for the Psychiatric Study of Adolescents in Swansea.

'At the moment people are saying it is the worst it has ever been, but that is unlikely.

'You get little blips where people become more violent. We are going through one at the moment where violence is certainly more serious, more noticeable and more popular. But it is not worse than in the past.'

Mr Wells picked out the 'razor gangs' of the early 1950s as typical of an earlier period where violence was a factor.

The Mods and Rockers of the 1960s and the original skinheads of the early 1970s were the products of other surges in violence.

'I do not believe the current wave is any worse than that experienced at the time of the razor gangs. They were as horrific at the time as the present problems are.'

He said there was a new work ethic in schools and universities, and the GCSE system was giving children more training for life.

'I can see reasons for optimism. Aids may be an ill wind which will push people back towards stable relationships, and the dip in the birth rate will provide fuller education and job opportunities.

'I am not saying it is not bad at the moment. Some of the violence is alarming and mindless, with people who are perfectly rational on a Thursday afternoon becoming wild on a Saturday night. But we must not lose sight of what has happened before.'

From: *The Daily Telegraph,*
18 July 1988

Source B

BRITAIN'S VIOLENT WEEK

David Rose finds a disturbing new factor behind the violence in Oxford and Cardiff.

Charles Pollard, Chief Constable of Thames Valley in which Oxford falls, said: 'There is a general erosion of respect for authority, epitomised by young people taking on the police and the criminal justice system as a whole, maximising every loophole to avoid prosecution, conviction and being sent to prison.'

In his book *Hooligan*, sociologist Geoffrey Pearson found that claims that 'respect for authority' was diminishing among the young have been made in virtually identical terms for more than a century: statements such as that of Mr Pollard could be found in newspapers quoting police chiefs at the time of the 1950s teddy boy craze, 1960s mods and rockers, or, for that matter in the 1890s.

But this time there is evidence of a new, more violent edge to the relationship between police and young people, fuelled by a visceral hatred which has little to do with conventional socio-economic indicators.

From: *The Observer*,
8 September 1991

Source C

But most of the day-to-day confrontations between the gangs were far more male-dominated and aggressive. Ray Rochford remembers the street battles between rival gangs in Salford during the inter-war years [1918–39]:

> You could never venture outside your street by yourself, you'd be too frightened; you'd be chased away or just beaten up. You had your territory, and the other streets had their territory. You had to be in a gang or you were nobody. And, every so often, the word would go round that a gang from another street or another neighbourhood was coming around for a fight. Everyone armed themselves with sticks and stones and bricks. It was mostly the boys, but you'd get a few girls there in the front line. Most of them, though, were weapon carriers. You wouldn't believe the violence, it was like the Battle of Crécy. There was bricks flying everywhere, broken glass, fists flying. I was terrified but you daren't show it; if you showed yourself to be a coward your life wasn't worth living – you'd be shunned. There'd be some injuries, broken noses, broken arms. I know I ended up in the infirmary sometimes, but amazingly nobody was killed. The other strange thing was that nobody tried to stop you: the police let you get on with it and the adults watched from their windows. They must have seen it as good entertainment!

S. Humphries, J. Mack and R. Perks,
A Century of Childhood

a. What reasons for optimism has the 'police chief' got in Source A?
b. What reasons for pessimism has the police chief got in Source B?
c. Taking account of Sources A, B *and* C, which police chief do you think is right and why? *Or*, if you think both are wrong, say why.

9 ADDITIONAL ASSIGNMENTS AND INVESTIGATIONS

1 Source B is a good example of how reports in the press can be misleading. The report claims that 'crime and unemployment go hand in hand' and yet the evidence in Source A might be used to prove the opposite. Devon and Cornwall have a very high unemployment rate, but a very low crime rate.

Source A

How your home rates

Are you in a break-in blackspot?

	POLICE REGIONS	TOTAL OFFENCES PER 100,000 POP.	UNEMPLOY-MENT RATE
1	Gt. Manchester ...	10,577	15.5
2	Northumbria	10,515	17.4
3	Merseyside	10,350	21.2
4	London	10,000	10.2
5	W. Midlands	9,031	18.8
6	Cleveland	8,052	22.8
7	Notts	8,896	13.4
8	W. Yorkshire	8,203	14.1
9	Humberside	7,027	17.5
10	Wales	7,480	16.6
11	S. Yorkshire	7,080	17.2
12	Durham	7,050	18.7
13	Bedfordshire	6,956	10.7
14	Northants	6,245	12.8
15	Gwent	5,912	17.3
16	Lancashire	5,761	14.8
17	Thames Valley	5,603	8.0
18	Derbyshire	5,537	13.0
19	Hampshire	5,501	10.3
20	Avon & Som.	5,491	11.2
21	Dorset	5,440	12.3
22	Cumbria	5,263	12.8
23	N. Wales	5,221	19.0
24	Cambs	5,180	10.2
25	Leics	5,180	10.8
26	Gloucs	5,066	10.4
27	Staffs	5,020	14.2
28	Wilts	4,997	10.4
29	Lincs	4,940	14.9
30	Norfolk	4,862	12.8
31	Sussex	4,857	12.4
32	W. Mercia	4,856	13.0
33	Herts	4,830	7.5
34	Cheshire	4,751	13.7
35	Kent	4,733	12.0
36	Essex	4,635	12.8
37	N. Yorks	4,621	11.0
38	Warwicks	4,581	12.8
39	Devon, Cornwall ..	4,483	16.7
40	Suffolk	4,163	10.0
41	Surrey	3,959	—
42	Dyfed, Powys	3,575	15.9

● Surrey unemployment data unavailable. Calculations do not work because less than 75 per cent of people do not both live and work there.

from: *Sunday Mirror*,
24 March 1985

Source B

BRITAIN today is a crime-torn nation. A shocking Sunday Mirror survey reveals how crime and unemployment go hand in hand – splitting the country.

There is a crime epidemic in the depressed North.

The better off South is not offence free – but your home is four times more likely to be burgled in unemployment blackspots like Liverpool and Manchester than in Surrey and Hertfordshire.

ibid.

Source C

HOW OFFENCES HAVE RISEN

Notifiable offences recorded by each force
(July 90–June 91)

	Offences	% rise		Offences	% rise
Avon/Som	145,945	33.0	Met Police	881,260	11.3
Beds	57,910	24.4	Norfolk	58,528	17.4
Cambs	50,870	24.4	Northants	53,918	25.0
Cheshire	58,838	15.0	Northumbria	215,117	10.5
Cleveland	75,303	13.3	North Yorks	49,037	23.0
Cumbria	39,503	32.1	Notts	143,873	21.2
Derbys	67,656	25.3	South Yorks	115,148	14.0
Dev/Cornwall	101,366	23.0	Staffordshire	79,470	21.8
Dorset	51,018	16.0	Suffolk	39,148	14.4
Durham	60,489	20.9	Surrey	47,639	30.6
Essex	103,154	23.0	Sussex	104,625	24.3
Glos	46,569	21.0	Thames Valley	169,117	27.3
Gtr Man	366,170	18.1	Warwickshire	36,697	26.7
Hampshire	132,569	21.5	W Mercia	67,225	16.0
Hertfordshire	51,141	18.2	W Midlands	280,061	13.1
Humberside	110,024	9.4	West Yorks	267,051	27.3
Kent	121,108	30.5	Wiltshire	36,989	22.2
Lancashire	114,634	13.0	Dyfed-Powys	24,239	33.8
Leicestershire	82,387	29.5	Gwent	35,420	29.9
Lincolnshire	42,840	15.3	North Wales	41,026	16.1
London, City	7,621	4.5	South Wales	151,791	19.1
Merseyside	144,182	6.2			

From: *The Daily Telegraph,*
14 September 1991

a. What evidence is there in Sources A and C which helps
   i. to support the claims in Source B?
   ii. to disprove the claims in Source B?

b. Why is the information in Source C inadequate if you are trying to decide which parts of the country are the most crime prone?

c. Using the information in Sources A and C, consider whether there appears to be a change in the behaviour that sociologists might traditionally have anticipated in urban and rural areas. If you consider a change is taking place, why do you think this is happening?

2 Source A

We live in a society where the motive force is competition and property. The ethic that everybody is brought up with is to compete against each other, get as much as possible. You have the same thing happening at every level. It is happening at the top on an enormous scale. You've got the sort of tax avoidance by the rich, for example, which makes social security fiddles at the other end of the scale look just like peanuts. And yet the social security offence is dealt with in a very harsh way while with tax avoidance they lean over backwards, especially if it's a company, to give the opportunity of paying it back.

… It's not merely a question of actual offences at the top level, it's when business is working as it is meant to work. It's a way in which people as a whole are being ripped off. And it's not surprising if all the way down the chain everyone is doing the same thing, all out for the easy buck. The people at the bottom are getting the prison sentences whereas all they are doing is competing in their own way, often in the only way they can compete.

The figures prove that prisons don't deter crime. We've got the largest prison population, proportionally, in Europe. And the crime rate is going up, not down. I think prison is a deterrent until that point when you pass through the gate. From then on it's a question of coming to terms with it. And prison could never be made so horrible that people couldn't come to terms with it, find some way of existing.

The problems that ex-prisoners come out to are the same problems they went in from, because nothing has been done in the meantime.

An ex-prisoner's viewpoint in Nance Lui Fyson and Sally Greenhill,
Investigating Society – People Talking

Source B

UK tops prisons league table

MORE people are sent to prison in the United Kingdom than in any other European Community country, according to figures released today by the National Association for the Care and Resettlement of Offenders.

From: *The Daily Telegraph,*
October 1988

HOW UK COMPARES		
(At 1 Sept. 1987)		
	Prisoners	Prisoners per 100,000 population
United Kingdom ..	54,384	95.8
England/Wales ...	47,105	94.1
Scotland	5,421	105.9
Northern Ireland ..	1,858	119.1
Luxemburg	353	95.5
France	50,639	88.9
West Germany	51,919	84.9
Portugal	8,270	84.0
Spain	27,278	70.2
Belgium	6,713	67.4
Denmark	3,190	62.0
Italy	34,838	60.8
Ireland	1,936	55.0
Greece	3,988	40.9
Holland	5,002	37.0

Source C

In 1984 Gallup conducted an international poll for *The Daily Telegraph*. The table shows the incidence of particular crimes (the numbers are per 1,000) in the years 1979–84 as reported to Gallup.

	Home broken into	Robbery of family member	Personal assault
Britain	16	25	5
Netherlands	10	30	4
France	17	17	6
Italy	13	32	4
Denmark	12	21	3
Spain	10	19	6
Switzerland	7	25	2
Sweden	6	24	3
Ireland	9	20	3
Norway	6	20	5
West Germany	7	13	2
Greece (Greater Athens)	5	12	2
Belgium	4	10	2

From: The Daily Telegraph, 1984

a. i. Which country listed has the largest prison population proportionate to total population?
   ii. What special reasons may account for this?

b. From the evidence available which country appears to have the most serious crime problem?

c. From the evidence presented does the size of the prison population accurately reflect the number of crimes being committed? Give reasons for your answer.

d. What factors make comparison of the evidence presented unreliable?

e. How effective is prison likely to be in reducing the incidence of crime?

3

Sign in a Chinese take-away, Brampton, South Yorkshire

ON SUNDAY YOU MUST EAT YOUR

FISH AND CHIPS HERE –

IT IS THE LAW   (Or is it?)

Shop opening hours were originally controlled to ensure that shop assistants were not required to work unreasonably long hours and to 'Keep the Sabbath day holy'. Legal variations have been permitted to accommodate differing religious beliefs, for example Petticoat Lane market in London on Sundays was permitted as it was originally a Jewish street market and the traders closed on Saturday instead.

Find out which shops can legally open on Sunday. Your local Chamber of Commerce should be able to help; if not, try the local police or Citizens' Advice Bureau. Having obtained this information, carry out a local survey of Sunday opening, noting which shops are acting legally and which illegally.

4 It is particularly difficult to obtain honest answers from respondents when the object of your research is personal behaviour. They may boast or seek to shock and thus exaggerate behaviour that might be regarded as anti-social and/or immoral. Equally they may be ashamed or concerned to hide law-breaking activities.

Provide a questionnaire that seeks to establish current behaviour among your peer group. Question people of the same age as yourself about the behaviour of people they know. For example: 'Do you know anyone who takes any of the following drugs...?' 'Has the fear of AIDS made any of your friends change their sexual behaviour as far as you know?'

Try giving the questionnaire to one group to complete privately and *administer* the questionnaire to another group (i.e. you ask the questions and fill in the answers). Consider:

- which set of responses appear the most reliable to you – and why they do
- whether if you were completing the same exercise again you would change the questions and/or your own approach.

9 OUTLINE OF AN APPROPRIATE GCSE INVESTIGATION/PROJECT

(For guidance, see 'Coursework for GCSE' on pages ix–xiv.)

Title   An investigation into whether what people believe to be deviant behaviour in Britain is really deviation from the norms and values of our society.

Hypothesis   Much of the behaviour which people claim to be deviant is not deviant.

In this investigation the hypothesis is vaguely expressed and you will have to decide how much 'much' represents. You will have to clarify what you mean by 'our society' – are you really going to test your hypothesis across the whole range of social class, age, gender, region and ethnic group? Probably not; it is for you to set your targets and ensure that the assessor understands both what you intend to do and why you intend to do it. For example, explain the problems that you would face in undertaking a truly representative survey; it is this knowledge of the methods and problems involved in undertaking a scientific study within society that is going to help you gain a good grade.

Secondary sources   *British Social Attitudes*, S.C.P.R. Gower, 1988

Social & Community Planning Research is funded by the Sainsbury Family Charitable Trusts and has produced a number of reports on changing values and variation in attitudes and beliefs among differing sectors of society (e.g. the 5th Report 1988–89 asked questions on such issues as employees fiddling expenses; milkmen overcharging; householders' claims in insurance). These reports might give you ideas for questions and give you some outcomes with which to compare your own research.

You might choose a range of newspapers and read editorials and leading articles to determine what their editors *think* the norms and values of our society are (e.g. in terms of violent crime; child abuse; social security fraud; abortion; single parents, etc.).

Primary sources   **Closed questionnaire**   In order to determine the behaviour which people regard as 'deviant' you may wish to design a questionnaire asking them their views on moral issues. This might be of the usual 'disapprove strongly/disapprove/neutral/approve/strongly approve' type or you could ask them questions based on what they would be prepared to do for £100, £1,000, £50,000, £500,000 (e.g. shoot a stranger, abandon their children, etc.).

Having established what your representative sample claims to be against their 'moral code' you may then proceed to compare what actually happens in society. (You may here wish also to use secondary sources such as *Social Trends* for statistical evidence.)

Participant observation   Studying the behaviour of the group of which you are part without their knowledge.

Interviews   'In-depth' interviews in which you try to determine how your interviewee actually behaves, as opposed to how they say people should behave. Ideally use your original sample, but do this part of your study first and well in advance of your closed questionnaire so that the connection is not obvious.

Remember to analyse your findings impartially and illustrate your evidence and results clearly using pie charts, bar charts and graphs where appropriate. You may be able to present taped or videoed material as part of your evidence (check on your Examining Group's regulations), but ensure that the actual results of this audio or video material appear in your written report.

 **GCSE QUESTION**

Note: GCSE questions often require answers using information from interrelated themes. This one is mainly, but not exclusively, concerned with deviance and social control.

Conformity, deviance and social control

Boys on a Saturday night in Sunderland, in a group, on a street corner, are aware that they are 'doing nothing' and are bored with it in their own minds, essentially wanting something to happen. They want to have an interesting or an exciting time.

Question: What do you do when you just knock around the streets?

Richard: Sometimes get into fights, or trouble, but mostly nothing much.

Question: Just try and give me an example.

Richard: Er . . . last Saturday we was hanging about and someone kicked a bottle over and it smashed. Then we all started smashing bottles.

Question: What do you do on an average Saturday evening?

Steven: Go in the Wimpy, or jump on some boys or something . . . kick them.

Question: Do you ever get into trouble for kicking boys?

Steven: If we are knocking about in gangs. The police pick on us for just knocking about in gangs. I've been down the police station twice for just knocking about in gangs.

Paul Corrigan, *Schooling the Smash Street Kids*, Macmillan, 1979

(a) Are the boys described in the source material behaving in a *deviant* way? (4)

(b) Most people conform to what is expected of them in society. How is this conformity and social control achieved? (7)

(c) Young working-class males are the group which is most likely to get into trouble with the police – why? (9)

MEG, Sociology Paper 2, 1991

 SELF-TEST QUESTIONS

(Answers on page 293)

1. What is the difference between formal and informal social control?

2. What is a sub-culture?

3. What is a deviant?

4. List the four usual motives for punishing a person.

5. Which political group believes there should be no rules?

6. What sort of behaviour is *sanctioned* by a society?

7. Why do most people obey the rules of their society?

8. When was abortion legalised in Britain?

9. What does 'secularism' mean?

10. Give two examples of religion being a contributory cause of strife.

APPENDIX

Answers to self-test questions

Note: Longer answers are in summary form.

Unit 1   Counting people

1. a. None.
   b. Over 100.
2. The number of people dying each year roughly equalled the number being born. This was caused particularly by high infant mortality, a high rate of maternal death in childbirth and a generally higher mortality due to malnutrition, poor hygiene and endemic diseases.
3. A desire for the company of one's own kind, particularly to be an integral part of a group.
4. A group of people of equal status who are presumed to have an identity of interest. It is particularly used to designate a group of people of about the same age.
5. a. Protection against other people.
   b. Care if ill, injured or old.
   c. Co-operation to improve chances of obtaining food.
6. Three from each of the following:

Primary industry:	Farming, fishing, mining, quarrying, forestry.
Secondary industry:	Any manufacturing industry such as steelmaking, furniture manufacturing, pottery or glassmaking could be given, or any of the building trades.
Tertiary industry:	Any non-productive employment areas could be given such as doctor, teacher, postman, lorry driver, shop keeper.

7. An urban community is a term used to denote people dependent one upon the other living in towns. It is particularly used to describe a group of people with a common identity whose behaviour and attitudes are influenced by the fact that they live in towns.
8. Because animals in jungles do not behave like people living in towns (e.g. become fat, murder their own kind, get ulcers), but animals living in zoos do have some of these characteristics.
9. The length of time a person can still expect to live on average at any given moment of time. For example, in 1981 a female at birth could expect to live 76 years; having survived to the age of 45 she could expect to live for another 33 years; if she was still living by the age of 80 she could expect another 7 years of life.
10. a. Static birthrate.
    b. A reduction in infant mortality.
    c. A falling death rate.

Unit 2   Family life

1. a. polygyny
   b. polyandry
   c. monogamy
   d. polygamy
   e. bigamy

2. a. They increase his workforce themselves.
   b. They provide children who work and increase his wealth.
   c. The marriages allow the formation of alliances between different families for political and economic purposes. (Added 'status' is a possible alternative reason.)

3. Four from:
   a. child rearing
   b. providing an economic framework
   c. companionship
   d. protection
   e. regulation of sexual behaviour

4. Long-established working-class communities (particularly in the North of England, Northern Ireland, Wales and Scotland) and among Indian and Pakistani communities.

5. Four from:
   a. increased educational opportunities leading to a need for job mobility
   b. improved transportation
   c. new housing estates
   d. improved welfare leading to less dependency
   e. regulation of family size

6. Increased expectation, uncertainty about roles, more stress, more time spent together, fewer relations to rely on, easier to obtain divorce.

7. a. Unless she is very rich the mother is now expected to perform all the roles connected with homemaking. However, with reduced family size it is now a transitory phase and as such does not command the same status as it did in the past and this reduces satisfaction. The nuclear family concentrates the maternal role and isolates the modern mother. Labour-saving devices and convenience foods reduce physical pressures on modern mothers but may also reduce 'professional' satisfaction; although these permit the mother to combine her mother role with a job, this will often cause 'role conflict'.
   b. The father's role is becoming increasingly home and family centred. Just as many mothers now combine motherhood with a job, most fathers share in the household tasks and the division of labour in the home is becoming more diffuse. With the reduction of economic dependency and increased education the modern father is not awarded automatic respect and his role as a disciplinarian is much reduced.

8. A name given to the supposed difference in attitudes and behaviour of adults and teenagers (or parents and children). It is sometimes suggested that there is a separate 'youth culture'. Some research suggests that this 'gap' is much overstated and that there is a greater correlation between the attitudes of parents and young people within the same family than between the young people concerned and young people from a different social background.

9. Three from: television; car ownership and family trips; longer education

with longer dependency; longer holidays for parent(s); shorter working hours for parent(s); more danger out of doors for young children; more homework for more children; high-rise flats confine children.

10. Death of one of the partners; accidental illegitimacy and a decision to rear the child by the mother; a decision to have a child, so as to rear it without male support.

Unit 3   Learning for life

1. a. A standard of behaviour shared by a group and acceptable within it.
    b. A general principle accepted by a group as the standard by which conduct can be judged.
    c. The part that a person plays in a given situation and the pattern of behaviour associated with that part.

2. A society of the South-West Pacific (the 'Marquesas') – a great number of other possibilities exist although not covered in the text, for example Iroquois, or Tchumbuli of New Guinea.

3. Studies of identical twins.

4. The score resulting from a test which has been validated with a control group so that the person of average intelligence will score 100. If they score under 70 they would have difficulty learning anything and if they score over 120 they are potentially of university standard.

$$IQ = \frac{\text{Mental age}}{\text{Chronological age}} \times 100$$

5. All the influences that surround us, both physical and psychological.

6. Secondary modern schools, grammar schools and technical schools.

7. Three from:

For	*Against*
● Less socially divisive.	● Often too large.
● Wider syllabus is provided.	● The most able are held back.
● There are opportunities for all to develop.	● The less academic influence the others.
● Academic standards for most are increased.	● Wider social contacts may be reduced.
● Specialised equipment is provided.	● The poorly behaved influence others.

8. The number of pupils to each 'teaching' teacher within a school or area.

9. ● Greater value is placed on education because parents have been successful within it.
    ● There are more books in middle-class homes.
    ● Teachers are middle class and their speech and expectations are middle class.
    ● There is more likely to be a quiet place for study in the home, because the house may be larger.
    ● Private lessons and educational trips can be afforded.
    ● Parents are more likely to encourage deferred gratification.
    ● Parents are more likely to be able to help their children academically.

10. A college that combines all kinds of non-advanced post-16 education (for example, offering City and Guilds qualifications for technicians, 'A' levels and commercial qualifications).

Unit 4   Us and them

1. Discrimination (persecution or prejudice acceptable).
2. a. religion
    b. dress
    c. values
    d. language
    (Prejudice also acceptable.)
3. Ethnic group.
4. a. Mongoloid
    b. Caucasoid
    c. Negroid
5. Discrimination on the grounds of colour or ethnic origin in employment, housing, advertising, insurance, the provision of goods and services or places of entertainment.
6. a. Jews (or more recently 'Asians' or similar term)
    b. Huguenots
    c. Irish
    d. West Indians
    e. Asians (a specific Asian group acceptable)
7. a. ascribed
    b. achieved
8. A top group (or 'élite') in society, the members of which have achieved their position through their own efforts.
9. Any three from: stocks and shares; bank deposits; cash; building society investment; consumer durables; dwellings net of mortgage debt; national savings; other buildings; land or trade assets.
10. Any four from:
    - differential access to power
    - differential access to educational opportunities
    - differential access to health provision
    - different standards of living (housing, holidays, etc.)
    - differing culture (one example of entertainment/dress/food/speech, etc.)
    - differing life expectancy
    - differing occupations, including working hours, benefits, pension rights, etc.
    - differing status

    (This list is not exhaustive.)

Unit 5   A better life?

1. Relative poverty is the situation in which some people have considerably less material possessions and opportunities compared with others within the same culture (or 'reference group'), even though these people may appear well off to people of other cultures.
2. The situation in which loss of benefits as a result of higher earnings or entry into employment results in no, or little, consequent increase in living standards.
3. Social Class V/unskilled manual workers.
4. a. Old Age Pensions
    b. Labour Exchanges
    c. Illness and Unemployment Insurance

  5. Beveridge Report.
  6. Three from: Child Benefit, Income Support, Sickness Benefit, Unemployment Benefit, Retirement Pension. (Others not included in the text are possible.)
  7. a. 40
     b. 79
  8. Mercy killing.
  9. Three from:

     • People may feel lonely away from family and friends.
     • Communities may be unbalanced in terms of the residents' ages.
     • There is less entertainment than in the inner cities.
     • They can look raw and uninviting ('soulless').

     (Others not included in the text are possible.)
 10. Two from: introduction of Clean Air Zones; banning lead in petrol; replacing lead pipes; reducing the risk from asbestos; treating sewage; stopping the discharge of chemicals into rivers and canals. (Others not included in the text are possible.)

Unit 6 Changing the rules

  1. An autocracy, a dictatorship, a totalitarian state.
  2. Rule by the people.
  3. Any three from:
     a. With certain limitations to prevent injustice, we can say what we like.
     b. We can join any non-criminal organisation.
     c. We cannot be arrested without just cause and if arrested we expect a fair trial.
     d. We choose those that govern us.
  4. A group within society which has considerable control and influence. It is sometimes used to refer to the most powerful group within a particular category of a society.
  5. Liberal Democratic Party.
  6. 651.
  7. a. The single transferable vote is based on multi-member constituencies. Electors vote for candidates in their order of preference. The number of votes is divided by the number of seats. Candidates achieving this quota, plus one more vote, are elected, surplus votes being transferred. Later preferences are then taken and assessed in order to allocate the remaining seats.
     b. The alternative vote is based on single-member constituencies. Electors number candidates in their order of preference. Candidates receiving more than 50 per cent of first preferences are elected. If no overall majority, the second preferences of those voting for the weakest candidate are distributed and go on until one candidate does obtain more than 50 per cent of the poll.
     There are a number of variations on the above systems: one is the 'party list' in which votes are cast for a political party rather than a person; another the 'second ballot' in which those who obtain more than 50 per cent of possible votes are elected but the remaining seats are voted for again.
  8. 1928.
  9. Oxfam, Age Concern, CND, Help the Aged, NSPCC, RSPCA, Consumer

Association, AA, Shelter, National Trust, British Medical Association, or many others. (Any trade union, church or political party could also be counted.)

10. Belgium, Netherlands, Luxembourg, Germany, France, Italy, the UK, Irish Republic, Denmark, Greece, Portugal, Spain.

Unit 7   The media and power

1. The ability to convey abstract ideas in the form of speech.
2. Rivers, mountains, seas, distance.
3. An international language.
4. Television, radio, newspapers (certain books, magazines, films, videos, records, or even tape recordings and advertising posters may be included in the category of mass media if they are reaching large numbers of people).
5. a. *Advantages* – it can: improve standards (by spreading knowledge and raising expectations); warn us of common dangers; help to establish a common identity (e.g. we may feel responsible for famine among other human beings).
   b. *Disadvantages* – it can: encourage stereotypes; present an unreal picture by selection of facts (or dramatisation); reduce sensibility (i.e. make us accept violence as normal).
6. The Press Council.
7. 94 per cent.
8. The less intelligent 13- to 14-year-old.
9. a. *Advantages* – five from: it informs us of new products; it boosts demand and hence production and employment; it reduces costs by encouraging mass production; it provides information (e.g. of dangers); it reduces the cost of newspapers and magazines; it increases competition; it increases expectations and hence standards; it helps charities; it adds colour to life.
   b. *Disadvantages* – five from: it increases vanity, envy and snobbery; it devalues sex; it increases expectations and hence discontent; it increases costs to the consumer as it must be paid for; it encourages overspending on unnecessary items; it often misleads; it is a nuisance (e.g. breaks continuity of TV programmes); it encourages health damage.
10. It is an offence to publish items which fall within any of these definitions.

Unit 8   Earning our living

1. The means by which thinking processes are performed by computer so that machines can be instructed by them in many or all of the production processes.
2. Three out of:
   - families are smaller and women are released from child rearing earlier
   - increased educational opportunities
   - pressure for higher living standards
   - less reliance on the extended family/more divorce
   - expectation that they should.
3. Two out of:
   - jobs in the wrong place

- the working hours are unattractive
- the jobs are poorly paid
- people available may not have appropriate skills.

4. Three out of: convenience foods; modern home equipment; smaller families; automation; legislation; influence of trade unions.
5. Three out of: shorter working hours; longer holidays; early retirement; reduction or abolition of overtime; later start to working life; ban on 'moonlighting' (having more than one job). (A legal right to educational leave, or 'sabbatical' also acceptable.)
6. Watching television.
7. Three from: car driving; foreign holidays; camping/caravanning; gambling; visiting discotheques/stately homes.
8. Cinema attendance or cycling. (Cycling has recently started to revive.)
9. Two from:

- more white-collar jobs
- decline of heavy industry and other unionised manual work
- open-plan offices like factories
- mechanisation/computerisation reducing clerical skills to operative level
- fewer opportunities for promotion for clerical workers.

(Others possible.)

10. Three from:

- increased unemployment
- decline in numbers in heavy industry
- a reduction of public service employees (e.g. civil service, teachers)
- new industries (e.g. computer technologies) tend to be smaller units
- growth of self-employment
- legislation (e.g. restriction on 'closed shop').

Unit 9 Keeping the rules

1. Formal social control is that laid down by rules and laws with officially sanctioned punishments and rewards (e.g. prison, or a knighthood). Informal social control is based on disapproval of those who do not abide by the group norms.
2. A culture differing from the dominant culture within the society and rejecting (or possibly inflating) the norms and values of the dominant culture (e.g. a criminal 'sub-culture'; a 'Hell's Angels' sub-culture).
3. Someone who does not accept the values and/or norms of the dominant culture and whose behaviour reflects this 'deviation'.
4. Retribution, reform, deterrence of others, prevention of repetition.
5. Anarchists.
6. Behaviour which is approved of in that society.
7. Fear of disapproval; fear of punishment; rewards for those who obey; socialised to do so.
8. 1967.
9. The belief that man invented God to explain things not understood. ('Secularisation' describes a general decline in the practice and significance of religion.)
10. Two from: Crusades, Inquisition, 1947 India/Pakistan partition, Northern Ireland today, 1979–80 Iranian Revolution, Indian Mutiny. (There are also other possible answers.)

INDEX

abortion, 48, 259–60
Abortion Act (1967), 259
absolute poverty, 126–7
achieved role, 59
achieved status, 107
advertising, 200, 207–9, 212, 214, 219–20
alienation, 227–9
anarchy, 185, 258
aristocracy, 108, 111
armed forces, and politics, 158, 160
ascribed role, 59
ascribed status, 107
Asians, 101–3
assimilation, 92
attitudes, 45–6
autocracy, 160–1, 163
automation, 225–6, 229, 243–4

Beveridge Report, 132
bias, 33, 86
bigamy, 31
birth control, 14, 16
birth rate, 2, 13–14, 21
blue-collar workers, see working class
British Nationality Act (1981), 105
Bullock Report, 224–5, 239
Butler Act (1944), 69

capital, 108
capitalism, 222
caste, 107
Catholic Church, 92, 260
censorship, 209–11, 212
census, 65
charisma, 161
child benefit, 132, 133
children
  influence of media on, 202–3, 204–5, 272
  rights of, 40–1, 45, 75

cinema, 247
class, social, 107–15
  classification of, 65, 108
  constitution of, 108
  definition criteria, 108–10, 123
  discrimination and, 117–18
  education and, 63–5
  life style and, 109, 110
  middle, see middle class
  mortality and, 118, 129–30
  newspaper readership and, 216
  power and, 111
  speech patterns and, 64, 115
  upper, see upper class
  working, see working class
  see also poverty
class consciousness, 108
class differences, 63–4, 108–9
classless society, 108, 118
closed shop, 240
coalition, 177
cohabitation, 31, 37–9
colonisation, 17–18
Commonwealth immigrants, 101–6
Commonwealth Immigrants Acts (1962, 1968), 105
communication, 6, 195–6
Communist Party, 166
community, 2–4, 8, 11, 24
commuters, 25, 143–4
conformity, 285
conjugal roles, 50

Conservative Party, 165–8
  aims of, 167
  financial support for, 165
  Members of Parliament, 166, 187–9
  votes for, 165–6, 171
conspicuous consumption, 110
conurbations, 9–10
corporal punishment, 81
crime
  causes of, 18, 20, 266, 277, 278–9
  class and, 280
  gender and, 269, 272–3
  juvenile, 4, 198–9, 266–9, 276–7
  statistics and, 12, 273, 278–9, 280, 281
culture, 7, 94
culture of poverty, 128
cycle of deprivation, 128

death rate, 2, 13
  decline of, 137–8
deferred gratification, 63
delinquency, see crime
democracy, 163–4, 193
deviance, 269, 271, 283, 285
dictatorship, 160–3
discrimination, 92–4
division of labour, 229
divorce, 36–8, 41
Divorce Law Reform Act (1969), 36
divorce rate, 36, 37
drug taking, 247, 275

earnings, 234–7
economy, 222–4

education, 58–72
  achievement in, 61, 63–7
  bipartite, 69
  comprehensive, 70–1
  development of, 67–72
  discipline in, 70, 81
  elementary, 68
  environment and, 63–5
  gender and, 67
  and grammar schools, 68–9
  home background and, 63–6, 86–7
  language and, 64
  primary, 69
  and public schools, 68, 71
  race and, 66
  and secondary modern schools, 69
  social class and, 63–5, 69
  system of, 67–70
  tripartite, 69
  unemployment and, 72
Education Acts (1870, 1902, 1944, 1988), 68–9, 71
egalitarian relationship, 41
elderly, welfare of, 21–2, 133–4
elections, 165–6, 169–77
elites, 108, 164
emigration, 106
employment
  children and, 228, 250
  ethnicity and, 100
  women and, 226, 230–4, 244
  see also work
Employment Protection Acts (1975, 1978), 234

endogamy, 28
environment, 2, 61, 63–6, 146–8
see also education
Equal Pay Act (1970), 232
esperanto, 196
ethnic groups, 94–107
European Community (EC), 181–4
EEC referendum, 165, 184
euthanasia, 137
evidence, 83
exogamy, 28
expectation of life, 9, 136

family, 27–47
egalitarian, 41
endogamous, 28
extended, 35–6
functions of, 29–30
home-centred, 40–1
man's role in, 30, 40–1, 50
matrilineal, 41
nuclear, 35–6, 40
patriarchal, 41
size of, 13, 36
symmetrical, 41
woman's role in, 30, 35, 40–1, 50, 232, 260
work and, 232
family companionship, 41
family patterns, 31–3, 41
family relationships, 4
family roles, 40–1
feudalism, 107

gender, 40, 59–61, 81, 83–4, 88–9
general elections, 164, 165–6, 169–77
generation gap, 45
ghettos, 141
government
British system of, 165–77
democratic, 163–4, 193
pressure groups and, 177–80
totalitarian, 160–1, 163
grammar schools, 68–9

health improvements, 136–7, 139

heredity, 62
holidays, 244, 247
House of Commons, 166
households, 34
housing, 140–4
hypothesis, 24, 85, 120, 152, 191, 217, 283

illegitimate births, 42, 48
Immigrants Act (1971), 105
immigration, 96–7, 99, 101–6
Irish, 93, 96–7
legislation and, 105
restriction of, 105–6
incest, 28
income, *see* earnings
income support, 133, 134
industrialisation, 8
infant mortality, 133, 136–7
inflation, 223
intelligence, 61–2
interest groups, *see* pressure groups
interviews, 24, 80, 84–5, 121, 192, 218, 254, 284
Irish immigrants, 93, 96–7

job satisfaction, 227–9

Kibbutz, 29

labelling, 64, 91, 272
Labour Party, 165–8
aims of, 167
financial support for, 165
Members of Parliament, 166, 187–9
votes for, 165–6, 171
law, the, 259–60, 264, 270, 281
leisure, 243–8, 252
Liberal Party, 165–8
aims of, 167
financial support for, 165
Members of Parliament, 166, 187–9
votes for, 165–6, 171
see also SLD

life expectation, 9, 136
lobbying, 178–9
lone parents, *see* single parents
longitudinal surveys, 46–7

Malthus, T. R., 16
manual workers, *see* working class
marriage, 27–33, 36–8
arranged, 53–5
bigamy, 31
monogamy, 31
polyandry, 31–2
polygamy, 31–3
polygyny, 32–3
mass media, *see* media
mechanisation, 225, 244
media, 196, 197–220
advertising expenditure, 200, 209
aggression and, 206
crime and, 198–9, 203
influence on children, 202, 204–6, 208, 212–13
politics and, 201–2
social class and, 206
Members of Parliament, 170, 174–5, 187–9
education of, 189
selection of, 174–5
meritocracy, 108
middle class, 108
education and, 63–5, 69
as voters, 168
migration, 96–7, 99–106
mobility, geographical, 35–6
morality, 258–60, 262, 274
mortality, *see* death rate
Muslims, 92, 260

National Health Service Act (1946), 132
nationalists, 171
negative sanctions, *see* punishment
new towns, 144–6
newspapers, 200–2, 215–16
norms, 58, 264
Northern Ireland, 164, 264

objectivity, xiv
observation, 86, 121, 191, 254
old age pensions, 131, 133
old people, 21–2, 133–4
oligarchy, 160

participant observation, 5, 284
peer groups, 3
pie charts, 34, 284
Plaid Cymru, 171
political levy, 240
political parties, 165–9
politics, 158, 160–79
effect of age on, 167
effect of education on, 168
effect of gender on, 168
effect of religion on, 168
pollution, 146–8
polyandry, 31–2
polygamy, 31–3
polygyny, 32–3
population, 2, 8–10, 13–16, 18, 19–20
ageing, 21–2
and birth rate, 2, 13
of Britain, 1–2
data on, 14, 15
and death rate, 2, 13
distribution of, 1
growth of, 16
infant mortality and, 133, 136–7
and migration, 99–107
population density, 15
poverty, 126–30, 132, 150–1
culture of, 128
cycle of (deprivation), 128
function of, 127–8
relative (deprivation), 127, 154–5
poverty trap, 129
power, 157–64
prejudice, 96–7
press, influence of the, 199–203, 215–16
pressure groups, 177–80, 191
prestige, 158, 266

primary sources, xiii, 24, 191
prison, 270–1, 280–1
privatisation, 222
proportional representation, 171–4
public schools, 68, 71, 189
punishment, 270, 280

questionnaires, 24, 33, 47, 50–1, 80, 86–7, 120–1, 152, 254, 282, 283–4
interviewer and, 80, 282
postal, 24

race, 94–107
race relations, 97
Race Relations Acts (1965, 1968, 1976), 98
racial prejudice, 92–4, 96–9, 116–17
random sampling, xiii, 33, 60
recidivists, 271
reference groups, 127
referenda, 176
relative deprivation, 127
religion, 260–3
change and, 262
functions of, 262
legitimation and, 262
secularisation and, 262–3
social control and, 260
state and, 260–3
religious beliefs, 260
religious groups, 262

representative sample, 24, 47, 121, 254
research methods, 5, 24, 33, 50
role model, 59–60
roles, 59
children's, 45–6
men's, 30
women's, 30, 35, 40–1, 232, 260

samples, xiii, 24, 33, 43–4, 47, 121, 254
sampling frame, xiii–xiv, 33, 50, 121
sanctions, 258
schools, see education
scientific method, 87
secondary modern schools, 69
secondary sources, x–xi, xiv, 24, 120, 191, 217, 283
secularisation, 262, 263
Security Council, 180–1
Sex Discrimination Act (1975), 232, 234, 250
shop stewards, 240
single parents, 27
SLD, 165–7
social class, 65, 107–15
see also class, social
social control, 265–72
law and, 269
media and, 198–9
peer group and, 266–7
religion and, 260–2
Social Democratic Party (SDP), 166
Members of Parliament, 166, 187–9
socialisation, 29

socialism, 222
sociology (as a science), 4
statistics, 192
status, 107, 110, 158, 159, 266
status symbols, 110
stereotypes, 91–2, 197, 272
stratified sample, 43–4
strikes, 242–3
sub-cultures, 74, 269
subsistence economy, 222
suburbanisation, 25, 143–4
suicide, 260

taboos, 28
television, 204–6, 246
see also media
totalitarian governments, 160–3
town planning, 142–3
trade unions, 237–43
Acts concerning, 237, 239
function of, 237
influence and power of, 238–40
members of, 238
size of, 238
strike action and, 242–3
types of, 238
women and, 238

unemployment, 133, 226–7, 251, 278–9
United Kingdom, 2
United Nations, 180–1
upper class, 108, 111
urban villages, 8

urbanisation, 7–13, 18

values, 258, 264
violence, 265, 271, 272, 276–7
voluntary organisations, 134, 135, 180
voting, 163–4, 165–8

wages, see earnings
wealth, 111–13
welfare state, 131–4
West Indians, 103–5
white-collar workers, see middle class
women
employment of, 226, 230–4, 244
family role of, 232, 260
as voters, 168
see also gender
work, 225–55
effects of, 228–9, 233
'extension' in, 253
family and, 232
leisure and, 244
motivation for, 229
nature of, 253
'neutrality' in 253
'opposition' in, 253
types of, 8
women in, 226, 230–4
worker participation, 224–5
working class, 108
education and, 63–5
health and, 129–31
working hours, 243–4

youth culture, 45–6, 73–80
youth employment, 72, 75